Education and Fascism:
Political Identity and Social Education in Nazi Germany

Edited by

Heinz Sünker and Hans-Uwe Otto

 The Falmer Press

(A member of the Taylor & Francis Group)
London • Washington, D.C.

UK   Falmer Press, 1 Gunpowder Square, London
USA   Falmer Press, Taylor & Francis Inc., 1900 Frost Road, Suite 101,
        Bristol, PA 19007

First published in 1997

A catalogue record for this book is available from the British Library

**Library of Congress Cataloging-in-Publication Data are available on
request**

ISBN 0 7507 0598 1 cased
ISBN 0 7507 0599 X paper

Jacket design by Caroline Archer

Typeset in 10/12 pt Times by
Graphicraft Typesetters Ltd., Hong Kong.

*Printed in Great Britain by Biddles Ltd., Guildford and King's Lynn on
paper which has a specified pH value on final paper manufacture of not
less than 7.5 and is therefore 'acid free'.*

Education and Fascism

Contents

Foreword

Heinz Sünker and Hans-Uwe Otto

Can we learn from history? Can we learn from social history and the effects on people living today of National Socialism, the German form of fascism, in areas not connected with these historical events? What does this history mean for us today? If we currently speak of the rising danger of racism and fascism, particularly in the USA, and also liberal circles, this indicates a social situation which, as a product of Reaganism — Thatcherism in Britain — is for many observers characterized by a destruction of the basic elements of that which is classically known as 'civil society' or of society at all. The devastation of sociability, forms of interaction and social relations which underpin society is important because it places in doubt the liberal model of society, a model which, following the Enlightenment tradition, assumes the existence of citizens who are actively competent, intervene into social situations and understand socio-political problems as their own. This is of crucial significance for the analyses collected in this book; it shows how social education in all areas of National Socialist society operated, and how it functioned in terms of an interest in political formation and social discipline. And this is not only the question of the perpetrators of Nazi crimes and murder but of the vast majority of the German people. In this way, relations between the character of National Socialist society, social policy and education policy and praxis are revealed and analysed in a concrete way, such as has never been achieved before. What is then made clear is the manner in which the pedagogization of all areas of life, was an attempt at complete social control, an unceasing incorporation of the whole lives of all 'people's comrades' — as they were called under National Socialism — from the cradle to the grave. At the centre of all these practices stood a process which was meant to lead to a particular formation of identity. The background to these practices constitute the ideology of the 'folk community', for which the catchword was: 'You are nothing, the people are everything'. The formative significance of this ideology of folk community, which, together with the transition from the welfare state to the National Socialist 'training state' — including in the self-understanding of its ideologues — was central, manifests itself in all social institutions and fields of social action. These contributions provide new types of information about ideological frameworks and real practices: including camp pedagogy, the Hitler Youth, the association of German maidens, social work as 'social education', on the constitutive conditions of the ideology of folk community. The identity-constituting/forming character of the ideology of folk community, however, also becomes clear when one examines the distinction between the social basis (anti-capitalist ideology of the *petite bourgeoisie*) and the social function of National Socialism (maintenance of the capitalist mode of production). At the same time, an analysis of the ideology of folk community makes it possible to clarify how education and social work, which were referred to as 'folk care', were used for 'selection processes' among the members of this society: the splitting of the population into those worthy and unworthy of 'selection', into suited and unsuited to community, had, in the context of ideologics of racial hygiene and eugenics and concepts of social education, outcomes ranging from exclusion to elimination and murder in a variety of forms.

Our engagement with the history of National Socialism must today investigate the relations between identity-formation, political culture and pedagogic activities. In this context, the question of the causes of National Socialism and its instigators, and also of its political/pedagogic traditions, orientations, classes and social milieus, takes on a special meaning which can be significantly extended by analyses of the expansion and maintenance of National Socialist domination. The title *Education and Fascism: Political Identity and Social Education in Nazi Germany* itself indicates the orientation to the articles in this collection: they are concerned with the possibilities of unravelling and analysing the social framework of National Socialism. Of particular importance here is the mediation between terrorist domination and an everyday life suggestive of normality, which is given pedagogic and political support in its human consequences. The formative capture of all members of this society succeeds essentially through an 'education towards folk community'. When the ideology of folk community encourages processes of social integration and exclusion, when it is a matter of 'human selection', when it concerns culprits, victims and accomplices, the decisive question becomes: how can an ideology, essentially mediated by pedagogic practices, operate so effectively that it apparently provided many in National Socialist Germany with a 'functioning' identity. The contributions in this volume aim to develop answers to this question, in order to prevent any repetition of this history.

We wish to thank the translators for their work on this book. Elizabeth Harvey naturally gave us an English text. Robert van Krieken translated the texts of Heinz Sünker and Hans-Uwe Otto and the Editors' chapter entitled 'Social Work as Social Education'. All the other texts were translated by Jonathan Harrow.

1 Political Culture and Education in Germany

Heinz Sünker

Introduction

One must not, therefore, estimate the particularity of people too highly. Rather, one should see as an empty fable the claim that teachers direct themselves carefully to the individuality of every one of their pupils, to encourage the same in study and education. They do not have any time for it. The particularity of children is suffered in the family circle; but with schooling begins a life according to a general order, according to a collective rule; there the spirit must be led to rid itself of its peculiarities, to the knowledge of, and desire for, the universal, to the absorbtion of the existing general education. This reformation of the soul — only this is education. The more educated a person is, the less their conduct reveals anything characteristic of only them, anything coincidental. (Hegel, 1970)

The question of the consequences of the non-linear, contradictory interdependence of constitution of society and educational institutions (Heydorn, 1980a, p. 99) for the determination of relations between educational systems and social history, for the social determination of the form of educational processes and their realization in empirical individuals, is here examined through a sketch of the particular developments in Germany. This examination of the connections between political culture and institutionalized education will also enable an analysis of problems of both structure and action.

Since studies of political culture are concerned with questions of the social relations, the conditions of political developments against the background of political-cultural frameworks of action and meaning, the regulation of political action through ideas, value systems and institutions; they investigate political culture as the expression of historical traditions, ideologies and mentalities (Pye and Verba, 1965). Political culture can thus be conceptualized as the interconnection of micro- and macro-politics (Reichel, 1981, p. 40; Sünker, 1989c). Germany is usually treated as a particular case in studies of political culture, because of the contradiction between its socio-economic modernity, the elements of which include — arising from the correspondence between the labour market and the education system in the service of increasing industrial competitiveness—the school system (Friedeburg, 1989, p. 334f.;

Meyer, 1976, p. 12f.), and its catastrophic political history — represented by Auschwitz (Almond and Verba, 1963; Sünker, 1994a).

In the context of educational theories, which are united by their use of a critical theory of society — related to history and the present — and their determination by the concept of the practical relevance of human action for social developments (Benner, 1982; Lenhart, 1987; Scherr, 1992), it is always important to bear in mind the mediation between education and the socio-historical context. Central here is the concept of a dialectic of the institutionalization of education, which emphasizes the contradiction it contains between domination and emancipation, so that although the analysis of hegemonic structures in the context of political culture remains crucial, the assessment of the total situation does not disappear within it, but rather requires historical specification.

The fact that under these auspices it is possible to make relatively unambiguous statements about wide-ranging lines of development in German history, with its traditions bound up with the dominant political culture, and the education system, demonstrates not least von Friedeburg's view in his 'Educational reform in Germany', where he concludes:

> The history of educational reform still shows that its development was determined not by pedagogic insights and organisational concepts, but by social relations of power. Over the centuries in the German lands they led to the extraordinary stability of the structures of public education and thus to a unique continuity in problems and polarisations. No matter how great the economic and political upheavals, the interest in particular forms of social inequality allowed new groups to tread in the footsteps of the old, to maintain the education system ... The underlying preconditions for structural reform improve when greater labour power is again required, particularly qualified and capable of further education. The individual demands increase, despite overwhelming status differentials. Continuous educational expansion undermines/hollows out the system of credentialisation. The social instrumentalisation of public education becomes increasingly difficult. Educational reform is still on the agenda. (Friedeburg, 1989, pp. 476–7; Sünker, Timmerman and Kolbe, 1994)

The notion of the socio-political instrumentalization of public education[1] captures an essential *leitmotiv* in the context of the approach being adopted here; beyond simple assessments of the reproduction of social relations and thus social inequality, which to a decisive extent always operates with the help of the education system,[2] we are thus led to the question of the complex mediations between hegemonically constructed social relations of power, political culture and institutionalized education (here in the form of the school system).

Against the background of German history, in which it is common — particularly in Prussia, i.e., under Prussian rule — to equate the school with the army barracks (Meyer, 1976, p. 11f.), the question of the chances of a democratic, i.e., a non-coercively structured society represents a remarkable goal.

For the exponents of the dominant fraction of the dominant class (Bourdieu, 1984) the connection between pedagogy and politics in German history was always very clear: it aimed for the construction of subjects obedient to authority in Frederich Wilhelm IV's speech to seminary directors in 1849, when he outlined his worldview:

> All the misery which has overcome Prussia in the distant past is your, only your fault, the fault of the rotten education, the irreligious mass knowledge, which presents itself as real knowledge, . . . (Heydorn, 1979, p. 124)

This was ensured in institutional political terms with the Stiehl Ordinance in 1854 on the material standardization of the curriculum, the methodical standardization of pedagogic forms and teacher education (Meyer, 1976, p. 35ff.; Heydorn, 1979, p. 181ff.; Kolbe, 1994).[3]

Even when one attempts to go beyond functionalist approaches, holding to the dialectic of the institutionalization of education, it cannot be overlooked that political and social disciplining, social integration qua indoctrination, stand — not just in this period — in the foreground of the development of schooling (Meyer, 1976, pp. 39, 192; Heydorn, 1979, p. 80; Koneffke, 1973, p. 279f.).

The Empire (Kaiserreich)

If one observes these constellations in modern German history, it becomes clear why H.-U. Wehler begins his mammoth *Deutsche Gesellschaftsgeschichte* (German Social History), devoted to the development of Germany since the eighteenth century, with the sentence, 'In the beginning there was no revolution'.

> While the history of England, France, the United States of America are characterized in such a fundamental sense by their revolutions in the 17th and 18th centuries, that any account of their modern development can commence with this turning point, Germany history at all times lack a similar dramatic break. (Wehler, 1987, p. 35)

Here Wehler is not simply identifying a decisive difference between German history and that of other important European and non-European nations, this deficiency also connects with a specific German problem in the realm of theory, practice and thence experiences of democracy.

Beyond the controversy, which will not be examined in detail here, over the question of how bourgeois — because of the absence of a revolution — the German Empire after 1871 really was (Wehler, 1988; Eley, 1991) and further, whether National Socialism with its policy of annihilation should be assessed as the consequence of a specific pathology of German history — deriving from its pre-modern orientations — or as the consequence of modernization processes which can be understood as the dark side of modernity (Wehler, 1988; Eley, 1991; Peukert, 1991; Bajohr *et al.*, 1991), it remains decisive for the lines of development of German history.[4]

A central problem in Germany has, following the consequences of a long period of undemocratic society, been the absence of a self-conscious bourgeois liberalism in the fledgling German nation-state after 1871 (Wehler, 1988, p. 38f.) as well as the class symbiosis of Junkerdom and bourgeoisie (Machtan and Milles, 1980). This led *inter alia* to the militarization of everyday life in the Wilhelmine Empire, which in turn encouraged hierarchical thinking and a subordinated spirit as well as a preference for violent resolutions to social conflicts.[5]

The Stiehl Ordinance of 1854, according to Heydorn, prepared the way not only for one of the half-revolutions's consequences for the organization of education; it was more the case that the State took over the popular content of mass education far more than in the previous period, for which pedagogic liberalism has prepared it. It effortlessly stripped away the rational-emancipatory elements of this liberalism; an early communication between liberalism and reaction can be recognized, since liberalism itself contains reactionary elements, which now have to be set free (Heydorn, 1979, p. 182f.). It is thus no wonder, that the early liberal-emancipatory nationalism of the German bourgeoisie was already in the late 1870s replaced by a conservative nationalism, which rises to the task of working as this period's ideology of integration (Wehler, 1988, p. 198). It is from this point that one can date the beginning of the fatal pathogenesis of the bourgeoisie in Germany: Under the new conditions, extreme nationalism and right-radicalism found their entry points, illiberalism flourished, hatred of outsiders grew (Wehler, 1988, p. 114).

In this way the suprising modernity of the Empire in many areas, which to a large extent embodied a bourgeois achievement, was accompanied by the pathology of various bourgeois social formations which began in this period, reaching their nadir in National Socialism (Wehler, 1988, p. 192).

Weimar

It is not only for the bourgeois class that National Socialism constitutes the reference point for the preceding epochs, for the aristocracy too — as the other decisive bearer of the form and content of political culture — the following proves to be the case: its ability to endure, despite its catastrophic defeat of 1918, is revealed by its fatal role in the crisis situation of the Weimar Republic up to 30 January 1933. The discrete charm of the East Elbish aristocracy degenerates between 1914 and 1944 into a grubby political irresponsibility, to which the Nemesis responds with annihilation (Wehler, 1988, p. 203).

'Alliance problems' between the bourgeoisie and aristocracy also constitute the framework for analyses of educational history in the Wilhelmine and Weimar periods, as they were outlined by Koneffke resulting from the Reich school conferences of 1890 and 1920: The Prussian school conferences of 1890 and 1900 realized, in the most powerful state in the German Reich, the necessary adaptation of the education system to the needs of the aggressive imperialism of the ruling class, and the school system was marvellously adapted to these needs. The primary interest in this adaptation, that of grandiosely puffed-up monopoly capital, found itself robbed of its feudal-aristocractic allies through the loss of the World War, and was thus compelled to reorganize the lines of social division, not, however, to oppose itself, but only compelled to reflection on its methods and strategies (Koneffke, 1973, p. 242; Heydorn, 1979, p. 190ff.; Friedeburg, 1989, p. 120ff.; Bölling, 1986, p. 672ff.).

Under these conditions of ruling interests in schooling and its function in maintaining the State, as well as the competing interests in reform on the part of the labour movement and reformist pedagogies, the Weimer Republic is exemplary of the newly formed mediation between political culture and the education system.

The conflicts over the comprehensive school involved problems which refer on the one hand to changed socio-historical conditions and on the other to system-immanent — ideologically oriented — answers. The struggle over comprehensive schooling provides — despite all historical limitations in the determination of positions (Koneffke, 1973, p. 253) — the guideline for the potential for an educational politics which is not beholden to hegemonic powers. Koneffke refers to its socio-political embeddedness in the context of social dynamics:

> An analysis of the negotiations and development of problems at the Reich school conference must, therefore, if it is to get to the heart of the matter, include a complex of statements on the dynamic structure of the German *petite bourgeoisie* and on the social process which form the *petite bourgeoisie* and defines its dynamics. This is important not only for this reason, since there is still extensive work to be done in the study of the *petite bourgeoisie*, but also because the school reform debate, even in the 70s, establishes the continuity of the German *petite bourgeoisie* — how society, which raises this problem and objectively defines the stability of the German dream of structural reforms in school affairs. (Koneffke, 1973, p. 246; Bourdieu, 1984, pp. 574ff., 691ff., 714 ff.)

However, within the Weimar context, of great relevance is the ideological reformulation of the idea of the comprehensive school with the concept of 'rights', which works as a synonym for the entity 'society'. This reactionary conception of the school, with the concept of 'community' embedded within it, was the point of entry for the 'folk community ideology', which was to bring about the disappearance of the idea of the equality of all human beings.

Fascism

This constellation, which he still sees as bound to an ideology-critical destruction of dominant positions in reform pedagogy and the youth movement, leads Heydorn to the conclusion: 'In the realm of education Fascism required neither a new theory nor a new practice. The education system was effective, it functioned, even after the end of Fascist rule, for a long time nothing changed' (Heydorn, 1979, p. 211).

Against this background, it is no wonder that Rainer Lepsius comes to the conclusion that in the Kaiserreich a democratic political culture only existed among minorities which were unable to hold their own in the Weimar Republic and in the

National Socialist period were opposed in every way and suppressed (Lepsius, 1988, p. 63). At the same time one should note Wehler's analysis, who in his clear language establishes that under the pressure of crisis, especially after 1929, the ideologies of integration which had been in operation for half a century were so radicalized that a new right-radicalism steadily gained in attractiveness: 'To this extent 1933 also presents the reckoning for bourgeois conservatism and nationalism, for bourgeois indifference to the dangerous power play, for the deficit in liberal-bourgeois political culture, in successful bourgeois politics, in the bourgeois impression on state and society generally' (Wehler, 1988, p. 217).

With the reference point of Political Culture one can today connect with the classical social-historical study of National Socialism which Franz Neumann published around fifty years ago under the title 'Behemoth'. His estimation that National Socialism embodied a form of imperialistic expansion of crisis resolution, requires greater precision (Neumann, 1984, p. 60f.). If it is true, as Gerald Feldman has maintained, that the crisis of capitalism in the 1920s and 1930s was universal, but not the crisis in democratic governments (Feldman, 1986, p. 25), then one must also pose the question, how political culture, relations of domination as well as the forms and content of schooling not only supported this development, but promoted it and provided it with crucial encouragement.

Thematically the question becomes both that of the mass basis of National Socialism — *inter alia* in the form of the tradition of a spirit of subordination, authoritarian character and inclination towards violence — and the politics of the elites. Their politics were, namely, as Peukert has established, decisive for the direction of politics and thus political culture in 1933 Germany.

> Hindenburg offered the government of national concentration that was formed on 30 January 1933 the opportunity of calling new elections to obtain a parliamentary majority. The machinery of state would be put at the government's disposal and a generous flow of funds would be assured. In so doing, Hindenburg set in train the national revolution which, in the space of a few months, was to see the complete collapse of the old politicians' scenario. Instead of being tamed by being given a share of power, Hitler would demand all power for himself. In point of fact, the consortium of elite interests that had now been formed by industry, the army and the NSDAP was little affected by this revolution. Sharing the aims of destroying the labour movement, setting up a leadership state and pressing forward with rearmament, these institutions became the central components of the new power structure of the 'Third Reich' and played a central part in its future evolution . . . Nevertheless, whatever emphasis one chooses to place on the facts, it is undeniable that after the nation's political and social leaders had cast off the republican institutions and the democratic settlement of 1918 like a worn-out garment, Germany then consciously decided, in an attempt to find a way out of the crisis it had itself deliberately exacerbated, to give a free hand to the destructive force of National Socialism. (Peukert, 1991, pp. 270–1)

The alliance of elites (Fischer, 1979; Jasper, 1986), then, involves both the relation between economy and politics, which provided structural advantage of national-socialist society, and the dominating intervention, a 'combination of welfare and repression' (Mason, 1982, p. 40), into the lives of most groups and classes not part of the regime.

In relation to the development of what can be defined in a preliminary sense as political culture in this period, the ideology of the folk community' constitutes the most important reference point. It connected with the demands of nationalism, organic thinking, a fetishization of totalization, so that ultimately racism was bound up together with a repressive social order. Folk community as National Socialism's ideology of formation was the foundation of the fascist dictatorship; its precise operation still requires closer investigation. Precisely in relation to current developments in the area of racism and hostility towards newcomers, under the conditions of biographical uncertainty and experiences of social crisis, it is important to refer to Adorno, who dealt with the rise and spread of National Socialism, its appeal to tradition as well as its ability to resonate with people's personality structure:

> It [the Hitler period, H.S.] violently anticipated current crisis management, a barbaric experiment in state administration of industrial society. The oft-mentioned integration, the organization intensification of the social net, which caught everything, also guaranteed protection against the universal anxiety about falling through the holes and sinking away. For countless people the chill of their alienated condition seemed to be removed by the ever-manipulated and artificial warmth of togetherness; the folk community of the unfree and unequal was, as lie, at the same time also the realization of an old, indeed ancient bad bourgeois dream. Certainly the system offering such gratifications contained within itself the potential for its own destruction. (Adorno, 1977, p. 562)

The ideology of the folk community, which was the nucleus of what can be characterized as the political culture of National Socialism and the concretization of Adorno's cold truth, drives/steers processes of integration and exclusion, especially with the concept of community suitability. In the transcendence of the distinction between pedagogy and politics, the qualitative transformation of the Weimar welfare state into the fascist 'training state' (Schnurr, 1988), are translated into practice. Geneticism and racial hygiene concretize these process in addition as control, exclusion, persecution and murder.

Federal Republic

The history of the Federal Republic of Germany contained the chance of a new beginning, which was immediately given away: the actual mode of dealing with the past, which mostly took the form of suppression, demonization or presented National Socialism as an industrial accident in German history, the dealings with resistance against fascism, with those driven into exile, with the victims of persecution, murder and ethnic cleansing precisely in the post-War period and the early years of the Federal Republic, showed less the emancipatory potential of a democratic political culture, and more the reactionary lines of tradition which have already often characterized historical development (Mitscherlich and Mitscherlich, 1967).

This was already clear in the first West German government statement by Chancellor Konrad Adenauer in September 1949: War prisoners, displaced persons, deportees, separated families now take up considerable space, the claims on the isolated eastern regions of the former Reich are legitimized. Adenauer expresses, how difficult he finds it, to speak with the necessary impassionate restraint, when he thinks of the fate of the displaced persons, who had perished in millions. No mention of Auschwitz, Maidanek, Treblinka, no mention of guilt or shame in the German people. The Germans returned to the status quo *ante*, with a democratic constitution, clear western orientation, an even clearer view of the Soviets as the enemy and the overwhelming untouchability of an occupied status. The historical responsibility for the crime against Europe's Jews did not affect the opening of the first parliament in the new Germany . . . This first West German govenment statement showed that the political leadership in Bonn at the time of the foundation of the Federal Republic did not regard it appropriate to engage critically and self-critically with the German past and the crimes against the Jews of Europe (Stern, 1991, p. 307).

The so-called de-nazification largely ran aground; the concerns of the politically responsible focused primarily on convicted or accused war criminals. Beyond that the so-called currency reform of 1948 turned out to be dispossession of (primarily) small capitalists, for the value of productive assets (factories, land and soil, stocks) was not affected: the securing of economic property relations and the anchoring of the dominant social structures were thus complete. The reproduction of the social status quo also served, what in the context of educational politics — but not only there — can be regarded as impaired renewal (Tenorth, 1988, p. 261ff.), to maintain an orientation to reactionary positions — mediated by an ideology of ability and a complementary pedagogic anthropology.

As a result, the so-called Adenauer era was overwhelmingly a period of restoration, in the political-cultural realm as well as that of educational politics. Like in the Weimar period, those who were interested in the development of a democratic political culture found themselves in a minority position, which they could only slowly work themselves out of.

This required at least two preconditions, which are of central concern to the mediation between political culture and institutionalized education. First, in 1964 a discussion developed on educational reform, which was determined as much by Picht's lament about the school emergency and an accompanying sense of a technological window, as by Dahrendorf's — democratically founded — speech on citizenship based on education and equality of opportunity (Heid, 1988). The focus of the discussion was the social and economic dysfunctionality of the three-tiered school system.

Second, there appeared a new relationship between the generations in the

FRG, a result of the fact that ever-increasing numbers of young people experienced their decisive political socialization — and then also divergence from classical authoritarianism — in the Federal Republic itself (Lepsius, 1988, p. 83f.). Both developments provided support for the argument that there were improved chances for the development of a democratic political culture in the Federal Republic. This is linked to the question of a third bearer of politicial culture in German history, alongside the bourgeoisie and the labour movement. Concretely this refers to the role of republican German intellectuals. In relation to their opponents, the mandarins — the conservative designers and producers of ideology — intellectuals formed a minority up until 1968. The decisive lines of social conflict were as follows: the elite model of the Right together with the mandarins' conceptions of leadership and compliance opposed the call for a democratization of all areas of life; a privileged claim to knowledge, which linked wisdom, truth and — symbolic — power, was contradicted by the classical Enlightenment conception of the autonomy of reason, the educability of all; claims to dominance and power came up against universal principles, guaranteeing freedom and citizenship, of the participation of all in social significant decisions, also those concerning procedures (Brunkhorst, 1987).

In 1968 the hour of the intellectuals struck, according to Hauke Brunkhorst in his study *Der Intellektuelle im Land der Mandarine* (The Intellectuals among the Mandarins). Only hegemony, once achieved, is not stable and not neccesarily durable. The relation to the egalitarian and democratically discussed public sphere has to be constantly renewed — as current events show. For the relation to the public sphere involves at the same time an associated claim, that of the autonomy of participants, or their interest in autonomy. This indicates how political culture is linked to a democratic pedagogy (Adorno, 1977).

Political Culture and Education

The task of a conceptualization of a democratic pedagogy and a related democratic educational practice, remains on the agenda in relation to both educational theory and real social relationships. Above all, apart from a few regional exceptions, there have been no structural changes which altered the traditional school selection processes. The extensive structural changes which can be observed in the FRG in the last twenty years operated within the framework of traditional schooling (Klemm, 1981, p. 148).

Without wanting to attribute total responsibility to the school as an essential form of institutionalized education, the consequences of educational politics and school pedagogy remain central when the empirical research into schooling shows that the current organization of education leads to almost a third of all pupils developing an ongoing learning aversion, often a learning neurosis. For around 20 per cent of pupils, going to school implies an ongoing tale of suffering with feelings of inadequacy and a long chain of experiences of intimidation (Fend, 1980, p. 364f.).

Equally important is what, in the context of political culture — and this means democratic participation — can be identified as the results of schooling: Conformist behaviour is established far more by the withdrawal of autonomous control over practical and cultural resources, without which personal expression is impossible. These resources of self-expression are to an increasing extent subordinated to the regularities of capitalist development. Not indoctrination, but expropriation of individuals' control over the conditions of their lives, becomes the foundation of social integration (Lenhardt, 1980, p. 83; Bowles and Gintis, 1987).

'Inequality for all' (Heydorn, 1979, p. 302) is the result of this situation, expressed in the transition of educated bourgeoisie to functional elite (Heydorn, 1979, p. 297). At the same time it is important to remember that pedagogy's original point of departure was a concept of education as a contract among people about their own freedom, as an attempt to end their delivery into coercion (Heydorn, 1979, p. 32).

If one approaches historical processes not in terms of a unity of the history of capitalism and that of bourgeois society, but in terms of processes with a dual character, in which the production and destruction of the social are combined (Sünker, 1995, 1996), then its principles can also be applied to social and educational history (Sünker, 1989a, 1989b, 1994); and it can be formulated as follows: Mass education stands today as a real appropriation of an autonomy aiming to transform history (Heydorn, 1979, p. 323).[6] Without giving up the distinction between pedagogy and politics, we can retain both the possibility and the task of their mediation (Adler, 1926, p. 78f.) this includes the task of conceptualizing the mediation of democratic political culture and democratic pedagogy. The realization of the school's — as a form of institutionalized education — and teaching's (Sünker, 1984, p. 204ff.) educational task raises two prerequisites for this: first, a theoretically inspired interest in the perspective of subjective autonomy — because it is the product of coercion-free educational processes; second, processes of recognition between subjects (Sünker, 1993).

Both realms thus need to be supported, political culture and education, by competent actors who experience democracy as integral to themselves, understanding themselves as subjects of the political process (Adorno, 1977, p. 559) and correspondingly intervene in an oppositional way in the authoritarian traditions of the German states. This involves the return of politics into society, into people's everyday life (Sünker, 1989a), and thus makes it possible to open up opportunities in Germany for a democratization and participatory re-orientation of political culture and institutionalized education,[7] along with consequences for the forms, content and profession of pedagogy. This is because it concerns the aim of the institution of education finally breaking free of domination and the genesis of a human pedagogy as part of the whole human struggle for liberation (Heydorn, 1980a, pp. 180, 164).[8]

Notes

1 Adorno provided a crucial analytical guideline: What education has turned into, sedimented as a sort of negative objective spirit, and not only in Germany, was itself derived

from social laws of movement, even from the concept of education itself. It has become socialized half-education, the ever-presence of the alienated spirit (1972, p. 93) and he concludes: 'If in the meantime the spirit only does what is socially correct, as long as it does not dissolve into society in an undifferentiated identity, anachronism is upon us: clutching to education after society has destroyed its foundations. But it has no other means of survival than critical reflection on half-education, which becomes essential for it' (1972, p. 121).

2   In relation to the discussion of reproduction, one can refer to Bourdieu: 'The education suse (system) is an institutionalised apparatus for classification, which represents an objective system, of classification and reproduces social hierarchies . . . ; in its apparent neutrality it transforms social classification in accordance with the results of education, and thus establishes hierarchies' (1984, p. 605; 210f., 242f.; Wexler, 1990; McLaren, 1993).

3   On the discussion of public education and the curriculum, see Apple, 1982; Englund, 1986.

4   On the representatives of the democratic German tradition, see Grab, 1984.

5   On the militaristic lifestyle of the bourgeois upper classes, see Binding (1937, p. 137f.).

6   In the context of his analysis of the dialectic of institutionalized education, Heydorn argues in general that: 'The general character which education has acquired [in the present, H.S.], indicates that the moments of education overcome their class-historical disintegration, and can become universal in a liberated species' (1980a, p. 291).

7   At the same time this perspective is not only a German one, but concerns a general problem in bourgeois-capitalist societies; see here the contributions headed Schooling, Cultural Politics and the Struggle for Democracy in Giroux and McLaren, 1989. The extent of the problem was already formulated some time ago by A. Siemsen: 'I see the cause [of the socio-political problems of this century, H.S.] far more in the fact that our consciousness is becoming exclusively technically oriented, aims for enormous success in the areas of control of nature and material technology, and correspondingly the area of social relations is completely neglected' (Siemsen, 1948, p. 5; 10, 93f., 146).

8   In opposition to anti-pedagogic sentiments Heydorn maintains: 'Liberation occurs where historical antagonism reaches its recognizable point. Only there can the solution appear. This means in practice, and in view of the normative character of institutionalised education, that the instruments required for appropriation, must themselves be appropriated. The learning demanded from the school [and this relates to the Hegelian formulation of education as becoming towards universality, H.S.] must then be rejected, if its dehumanising intent is made clear, [because the achieved level of a civilization . . . is objectively suppressed] the instruments necessary for the control of social processes are made available. Only when we have them at our disposal can we master these processes . . . Precisely this contradiction must be endured; expropriation and liberation are interdependent' (Heydorn, 1980a, p. 176).

References

ADLER, M. (1926) *Neue Menschen: Gedanken über Sozialistische Erziehung*, 2, verm. Aufl., Berlin, Mohr.

ADORNO, TH.W. (1972) 'Theorie der Halbbildung', in ABORNO, TH.W. *Gesammelte Schriften*, **8**, Frankfurt/M., Suhrkamp.

ADORNO, TH.W. (1977) 'Was bedeutet: Aufarbeitung der Vergangenheit', in ADORNO, TH.W., *Gesammelte Schriften*, **10**, 2, Frankfurt/M., Suhrkamp.

ALMOND, G. and VERBA, S. (1963) *The Civic Culture*, Princeton, University Press.

APPLE, M. (Ed) (1982) *Cultural and Economic Reproduction in Education*, London, Routledge (Education Books).

BAJOHR, F., JOHE, W. and LOHALM, U. (Eds) (1991) *Zivilisation und Barbarei, Die Widersprüchlichen*, Potentiale der Moderne, Hamburg, Christians.

BENNER, D. (1982) 'Bruchstücke zu einer nicht-affirmativen Theorie pädagogischen Handelns', *Zeitschrift für Pädagogik*, pp. 951–67.

BINDING, R.G. (1937) *Erlebtes Leben*, Berlin, Scherz.

BÖLLING, R. (1986) 'Schule, Staat und Gesellschaft in Deutschland', *Archiv für Sozialgeschichte*, **23**, pp. 670–87.

BOURDIEU, P. (1984) *Die Feinen Unterschiede*, Frankfurt, Suhrkamp.

BOWLES, S. and GINTIS, H. (1987) *Democracy and Capitalism: Property, Community, and the Contradictions of Modern Social Thought*, New York, Basic Books.

BRUNKHORST, H. (1987) *Der Intellektuelle im Land der Mandarine*, Frankfurt, Suhrkamp.

ELEY, G. (1991) 'Die deutsche Geschichte und die Widersprüche der Moderne: Das Beispiel des Kaiserreiches', in BAJOHR, F., JOHE, W. and LOHALM, U. (Eds) *Zivilisation und Barbarei, Die Widersprüchlichen*, Potentiale der Moderne, Hamburg, Christians.

ENGLUND, T. (1986) *Curriculum as a Political Problem*, Uppsala, Studentenliteratur Chartwell-Bratt.

FELDMAN, G. (1986) 'The Weimar Republic: A problem of modernisation?', in *Archiv für Sozialgeschichte*, **26**, pp. 1–26.

FEND, H. (1980) *Thorie der Schule*, München, Urban und Schwarzenberg.

FISCHER, F. (1979) *Bündnis der Eliten: Zur Kontinuität der Machtstrukturen in Deutschland 1871–1945*, Düsseldorf, Droste.

FRIEDEBURG, L.v. (1989) *Bildungsreform in Deutschland: Geschichte und Gesellschaftlicher Widerspruch*, Frankfurt, Suhrkamp.

GIROUX, H. and MCLAREN, P. (Eds) (1989) *Critical Pedagogy, the State, and Cultural Struggle*, Albany, Suny Press.

GRAB, W. (1984) *Ein Volk Muß seine Freiheit Selbst Erobern: Zur Geschichte der Deutschen Jakobiner*, Frankfurt, Büchergilde Gutenberg.

HEGEL, G.W.F. (1970) Enzyklopädie der philosophischen Wissenschaften III, Frankfurt/M., Suhrkamp.

HEID, H. (1988) 'Zur Paradoxie der bildungspolitischen Forderung nach Chancengleichheit', *Zeitschrift für Pädagogik*, pp. 1–17.

HEYDORN, H.-J. (1979) *Über den Widerspruch von Bildung und Herrschaft*, Frankfurt, Bildungstheoretische Schriften.

HEYDORN, H.-J. (1980a) *Ungleichheit für Alle*, Frankfurt, Syndikat.

HEYDORN, H.-J. (1980b) 'Überleben durch Bildung', in HEYDORN, H.-J. *Ungleichheit für Alle*, Frankfurt, Syndikat.

HEYDORN, H.-J. (1980c) *Zu einer Neufassung des Bildungsbegriffs*, in HEYDORN, H.-J. *Ungleichheit für Alle*, Frankfurt, Syndikat.

JASPER, G. (1986) *Die Gescheiterte Zähmung: Wege zur Machtergreifung Hitlers 1930–1934*, Frankfurt, Suhrkamp.

KLEMM, K. (1991) 'Entwicklung und Verlauf der Schulreform', *Zeitschrift für Sozialisationsforschung und Erziehungssoziologie*, **1**, pp. 147–53.

KOLBE, F.U. (1994) *Strukturwandel Schulischen Handelns: Untersuchungen zur Institutionalisierung von Bildung zwischen dem Anfang des 19. Jh. und den 1880er Jahren*, Weinheim, Deutscher Studienverlag.

KONEFFKE, G. (1973) 'Die Reichsschulkonferenz von 1920', in HEYDORN, H.J. and KONEFFKE, G. (1973) *Studien zur Sozialgeschichte und Philosophie der Bildung II*, München, List.

LENHARDT, G. (1980) 'Schule und Lohnarbeit', *Leviathan*, **8**, pp. 76–105.

LENHART, V. (1987) *Die Evolution Erzieherischen Handelns*, Frankfurt, Lang (Studien zur Erziehungswissenschaft 23).

LEPSIUS, R.M. (1988) 'Die Prägung der politischen Kultur der Bundesrepublik durch institutionelle Ordnung, in ders.', *Interessen, Ideen und Institutionen*, Opladen, Westdeutscher Verlag.

MACHTAN, L. and MILLES, D. (1980) *Die Klassensymbiose von Junkertum und Bourgeoisie: Zum Verhältnis von Gesellschaftlicher und Politischer Herrschaft in Preußen, Deutschland 1850–1878/79*, Frankfurt, Ullstein.

MASON, T. (1982) 'Die Bändigung der Arbeiterklassen im nationalsozialistischen Deutschland: Eine Einleitung', in SACHSE, C. (Eds) *Angst, Belohnung, Zucht und Ordnung: Herrschaftsmechanismen im Nationalsozialismus*, Opladen, Westdeutscher Verlag.

MCLAREN, P. (1993) *Schooling as a Ritual Performance: Towards a Political Economy of Educational Symbols and Gestures*, 2nd ed., London, New York, Routledge.

MCLAREN, P. and GIROUX, H.A. (1989) *Critical Pedagogy, the State, and Cultural Struggle*, Albany, New York University Press.

MEYER, F. (1976) *Schule der Untertanen: Lehrer und Politik in Preußen 1848–1900*, Hamburg, Hoffmann und Campe.

MITSCHERLICH, A. and MITSCHERLICH, M. (1967) *Die Unfähigkeit zu Trauern: Grundlagen kollektiven Verhaltens*, München, Piper.

NEUMANN, F. (1984) *Behemoth: Struktur und Praxis des Nationalsozialismus 1933–1944*, Frankfurt, Fischer.

PEUKERT, D.J.K. (1991) *The Weimar Republic: The Crisis of Class Modernity*, London, Allen Lane.

PYE, L. and VERBA, S. (Eds) (1965) *Political Culture and Political Developments*, Princeton, University Press.

REICHEL, P. (1981) *Politische Kultur in der Bundesrepublik Deutschland*, Opladen, Leske und Budrich.

SCHERR, A. (1992) 'Anforderungen an professionelle Jugendarbeit mit gewaltbereiten Jugendszenen', *Neue Praxis*, **2**, pp. 387–95.

SCHNURR, ST. (1988) 'Vom Wohlfahrtsstaat zum Erziehungsstaat: Sozialpolitik und soziale Arbeit in der Weimarer Republik und im Nationalsozialismus', *Widersprüche*, **8**, 26, pp. 47–64.

SIEMSEN, A. (1948) *Die Gesellschaftlichen Grundlagen der Erziehung*, Hamburg, Oetinger.

STERN, F. (1991) *Im Anfang war Auschwitz. Antisemitismus und Philosemitismus im Deutschen Nachkrieg*, Gerlingen, Bleicher.

SÜNKER, H. (1984) *Bildungstheorie und Erziehungspraxis*, Bielefeld, Kleine.

SÜNKER, H. (1989a) *Bildung, Alltag und Subjektivität*, Weinheim, Deutscher Studienverlag.

SÜNKER, H. (1989b) 'Heinz-Joachim Heydorn: Bildungtheorie als Gesellschaftkritik', in HANSMANN, O. and MAROTZKI, W. (Eds) *Diskurs/Bildungstheorie I*, Weinheim, Deutscher Studienverlag.

SÜNKER, H. (1989c) 'Politische Kultur, politische Sozialisation und Bildungstheorie', *Neue Praxis*, **19**, 5, pp. 416–23.

SÜNKER, H. (1993) 'Education and enlightenment, Or: Educational Theory Contra Postmodernism?', *Education*, **48**, pp. 39–57.

SÜNKER, H. (1994b) 'Pedagogy and politics: Heydorn's "survival through education" and its challenge to contemporary theories of education', in MIEDEMA, S., BIESTA, G., BOOG, B., SMALING, A., WARDEKKER, W. and LEVERING, B. (Eds) *The Politics of Human Science*, Brussels, VUB Press.

SÜNKER, H. (1994c) 'Germany today: History and future (or dilemmas, dangers and hopes), An Interview', *Intern. Jour. for Educational Reform*, **2**, pp. 202–9.

SÜNKER, H. (1995) 'Soziale Arbeit und Vergesellschaftung der Gesellschaft', in THIERSCH, H. and GRUNWALD, K. (Eds) *Zeitdiagnose Soziale Arbeit*, Weinheim, Juventa.

SÜNKER, H., TIMMERMANN, D. and KOLBE, F.U. (Eds) (1994) *Bildung, Gesellschaft, soziale Ungleichheit*, Frankfurt, Suhrkamp.

SÜNKER, H. (1996) 'Violence and society — Violence in society', in FRENSEE, D., HOM, W. and BUSSMANN, K.-D. (Eds) *Family Violence against Children: A Challenge for Society*, Berlin, New York, De Gruyter.

TENORTH, H.-E. (1988) Geschichte der Erziehung, Weinheim, Juventa.

WEHLER, H.U. (1987) *Deutsche Gesellschaftsgeschichte*, **2**, München, Beck.

WEHLER, H.U. (1988) *Aus der Geschichte Lernen?*, München, Beck.

WEXLER, P. (1990) *Social Analysis of Education*, New York/London, Routledge.

2   *Volk* Community: Identity Formation and Social Practice

Heinz Sünker and Hans-Uwe Otto

Introduction

The social reality of the German version of fascism, national socialism (Saage, 1987) confronts us continually with the need to discuss not only its causes and reasons but also how this social development 'functioned'. In this context, 'social development' summarizes an approach that aims to analyse overall social relationships; it aims to transcend both the restrictive structural-determinist approach and the positivistic perspective that would scratch only the surface of phenomena (Ziebura, 1979, pp. 11–12, 22). Social and sociohistorical analyses of national socialism that strive to combine social theory and social policy therefore address the relationship between politics, economics, and ideology[1] as well as the problems in identifying 'historical agents' (Baldwin, 1990, pp. 5–6).

Against this background, our first concern in this chapter is to reconstruct the growth of historiographic ideas on the '*development* of a society' (Ziebura, 1979, p. 17), in our case, national socialism. Then we shall link this to a social-theoretical analysis of societalization processes, and finally discuss the sociopolitical implementation and the breadth of '*Volk* welfare' based on the ideology of the *Volk* community, and examine how this ideology formed its individual members and relationships.

This makes it necessary to consider a point raised by Adorno (1977) when discussing the rise and impact of national socialism, its traditional components, and its ability to address the personality structure of human beings (Kilian, 1971, pp. 193–5):

> Violently, it [the world of Hitler] anticipated the contemporary dominance of crisis, a barbaric experiment of state control over an industrial society. The frequent demand for integration, the organizational strengthening of the social net, which caught everything, also provided protection against the universal fear of slipping through the net and becoming destitute. For innumerable persons, the coldness of their estranged state seemed to be abolished by the warmth of togetherness, although this was manipulated and contrived; the *lie of the Volk community of the unfree and unequal, simultaneously also the fulfillment of an old, and always evil dream of the*

citizen. Indeed, the system offering such gratifications contained the seeds of its own downfall. (p. 562, translated, emphasis added)

Adorno touches on a problematic issue in the sociohistorical causes of national socialism, and also raises an issue regarding the implementation of ideology that has become controversial in recent historiographic literature. For example, Kershaw (1989) summarizes his argument as follows:

I have argued that the exceptionality of the Nazi state say not only in the conditions which allowed an 'outsider' such as Hitler, fronting an unusual political force, to come to power, but also in the extraordinary character, in a modern capitalist state, of the type of power he exercised. This gradually culminated in the dominance of purely ideological goals which ultimately ran counter to the reproduction of the socio-economic order and, indeed, of the political system itself. Not only destruction on the grand scale, but self-destruction was arguably immanent to the Nazi 'system' of rule. (Kershaw, 1989, p. 66)

From another perspective, Mason (1995a) works out Kershaw's attempt to conceptualize 'political theology', when discussing the difficulties involved in a historiography of national socialism and proposing some solutions to these difficulties in his criticism of intentionalists and functionalists. He notes that marxist historians and political theorists have paid little attention to the debate between the two schools of liberal historians, but also that they have written little about Nazi genocide. However, this is precisely the object that most clearly reveals the question of agency and structure:

There is no compelling reason for this. Marxism offers a dynamic theory of the development of all modern industrial capitalisms, which incorporates, or rests upon, a structural (some would argue 'functional') analysis of these systems. The dynamic element introduces human agency, and human agency is central to Marx's writings: Men do make their own history, but they do not make it as they please, not under conditions of their own choosing, but rather under circumstances which they find before them, under given and imposed conditions. This sentence ought to introduce all biographical studies of Hitler! It formally encapsulates intentions and structures, and suggests the necessity of relating the two in historical writing. (Mason, 1995a, pp. 226–7)

However, while the intentionalists so frequently misunderstand the given and imposed conditions, marxists have paid insufficient attention to the fact that human beings make their own history and, instead, they have concentrated too exclusively on dominant classes and balances of power.

This deficiency in giving an account of intentions and actions is a weakness in marxist work on fascism; but the weakness is not inherent in the theory as such, for the challenge can be met by further research along the lines of the various non-literal ways of reading sources referred to above. It is an urgent task, for studies which exhaust themselves with the conditions which 'permitted' certain developments, or made certain policies 'possible' or 'necessary' fall short of historical explanation; they cut off before reaching those human actions which actually require explanation-mass murder. But it is the stopping short which is mistaken, not the original effort. What was permitted by conditions, or was possible, must be analysed, and it is here that marxism offers a more comprehensive framework than an approach which concentrates heavily upon political institutions and decision making processes (p. 227).

Social Analysis and Social Theory

If we summarize these ideas, we find that we are confronted with the task of relating intentions and structures in a way that reveals a developmental logic for the German bourgeois society. This should provide information on the continuities and disruptions in German history that were the prerequisite for the establishment and implementation of national socialist rule.

This calls for a reappraisal of the classical sociohistorical study of national socialism, Neumann's *Behemoth*. His view of national socialism as an imperialist expansion to resolve crises (Neumann, 1984, pp. 60–1) now needs to be extended. This certainly makes it necessary to consider elements of a psychological history of German development that address the unique sociohistorical quality of national socialism. If, as Feldmann claims, the crisis of capitalism in the 1920s and 1930s may well have been universal, but not the crisis of democratic governments (Feldmann, 1986, p. 25), it will also be necessary to consider hypotheses that address the *peculiarly German* aspect of national socialism (Gay, 1987, p. 13; Butler, 1941; Bloch, 1970; Elias, 1989; Otten, 1989) from different perspectives: psychohistorical, culture-historical, or even civilization-theoretical. Almost fifty years ago, Neumann (1984) had already pointed out that national socialist rule was based on two organizational principles:

> The pluralistic principle is replaced by a monistic, total, authoritarian organization. This is the first basic principle of the national socialist organization of society. The second principle is the atomization of the individual. Groupings such as the family and the church and the solidarity that arises from working together in factories, businesses, and offices are broken consciously. (Neumann, 1984, pp. 464–5, translated)[2]

The resulting ruling mechanism of direct control over the members of national socialist society that Neumann (1984, p. 543) confirms represents an inversion of the accepted constitutional principle of bourgeois society.

This theory of bourgeois society developed by Hegel in his *Philosophy of Law* clarifies vividly that the form and content of the relations between the members of this society result from an externally imposed relation between them. As a result, they only relate to each other formally and therefore exist only as exceptional, particular individuals (Hegel, 1955, par. 182–8). As Theunissen (1982) states:

> In the same way that Hegel conceived the entire bourgeois society in a reflexive logic, he also conceived the autonomy that individuals possess in society as the characteristic reflexive autonomy that has to be differentiated from an ontological existence for oneself. This autonomy results directly from the dependence of individuals on each other. It is a dependence of all on all; the bourgeois society as a joining together of autonomous individuals, a 'system of all-sided dependence.' (Theunissen, 1982, p. 371, translated)

The reality of the 'pure society' that grows out of the dissolution of 'natural' communities leads to a dynamic change in the relationship of the individual to his or her environment. 'The more continuously the individual must assert his or her "ability to live all life long", the less complete the acquisition of the world when entering into adulthood' (Heller, 1978, p. 27, translated). Hegel (1955) describes the consequences of individual existence and the struggle for survival: 'In these contradictions and their complications, bourgeois society represents both the drama and the dissipation of misery as well as the physical and moral decline that they both share' (par. 185, translated).

'Solutions' to the crises of bourgeois society grow out of an educational process in which the individual passes through the contradictions of the bourgeois society toward true individuality, that is, the perspective of the association of free individuals,[3] or out of a process in which social decline is countered through recourse to 'community' — in different forms.

One societalization process does not exactly encourage the educational process of the individual. Following Lefebvre's analysis, this is separated into a threefold movement: Societalization in the form of a 'totalitarization of society' that, with regard to individual development, takes on the forms of 'extreme individualization' as well as 'particularization' (Lefebvre, 1978, p. 340). This results in a social situation that is determined by a dissolution of life contexts and by general integration into the societal totality:

> The trend toward totalization and 'integration' (in the social ensemble, i.e., the State) conceals these separations. The fragmentation of everyday life, more comprehensive than that of working life, veils the unification from above and the suppression of the original differences. (Lefebvre, 1978, p. 146, translated)

The rise of a form of individualism that should not be mistaken for the formation of individuality but ends in the privatism of the bourgeois existence thus corresponds eventually, in ideological and pragmatic terms, to antibourgeois emotions of a different kind that, in the case of national socialism, take the form of the ideology of the *Volk* community.

Although Grunberger (1971) describes essential elements of the historical and social roots of the ideology of the *Volk* community, his work simultaneously reveals the need for further explanation. As a result of the experiences or rather the adventure of World War I[4] and the fundamental social disorientation arising from the depression during the Weimar republic, he interprets the yearning for a return to the 'womb of the community' as a collective infantile regression characterized by the wish to overcome all social contradictions and conflicts. The national socialists exploited this yearning for '*Volk* community' and developed a specific synthesis of quasi-socialist promises and quasi-capitalist fulfilment (Grunberger, 1971, p. 44).

The theoretical strategy underlying Grunberger's comments recalls Lefebvre's ideas on the possibilities of social analysis in developed capitalist societies. Lefebvre maintains that, over the course of capitalist development, neocapitalism has become increasingly concerned with everyday life rather than the economic sphere (Lefebvre, 1974, p. 69), and that the criticism of everyday life includes and supersedes the criticism of the political economy in the marxist sense. Therefore, research on everyday life becomes a '*guideline for understanding modern life*', and it includes a destruction of ideologies beyond one-dimensional procedures; because there can be:

No knowledge of the (global) society without critical knowledge of everyday life in the way that it implants itself — with its organization and its privation, with the organization of its privation — in the middle of this society and its history. No knowledge of everyday life without critical knowledge of the (entire) society. (Lefebvre, 1987, p. 353, translated; see Sünker, 1989b)

Volk Community and Identity

Adorno's rhetorically skilful and analytically rich remark on the '*Volk* community of the unfree and unequal' as the fulfilment of the old 'evil dream of the citizen' provides various levels and dimensions for dealing with the '*Volk* community'. It clarifies sociohistorical implications of the formulation and implementation of ideology, so that the question of the rise and hold of ideology can be posed. The socially formative character, thereby the essential influence of the ideology of the *Volk* community on everyday life and the social organization of life, can be understood only when both the apparent and the powerfully real aspects of this ideology become clear. At the same time, this means that the functionality of this ideology for the implementation and maintenance of the national socialist system of rule has to be reconfirmed repeatedly, without this system of rule becoming lost within it or the ruling elite being freed from their responsibility for this system:[5] Totalitarian state, the *Führer* principle, and the ideology of *Volk* community are inseparably intertwined (Neumann, 1984, pp. 75, 429, 466).

Marcuse had already summarized the ideopolitical 'underlining' of this programme in 1934:

> If we ask the programmers of the new world view what they are attacking in their fight against liberalism, we hear about the 'ideas of 1789', of soft humanism and pacifism, Western intellectualism, self-obsessed individualism, subjection of the nation and the state to the struggles of certain social groups for their own interests, abstract egalitarianism, political party system, hypertrophy of the economy, subversive mechanization and materialism. (Marcuse, 1979, p. 11, translated; see Herf, 1984)

Extending this presentation of the programmes that focus on the idea of transforming the class society into the *Volk* community leads to issues that address their ability to connect, their implementability, their effects, as well as their demands on social policy. This issue of connectability and implementability already points to the peculiar ways in which the 'concept of community' was dealt with in and by national socialism. Whether *Volk* community is understood and interpreted as a 'sham' (Mommsen, 1988, pp. 9–10); as essentially ideological (Grunberger, 1971, p. 53); as a 'myth' (Winkler, 1977a); as an ideal claim compared to real social contradictions and tensions (Baldwin, 1990, p. 22); as a 'ritual of classlessness, without affecting the relationships of the classes' (Elfferding, 1980, p. 225); as 'more than propaganda or a mobilization lie' (Spurk, 1988, p. 62); as a pragmatic and partially achieved programme (Prinz, 1985, p. 336); or as the basis for the popularistic character of the national socialist regime (Broszat, 1983),[6] it should never be forgotten that this concerns not only the link between *Volk* community and racism but also a specific conceptualization of labour policy.

It concerns, as Krieck's book on *National Political Education* has shown, the link between community and racial policy, 'the *Volk* population of the coming Third Reich', and in his version this means:

> With this revolution, blood rises up against formal rationality, the race against the national striving for purpose, honor against profit, commitment against the 'freedom' also called randomness, the organic whole against the individualistic separation, physical fitness against bourgeois safety, politics against the primacy of the economy, state against society, *Volk* against the individual and the masses. (Krieck, 1932, p. 68, translated)

The *Volk* concept (see Boehm, 1935, p. 13; Scheele, 1939) received its foundation in racial policy through naturalistic references as well as a radicalization of organological ideas on wholeness and corresponding parts (see Bloch, 1970, p. 174; Schleicher, 1939, p. 29) — condensed, for example, in the talk about 'transforming the *Volk* into a community' (Scheele, 1939, p. 110, translated). Both find their frightful end in 'racial hygiene' with its policy of segregation and murder (Kaiser, 1989, pp. 316–90; Peukert, 1982, pp. 246–79; Weingart, Kroll, and Bayertz, pp. 371–2, 399–406). If the function of social policy in bourgeois-capitalist societies is described classically with the thesis of the 'transformation of the people into wage-earners' (*Verlohnarbeiterung*, see Sünker, 1992, pp. 205–6), which deals with the problems of integration as well as the ascertainment of legitimacy and loyalty, then the reference to *Volk* community in national socialism should fulfil these functions within the framework of workers' and labour policy in general — also by suggesting shared interests that 'transcend class and political party' (Elfferding, 1980, p. 200; SOPADE, 1935, p. 883). The basic analyses of Mason in his *Arbeiterklasse und Volksgemeinschaft* (1975) and *The Containment of the Working Class in Germany* (1995b), just like further contributions from other social historians, point to this complex. The speeches on the 'nobility of work' and 'service to the *Volk* community' are products of the idea that *Volk* community instead of class struggle should determine social reality (Seldte, 1939, p. 7; Siegel, 1988, p. 108; Voges, 1982). 'The struggle for the soul of the German worker', which Bons (1989) cites from the national socialist newspaper, the *Völkische Beobachter*, is accompanied by the resurrection of procommunity terms such as 'honour' (Seldte, 1939, p. 10), which actually means honour instead of wages (SOPADE, 1935, pp. 866–7), and 'loyalty' (Brucker, 1934, p. 8). The social disadvantages of the working class (Herbert, 1989, p. 332), the dismantling of social welfare (see SOPADE, 1935, pp. 834–6), should be compensated by membership in the *Volk* community in which 'attitudes' (Mommsen, 1988, p. 14) were the decisive factor.

Correspondingly, the ruling system of national socialism formed:

> For wage-earners the Third Reich represented a political synthesis of workhouse and supermarket — a remorselessly demanding and threatening construction which generated its own strong pressures upon the inmates both to consume at least a few of the political commodities on display and not to think about the connections between them. The regime incessantly claimed the total loyalty and enthusiasm of the German people. (Mason, 1995b, p. 265)

In addition, a 'welfare affectation' of the regime, which actually involved the combination of 'welfare and repression' (Mason, 1995b, pp. 259–61), was designed to conceal the social reality that this development focused on the idea of the *Volk* community as a 'performance oriented community' (*Leistungsgemeinschaft*) (Brucker, 1934, pp. 9, 18; Mason, 1995c, p. 93; Siegel, 1988, p. 109).[7]

Herbert (1989) has pointed out that 'one of the important conceptual advances in recent research' (p. 333, translated) has been the linking together of previously separate research on labour policy and social policy, on the one hand, and extermination policy and racism on the other hand. The constitutive political economy of the labour force in bourgeois-capitalist social development underwent an extension and radicalization in national socialism that did not just seem to encourage the general validity of the achievement concept by promoting competition and achievement (Broszat, 1983, p. 68; Peukert, 1982, pp. 43–6). It was much more decisive to use the achievement concept[8] to tackle the dissemination of racial policy, labour policy, and extermination policy.[9]

One sociopolitically functional aspect in the implementation of the national socialist idea of the *Volk* community was to link predominantly industrial differentiations of achievement to racist ideas and perspectives or concepts of racial hygiene. As Herbert (1989) has pointed out:

> The achievement hierarchy did not just point to the strong achievers who should receive particular support and reinforcement but also, at the other end of the scale, to the 'rejects', those who are unable or unwilling to achieve, who should now be punished not just through social disadvantage — as before — but through persecution and segregation. (Herbert, 1989, p. 333, p. 358; see Geyer, 1989, pp. 383, 391–2)

If social policy was supposed to gain a new role by being guided through reference to the '*Volk* order' (Boehm, 1935, p. 110), then its focus on labour policy additionally offered a gateway for the claims to power of the Labor Front (*Deutsche Arbeitsfront*, DAF), 'which felt itself to be the guardian of the national socialist ideology of the "*Volk* community"' (Winkler, 1977b, p. 6, translated; Siegel, 1988, p. 130). The general goal after the seizure of power was to transform the middle class, which, because of its interests and motivation, embodied decisive elements of the social basis of national socialism (see Broszat, 1988, p. 276), into an 'unnecessary class' (Winkler, 1977b).

Politics of Inclusion and Exclusion

This triad of social policy, labour policy, and welfare policy, which has to be confirmed in terms of social theory and social policy, forms the basis for the most pronounced and also most provoking judgments on the social reality of fascist ideas and the potentials for their realization. These have to be reconstructed in a critical approach to ideology: 'Far-reaching societal plans of the most modern standard [were] directed toward a racist utopia of the final solution of social issues' (Peukert, 1988, p. 25, translated). Despite differences in analytical orientation, this links up with Aly and Roth's (1984) sociopolitically oriented appraisal in their study *Die restlose Erfassung* (total registration):

> Even at its decisive beginning, its conception, the 'final solution to the Jewish issue' was part of a 'final solution' to the social issue. It was intended to provide a sociopolitical action scope . . . The racial hygiene of the Third Reich, which was directed particularly toward the German Jews and the people of Eastern Europe, had its internal correlate in genetic hygiene. It was a technology of scientific mastery for splitting, dividing, and selectively threatening. (Aly and Roth, 1984, p. 142, translated)[10,11]

In a radical about turn from the basic welfare-state principles of bourgeois societies, the *final solution to the social issue* (Wagner, 1935, p. 30) was justified in sociopolitical terms by seeking to implement cost-effectiveness computations. As a contemporary doctoral dissertation in law expressed it, these would make the 'value of the needy to the *Volk* community' the sole criterion for allocating welfare (Schleicher, 1939, p. 34; Fenner, 1936, p. 19; Junk, 1940, p. 51; Kaiser, 1989, pp. 349, 359).

A sociopolitically induced 'change in the form' (Frauendiener, 1937) of social work could be implemented with the aid of a 'race-conscious welfare' system (Wagner, 1935), and, to a great extent, it could be carried on the judicial basis of the welfare legislation of the Weimar republic (see Schleicher, 1939, pp. 1, 27–8; on Weimar, see Abelshauser, 1987)[12] in a way that reversed and destroyed these laws. This trend, which casts a notable light on the relationship between politics and social work, was able to 'succeed' against the increasing professionalization of social work in the Weimar republic and expressed itself in part in that:

> . . . the practical experience of the new social-work professionals and the need to reflect scientifically on theories, methods, and findings in the professional field of social work had led to a rapid increase in knowledge and a notable qualification of the insights into the objects of social work: children, adolescents, their families, and their milieu. (Peukert, 1989, p. 319, translated)

The destruction of welfare state mechanisms, which were expressed in the general legal claims of individuals based on discourses in welfare policy, was supported by the radicalization of the 'criticism of the welfare state' (see Abelshauser, 1987, p. 10) that had already commenced during the Weimar republic.

The project of the welfare state, which was associated with the hated 'Weimar systems time' (Frauendiener, 1937, pp. 86–98; Junk, 1940, p. 13; Schleicher, 1939, pp. 1–3; Zimmermann, 1938–9, p. 13), was replaced with the model of the *Volkskörper* and *Volk* health centred on the ideology of the *Volk* community within which national socialist *Volk* welfare was labeled '*Volkspflege*'. Even the label reveals how ideas on racial policy were mixed up with ideas on the 'health control' of the German people (Hansen, 1991, pp. 156–78; Kater, 1983).[13]

The concept of *Volkspflege* consolidated ideas on the need and extent of social work,[14] on its form and content, so that it was used to justify the right to or the exclusion from welfare.

Although criticisms of the clientalization resulting from the prior practice of social work were linked to criticisms of the schematization and bureaucratization of public welfare, the 'achievement problem' finds its true focus in the issue of individual blame and use to the community:

> The judgment of a welfare case according to its significance in terms of the *Volk* community was unable to assert itself against the other [in the Weimar republic]. By abusing the regulations, it was often possible to enforce claims in opposition to a rational idea of welfare. For example, whether someone was to blame or not to blame for their situation was

generally regarded as irrelevant. As a result, in broad sectors of our people, the idea became lodged that the state was an institution that served the individual as a beneficiary, without the individual feeling any internal commitment to it. The duty of citizens to harness their own powers, to maintain their health, and to rear their children to be competent members of our people was thereby increasingly forgotten. (Reichert, 1935, p. 8, translated; see Schleicher, 1939, p. 30)

Ideological elements from genetic biology and racial hygiene played a central role in statements such as 'it does not concern the well-being of the individual but the entire *Volk*' (Althaus, 1937, p. 8, translated; see Hilgenfeldt, 1936, 1937; Wagner, 1935, p. 7) and that it has nothing to do with 'charity' (Junk, 1940, p. 107). And speeches on 'useless types of life' (Zimmermann, 1938/9, p. 17) and the need to segregate 'asocial elements' (Kirmeß, 1939, p. 43) led to the practice of selection; to selection processes that take the form of culling and eradication.

Planned race-improvement policy,[15] the selection of members of the *Volk* who are of value to the community, and the eradication — from expulsion to murder — of so-called '*Nichtgemeinschaftsfähiger*' (those who are unable to contribute to the community; see Guse and Kohrs, 1989; Harvey, 1989; Hepp, 1987; Kohlhase, 1940; Knüppel-Dähne and Mitrovic, 1989; Peukert, 1985; Wagner, 1988) interrelate in a way that clarifies that this framework did not involve questions of 'intentionality', but the realization of societal plans.

On the basis of a *Volkspflege* health policy, the developments that occur in this field range from a medically veiled diagnosis system in the framework of a so-called genetic health theory addressing population policy (Fenner, 1936, pp. 7–8) to concepts of social diagnostics (Aly and Roth, 1984, pp. 105–7). Because of the orientation toward, 'race improvement', 'breeding', 'value scales', and corresponding 'special treatments', the decisive issue of identity and difference in this 'concept' was drawn from a discussion in the human sciences at the turn of the century. This discussion was based on principles such as the distribution into 'values' and 'nonvalues', into 'highly valuable' and 'less valuable' (Weingart, Kroll and Bayertz, 1988).

The transformation of social policy on the basis of health policy, which materialized particularly crudely in the ideologies of '*Volk* community' and 'blood and land', supports Peukert's thesis that the resulting qualitative categorization of persons led to the crystallization of the abstract practice of selection based on a fictitious, racially defined whole, and the principle of a highly technological 'solution' based on the idea of cost-effectiveness. The 'final solution' within which the Jews were the largest group of victims should then be understood as a highly technological 'eradication' of 'non-values' that united the dichotomies of sick–healthy with reference to the '*Volk* body', normal–deviant with reference to the '*Volk* community', and *Volk*–alien with reference to nation and race (Peukert, 1988, p. 26).

If the connotations of *Volk* community offer a basis for the ideology and practice of '*Volk* welfare', because of the intended or achieved social homogenization in the form of a negative radicalization of a widespread discussion in the human sciences, this can simultaneously explain the turning away from the general view of the socially integrative function of social policy and social work, as well as the inversion of the theoretical approaches to problems in the profession that underlaid the discussion on welfare in the Weimar republic. This concerns the overlapping of the generalization of the educational concept in social work with what could be labeled the problem of the specific quality of welfare services. In a paper entitled *Die Problematik des Sozialbeamtentums* (the problems of a state social welfare system), Fischer (1954) attempted to organize the assistance concept as the basis for a mediation between education and welfare and also to counteract the rationalizing consequences of institutionalization processes in social welfare:

> For the first prerequisite of moral and mental assistance is the client's motivation to be assisted, and, related to this, the firm trust in this or that person that he or she is impartially and warm-heartedly capable and willing to provide this assistance. (Fischer, 1954, p. 319, translated; see Sünker, 1989a, pp. 95–7)

In this way, under the auspices of *Volk* community and *Volk* welfare, the access to the problems of professional activity in the field of social work became the task of forming the 'persons entrusted to it' (Martini, 1938, p. 56), as material support alone was not enough for the person in need. Martini linked this to the idea that educational work could only be successful within the context of a relationship of trust, an inner human commitment (Martini, 1938, p. 52), whereby, nonetheless, the third part of assistance and education revealed itself to be character formation and social disciplining, because 'education to *Volk* community' (Document 171, Vorländer, 1988) is education to willingness to make sacrifices (Hilgenfeldt, 1937, p. 11).

In '*Volk* welfare from the cradle to the grave', so the total concept in a preparation for a speech by Fiehler (Hansen, 1991, p. 332), whoever was defined and selected as healthy, genetically and eugenically useful, educable, and therefore as potentially valuable to the community, whoever additionally qualified themselves through 'good conduct' (Prinz, 1985, p. 235) on the basis of a cut-off on merit scales and therefore also payment claims (Leibfried, Hansen and Heisig, 1986) should be blessed. In addition, they should not just receive human closeness in '*Volk* welfare', not just understand themselves as an object of assistance, but feel themselves to be a member of the *Volk* community, as part of a larger whole, who has received support so that they would once more be enabled to fulfil their duties as citizens of the *Volk* (Schleicher, 1939, p. 35).

This motivational structure on the client side corresponds to that on the side of the helper: It concerns the disassociation of the helping process from individual feelings — of benevolence or sympathy — through insight into the duty to support the *Volk* community, above all, its military power (Hsiao, 1943) and the future maintenance of the *Volk* community in the form of a healthy *Volk* body (Fenner, 1936, p. 7; Hilgenfeldt, 1937, p. 9; Zimmermann, 1938/9).

This leads to the privatization of the helping process in two ways: The hypostatization of 'self-help' and 'welfare' (Hilgenfeldt, 1937, pp. 21, 27; Junk, 1940, p. 13; Schleicher, 1939, pp. 31, 34; Wagner, 1935, p. 5) corresponds to the conceptualization of 'help' as a concern of all 'citizens of the *Volk*' for all 'citizens of the *Volk*' (Schleicher, 1939, p. 35).

The sociopolitical instrument for implementing '*Volk* welfare' was the national socialist *Volkswohlfahrt* (NSV). This represented the drive shaft between party and '*Volk*'. As a mass organization linked to the party with 12.5 million members and approximately 1 million activists in 1939, its tasks were a 'complete assessment' (Zimmermann, 1938/9, p. 27) of all citizens of the *Volk* and to exploit '*Volk* welfare' as a 'polycratic battle cry' (Hansen, 1991, p. 352) in the demarcation dispute with both other associations (after the prohibition of the *Arbeiterwohlfahrt*, the exclusion of the Jewish welfare association, and the voluntary disbandment or absorption of the DPWV into the NSV, the DRK, the central committee for the inner mission of the German evangelical Church, and the German *Caritas* association belonged to the 'Working Community of the Leading Associations of Independent Welfare' under the leadership of the NSV) and public welfare (Hansen, 1991, pp. 93–104, 197–220) as well as in the power struggles within national socialism.[16]

Because of its organizational links to the NSDAP in the form of a national office for *Volk* welfare, its membership fees, its privileged position due, among others, to a monopoly of charity collections, its suborganizations *Winterhilfswerk* (winter assistance) and *Mutter und Kind* (mother and child), the NSV had an exceptional position in the national socialist hegemony that suggests that its activities should be interpreted as an attempt to present itself as an 'achievement of the *Volk* community' (Elfferding, 1980, p. 209).

In all, this development corresponds — also with reference to the popular character of national socialism — to the change from the welfare state to the functional education state (Schnurr, 1988). This was accompanied by a redistribution of welfare costs that principally represented a denationalization of social welfare on the basis of the ideology of the *Volk* community as a result of the nationalization of society.

Even when it can be confirmed that this involved the further development of an increasingly restrictively applied social policy — above all in terms of welfare payments (Homburg, 1985; Jaschke, 1982, pp. 91–4; Winkler, 1987, pp. 19–99) — that originated during the last third of the Weimar republic and was carried to an extreme during national socialism, we are still faced with the decisive question regarding how the computations of cost-effectiveness, in their different forms but always inhuman solutions — because even in cases of 'beneficiaries' they were determined racially on the basis of eugenic ideas — could be realized in social policy and social work. Under these conditions, the special historical role of '*Volk* welfare' along with the 'ideology of the *Volk* community' is underestimated when it is claimed that the Nazi regime retained the welfare state at a lower level up to World War II (Tennstedt, 1987, p. 157) or that we can only talk about the 'radicality of exclusion' (Hansen, 1991, p. 33, translated).[17] Without normative exaggeration, and only within the context of a social-theoretical and sociopolitical analysis, we consider that it is impossible to associate ideas on the welfare state with national socialism: Even today, the special historical role of '*Volk* welfare' has to be emphasized.

Notes

1 This approach is critical of Wehler (1987) who entitles his approach to a history of German society a 'History of Society as an Attempted Synthesis':

> Modern history of society understands its object as the entire society in the sense of the English 'society' or the French '*société*'; it attempts to assess as many as possible of the basic processes that have determined and perhaps continue to determine the historical development of a large-scale system that generally lies within national and political borders. Following the 'secular theories' and categories that Max Weber has developed for his universal historical studies in order — and this was the original driving force — to assess occidental types of society as precisely as possible through comparisons with other cultures, three equally important, continuous dimensions of society can be discriminated analytically. Power, economics, and culture represent these three simultaneously permeating and determining dimensions that are principally involved in the initial development of every society. (Wehler, 1987, pp. 6–7, translated)

At a later point, Wehler (1987) continues to follow the implicit problems here when he shows the difficulty of his undertaking:

> Naturally, after the comparatively marked independence of such developmental processes is admitted [those of economics, power, and culture], we are left with the completely central problem of viewing the interaction between them, the inner relationships, and the radiations that impact on other domains through the change in one area, in order to do justice to the *character of interdependence that characterizes the historical totality.* (op.cit. p. 333, translated, my emphasis)

2 There are already interesting indications on 'atomization' in 1935, in the '*Deutschland-Berichte*' of the SOPADE:

> The purpose of all national socialist mass organizations is the same. Whether one thinks of the labor front or of *Kraft-durch-Freude* (power through joy), of the Hitler Youth Movement or the '*Arbeitsdank*', overall the organizations serve the same purpose: to 'assess' or to 'care' for the 'citizens of the *Volk*', not to leave them to go their own way and possibly never arrive at the truth . . . The form of fascist power over the masses is compulsory organization on the one side and atomization on the other. (SOPADE, 1935, pp. 1375–6, translated; see pp. 869, 1447)

3 Hegel's discussion of the individual as the child of bourgeois society indicates the two-sidedness of his situation:

However, bourgeois society tears the individual out of this bond, alienates the members from each other, and recognizes them as autonomous persons. Furthermore, it substitutes the external nonorganic nature and the paternal basis, in which the individual had his or her subsistence, with its own nature, and subjects the existence of the entire family, the dependence on it, to chance. (Hegel, 1955, par. 238, translated)

4 The impact of World War I on world views, mentalities, and consciousness has been illustrated paradigmatically by Döblin (1978) in his novel *November 1918*. A short excerpt illustrating the world view of one of the protagonists is interesting in our context, the issue of the *Volk* community:

He talked about his encounter with the reds: 'There are competent fellows among them. But the movement lacks a core of ideals. They don't know Germany. They know no religion, they know only themselves, the proletariat, and that poorly. They talk about classes. It's a mania. They've closed off their minds. They want a new society without classes. What an idea! Some kind of heaven on earth. It will be a hard search to find the people to populate it.'

'And what do you want?'

'A healthy new Germany. People at the top who can rule and whom one can trust.' (Döblin, 1978, Vol. 4, p. 173, translated)

5 Peukert's presentation reveals the elite policy:

When Hindenburg gave the 'government of national concentration' formed on January 30th, 1933 the opportunity to wring a majority in new elections through the use of the state apparatus and the increasingly rich flow of contributions from industry, he triggered the dynamic process of the so-called 'national revolution' that, within a few months, used the taming principle to transform the transfer of power to the 'seizure of power'.

The recently established elite cartel of economy, the army, and the NSDAP were scarcely affected by this. They had formed the power structure and developmental dynamics of the 'Third Reich' under the common goals of the destruction of the labor movement, the establishment of the 'Führer state', and the drive toward rearmament. . . .

However, despite all differentiation, we are finally left with the fact that the German Reich, *after the politically and socially powerful members had discarded the republican institutions and the compromises of the establishment of democracy in 1918 like a cast-off skin, consciously sought a way out of the intentionally aggravated crisis that liberated the destructive dynamics of national socialism.* (Peukert, 1987, pp. 264–5, translated, my emphasis)

6 The relationship between the popular character of the regime and the Hitler myth will be mentioned only in passing (Broszat, 1983; Kershaw, 1988).

Even during the early stages of the 'movement', Krieck (1932) had pointed out that:

As a mass movement, it [national socialism] required the art of arousing the masses: Mass has to be fluid if it is to be shaped. Hitler's masterly practice of the art of mass arousal has not only increased the agitation and party leadership technology of the party state in its final conclusions but found essentially new elements and ways of arousing and leading the masses. (Krieck, 1932, p. 36, translated)

In the follow-up to Benjamin's thesis of the 'aestheticization of politics' — as the symbol of fascism — Stollmann (1976) has emphasized that the discontinuity of fascist public life, of the national socialist movement, too frequently let its brew of ideas decline into the verdict of deception, manipulation, and demagogics:

> This degraded the true energies, the enthusiasm, the power, the commitment, the desires, the hopes that Hitler's fascism could evoke to a 'subjective factor' and devalued them compared to the 'objective regularities'. It was then important to accept the 'false awareness of the situation' as a 'reality' that could not be altered sufficiently through the mere explanation of that which was socioeconomic. (Stollmann, 1976, p. 97, translated)

7 In our context, it is interesting that the 'underlining' of achievement ideas (Becker, 1938, p. 82) — on the basis of a 'Nordic metaphysics' — and '*Volk* morals' — as the legitimation of folk community (Larenz, 1938) — was also sought in a pseudo-philosophical perspective through a complete reversal of Hegel's philosophy.

8 Here the relation between the ideology of *Volk* community and 'Jewish policy' with its political and economic consequences should be pointed out: It is important to recall that in the cases of Jewish German citizens up to the Shoah, this essentially concerned 'the complete liquidation of their economic existence and the plundering of their wealth' (Barkai, 1988, p. 108, translated; see pp. 33, 61, 152, 189–203, 205; Ludwig, 1989).

9 In this context, we consider that the approaches in modernization theory that attempt to deal with national socialism should also be viewed critically (for a controversial discussion, see, e.g., Alber, 1989; Herf, 1984; Mason, 1975; Prinz, 1985).

In our opinion, the controversial estimations raised by Broszat's 'historization demand' also have a major basis in their modernization theory 'underlining', because Broszat calls for 'casting light on the social dynamization function of national socialism' — without suppressing 'the moral effects of the world view of the norm system of the Third Reich' — in order to insert 'the apparently only NS-specific . . . into the broader perspective of long-term changes in German society' (Broszat, 1988, p. 277, translated).

10 A possible link between the different accents of Aly and Roth and Peukert has already been suggested by de Witt (1978):

> Ultimately welfare would become obsolete, since the Nazis interpreted poverty as primarily a racial problem which could be solved through preventive health care and economic assistance for the racially valuable and politically reliable-citizen, therefore precluding welfare dependency. (de Witt, 1978, p. 260)

> The at least inherent economic aspect of the 'final solution of the social issue' is then finally reflected in the thesis of the economy of the 'final solution'. (Heim and Aly, 1987; see, also, criticisms in Browning, 1989)

11 The core of all discussions on the 'social issue' also includes estimations on the relation between economy and eugenics or genetic biology (Schwartz, 1989, p. 487) as well as the continuity or discontinuity of eugenics and racial hygiene. This concerns a discussion of the provocative suggestion of Schwartz (1989) that, seen as a whole, it is more the *possibility* of a synthesis of national socialist ideology and eugenics that should be accentuated:

. . . whereby, admittedly, more is said about national socialism, its programmatic eclecticism, and its intellectual vacuum than about eugenics. A closer
look at Hitler's goals would additionally reveal that he was less concerned
with the realization of scientifically acceptable 'race-improvement programs'
than the eugenic and thereby scientistically more superficially legitimated
propagation of a racist ideal of breeding . . . Only those who sovereignly attempt to ignore the restriction and radicalization of the eugenic spectrum
through the violent elimination of its 'left wing' in 1933 can perceive the
legitimate 'heir' of the eugenic goals and their allegedly inherent extremism
in NS race hygiene. (Schwartz, 1989, p. 475, translated; pp. 476–7)

12 See Abelshauser (1987):

Admittedly without using the term itself, the Weimar constitution based its
recognition of the welfare state on a number of sociolegal individual guarantees that expressed the principle of the social state with more intensity than
the constitution at Bonn . . . With this, the Weimar constitution placed all
economic activity under a 'social reservation' that although it was not as
powerful as the dominant principle of contractual freedom, nonetheless modified it essentially. Even when the Weimar republic was unable to fulfill the
majority of these guarantees in practice, these were nonetheless not just dec-
lamatory constitutional goals. They justified directly effective far-reaching
state rights of intervention, in some cases also the individual's legal duties
and rights to protection. (Abelshauser, p. 11, translated)

13 Of interest in this context is Fenner's (1936, p. 43) note that a proclamation was being
prepared that would change the title of *Volkspflegerin* (*Volk* welfare workers) to
Gesundheitspflegerin (health welfare workers).
14 These relationships were addressed clearly on the occasion of the establishment of a
'social scientific institute for *Volk* welfare' at the University of Berlin in 1937:

The tasks of this institute will include the attainment of the desirable clarity
in the basic commitment of welfare to the national socialist world view through
which its need is justified and through which it can simultaneously be limited
in its extent. (Vorländer, 1988, Document 182, translated)

15 Breeding and race-improvement ideology took a particularly 'strange' form at *Lebensborn*.
Treated as satire, there is an exquisite presentation of this in Hrabal's novel (1988,
pp. 165–217).
16 This also makes it clear why we cannot agree with Vorländer's (1988, p. 1) idea that
the NSV should be viewed as a welfare organization.
17 We consider that this lack of a special historical position also leads to misunderstood
formulations in Broszat (1988, p. 279) on the DAF's plans for a 'general *Volk* insurance
scheme' whose underlying ideas were later found once more in the social welfare
legislation of the Federal Republic of Germany.

References

ABELSHAUSER, W. (1987) 'Die Weimarer Republik: Ein Wohlfahrtsstaat?', *Die Weimarer
Republik als Wohlfahrtsstaat: Zum Verhältnis von Wirtschafts- und Sozialpolitik in der
Industriegesellschaft*, Wiesbaden, Steiner.

ADORNO, TH.W. (1977) 'Was bedeutet: Aufarbeitung der Vergangenheit?', *Gesammelte Schriften*, **10**, 2, Frankfurt/M., Suhrkamp.

ALBER, J. (1989) 'Nationalsozialismus und Modernisierung', *Kölner Zeitschrift für Soziologie und Sozialpsychologie*, **41**, pp. 346–65.

ALTHAUS, H. (1937) *Nationalsozialistische Volkswohlfahrt: Wesen, Aufgaben und Aufbau*, **3**, Überarbeitete Auflage, Berlin, Junker und Dünnhaupt.

ALY, G. and ROTH, K.H. (1984) *Die Restlose Erfassung: Volkszählen, Identifizieren, Aussondern im Nationalsozialismus*, Berlin, Rotbuch.

BALDWIN, P. (1990) 'Social interpretations of Nazism: Renewing a Tradition', *Journal of Contemporary History*, **25**, pp. 5–37.

BARKAI, A. (1988) *Vom Boykott zur Endjudung: Der wirtschaftliche Existenzkampf der Juden im Dritten Reich 1933–1943*, Frankfurt/M., Fischer.

BECKER, O. (1938) 'Nordische Metaphysik', *Rasse*, **5**, pp. 81–93.

BLOCH, E. (1970) *Politische Messungen: Pestzeit, Vormärz*, Frankfurt/M., Suhrkamp.

BOEHM, M.H. (1935) *Volkstheorie und Volkstumspolitik der Gegenwart*, Berlin, Junker und Dünnhaupt.

BONS, J. (1989) 'Der Kampf um die Seele des deutschen Arbeiters: Zur Arbeiterpolitik der NSDAP 1920–1933', *Internationale Wissenschaftliche Korrespondenz zur Geschichte der Deutschen Arbeiterbewegung*, **25**, pp. 11–41.

BROSZAT, M. (1983) 'Zur Struktur der NS-Massenbewegung', *Vierteljahreshefte für Zeitgeschichte*, **31**, pp. 52–76.

BROSZAT, M. (1988) *Plädoyer für eine Historisierung des Nationalsozialismus*, Nach Hitler, München, dtv.

BROWNING, CH.R. (1989) 'Vernichtung und Arbeit', *Konkret*, **12**, pp. 64–9.

BRUCKER, L. (1934) *Die Kommende Sozialpolitik im 3. Reich*, Berlin, Verlag für Sozialpolitik.

BUTLER, R. (1941) *The Roots of National Socialism 1783–1933*, London, Faber and Faber.

DÖBLIN, A. (1978) *November 1918*, 4 Bde, München, dtv.

EBBINGHAUS, A. (Ed) (1987) *Opfer und Täterinnen: Frauenbiographien des Nationalsozialismus*, Nördlingen, Delphi.

ELFFERDING, W. (1980) 'Opferritual und Volksgemeinschaftsdiskurs am Beispiel des Winterhilfswerks (WHW)', *Argument-Sonderband*, **62**, pp. 199–226.

ELIAS, N. (1989) *Studien über die Deutschen*, Frankfurt/M., Suhrkamp.

FELDMAN, G.D. (1986) 'The Weimarer Republic: A Problem of Modernization?', *Archiv für Sozialgeschichte*, **26**, pp. 1–26.

FENNER, K. (1936) *Mutter und Kind: Grundlagen und Aufbau der Fürsorge im Heutigen Staate*, Leipzig, J.A. Barth.

FISCHER, A. (1954) 'Die Problematik des Sozialbeamtentums', *Leben und Werk*, **3/4**, München, Bayerischer Schulbuchverlag.

FRAUENDIENER, F. (1937) *Der Gestaltwandel der Staatlichen Jugendfürsorge*, Berlin, Junker und Dünnhaupt.

GAY, P. (1987) *Die Republik der Außenseiter: Geist und Kultur in der Weimarer Zeit 1918–1933*, Frankfurt/M., Suhrkamp.

GEYER, M.H. (1989) 'Soziale Sicherheit und wirtschaftlicher Fortschritt', *Geschichte und Gesellschaft*, **15**, pp. 382–406.

GREBING, H. (1986) *Der Deutsche Sonderweg in Europa 1806–1945: Eine Kritik*, Stuttgart, Kohlhammer.

GRUNBERGER, R. (1971) *A Social History of the Third Reich*, London, Weidenfeld and Nicolson.

GUSE, M. and KOHRS, A. (1989) 'Zur Entpädagogisierung der Jugendfürsorge in den Jahren

1922–1945', in Otto and Sünker (Eds) *Soziale Arbeit und Faschismus*, Frankfurt/M., Suhrkamp.

HANSEN, E. (1991) *Wohlfahrtspolitik im NS-Staat: Motivation, Konflikte und Machtstrukturen im 'Sozialismus der Tat' des Dritten Reiches*, Augsburg, Maro.

HARVEY, E. (1989) 'Die Jugendfürsorge in der Endphase der Weimarer Republik', in OTTO, H.-U. and SÜNKER, H. (Eds) *Soziale Arbeit und Faschismus*, Frankfurt/M., Suhrkamp.

HEGEL, G.W.F. (1955) *Grundlinien der Philosophie des Rechts*, Hamburg, Meiner.

HEIM, S. and ALY, G. (1987) 'Die Ökonomie der Endlösung: Menschenvernichtung und wirtschaftliche Neuordnung', in *Beiträge zur Nationalsozialistischen Gesundheits- und Sozialpolitik 5: Sozialpolitik und Judenvernichtung*, Berlin, Rotbuch.

HELLER, A. (1978) *Das Alltagsleben: Versuch einer Erklärung der Individuellen Reproduktion*, H. Joas (Ed) Frankfurt/M., Suhrkamp.

HEPP, M. (1987) 'Vorhof zur Hölle: Mädchen im Jugendschutzlager Uckermark', *Ebbinghaus*.

HERBERT, U. (1989) 'Arbeiterschaft im Dritten Reich', *Geschichte und Gesellschaft*, **15**, pp. 320–60.

HERF, J. (1984) *Reactionary Modernism*, New York, Cambridge University Press.

HILGENFELDT, E. (1936) 'Die Volksgemeinschaft als Ausgangspunkt und Ziel im heutigen Deutschland', in ALTHAUS, H. (Ed) *Soziale Arbeit und Gemeinschaft*, Karlsruhe, G. Brann.

HILGENFELDT, E. (1937) *Idee der Nationalsozialistischen Wohlfahrtspflege*, München/Berlin, Zentralverlag der NSDAP.

HOMBURG, H. (1985) 'Vom Arbeitslosen zum Zwangsarbeiter', *Archiv für Sozialgeschichte*, **25**, pp. 251–98.

HRABAL, B. (1988) *Ich Habe den Englischen König Bedient*, Frankfurt/M., Suhrkamp.

HSIAO, Y. (1943) *Die Bedeutung der Formationserziehung für die Vorbereitung der Landesverteidigung in den Jugendorganisationen Deutschlands und Chinas*, Diss. Berlin.

JASCHKE, H.-G. (1982) *Soziale Basis und soziale Funktion des Nationalsozialismus*, Opladen, Westdeutscher Verlag.

JUNK, M. (1940) *Mädelberufe in Vorderster Front: Über Hauswirtschaft, Säuglings- und Krankenpflege zur Volkspflege*, Stuttgart, Union Deutsche Verlagsgesellschaft.

KAISER, J.-CH. (1989) *Sozialer Protestantismus im 20. Jahrhundert: Beiträge zur Geschichte der Inneren Mission 1914–1945*, München, Oldenbourg.

KATER, M.H. (1983) 'Die Gesundheitsführung des deutschen Volkes', *Medizinhistorisches Journal*, **18**, pp. 349–75.

KERSHAW, I. (1988) 'Hitlers Popularität: Mythos und Realität im Dritten Reich', in MOMMSEN, H. and WILLEMS, S. (Eds) *Herrschaftsalltag im Dritten Reich: Studien und Texte*, Düsseldorf, Schwann.

KERSHAW, I. (1989) 'The Nazi State: An exceptional State?', *New Left Review*, **176**, pp. 47–67.

KILIAN, H. (1971) *Das Enteignete Bewußtsein*, Neuwied, Luchterhand.

KIRMEß, A. (1939) *Von der Wohlfahrtspflege zur Volkspflege*, Diss. München.

KNÜPPEL-DÄHNE, H. and MITROVIC, E. (1989) 'Helfen und Dienen: Die Arbeit von Fürsorgerinnen im Hamburger öffentlichen Dienst während des Nationalsozialismus', in OTTO, H.-U. and SÜNKER, H. (Eds) *Soziale Arbeit und Faschismus*, Frankfurt/M., Suhrkamp.

KOHLHASE, F. (1940) *Die Kinderreichen in Bielefeld, eine Soziologisch-biologische Untersuchung als Beitrag zum Problem der Kinderreichen*, Diss. Freiburg.

KRIECK, E. (1932) *Nationalpolitische Erziehung*, **3**, Auflage, Leipzig, Armanen.

LARENZ, K. (1938) 'Die Bedeutung der völkischen Sitte in Hegels Staatsphilosophie', *Zeitschrift für Gesamte Staatswissenschaft*, **98**, pp. 109–50.

LEFEBVRE, H. (1974) *Die Zukunft des Kapitalismus: Die Reproduktion der Produktionsverhältnisse*, München, List.

LEFEBVRE, H. (1978) *Einführung in die Modernität*, Frankfurt/M., Suhrkamp.

LEFEBVRE, H. (1987) *Kritik des Alltagslebens: Grundrisse einer Soziologie der Alltäglichkeit*, Mit einem Nachwort zu dieser Ausgabe von Dewe, Ferchhoff and Sünker, Frankfurt/M., Fischer.

LEFEBVRE, H. (1989) *La Somme et le Reste*, Paris, Meridiens Klincksieck.

LEIBFRIED, ST., HANSEN, E. and HEISIG, M. (1986) 'Bedarfsprinzip und Existenzminimum unter dem NS-Regime: Zur Aufstieg und Fall der Regelsätze in der Fürsorge', in OTTO, H.-U. and SÜNKER, H. (Eds) *Soziale Arbeit und Faschismus*, Frankfurt/M., Suhrkamp.

LUDWIG, J. (1989) *Boykott, Enteignung, Mord: Die Endjudung der Deutschen Wirtschaft*, Hamburg, Facta.

MARCUSE, H. (1979) 'Der Kampf gegen den Liberalismus in der totalitären Staatsauffassung', in *Schriften*, 3, Frankfurt/M., Suhrkamp.

MARTINI, O. (1938) 'Die Aufgaben der öffentlichen Fürsorge nach Beendigung der Massenarbeitslosigkeit', in *Neue Familien- und Arbeitspolitische Aufgaben der Deutschen Wohlfahrtspflege, Bericht über die Tagung des Deutschen Vereins für Öffentliche und Private Fürsorge am 23. und 24.5.1938 in Würzburg*, Frankfurt/M., Heinrich Demuth.

MASON, T. (1975) *Arbeiterklasse und Volksgemeinschaft: Dokumente und Materialien zur Deutschen Arbeiterpolitik 1936–1939*, Opladen, Westdeutscher Verlag.

MASON, T. (1995a) *Nazism, Fascism and the Working Class*, Cambridge, Cambridge University Press.

MASON, T. (1995b) 'Intention and explanation: A current controversy about the interpretation of National Socialism', in MASON, T. *Nazism, Fascism and the Working Class*, Cambridge, Cambridge University Press.

MASON, T. (1995c) 'The containment of the working class in Nazi Germany', in MASON, T. *Nazism, Fascism and the Working Class*, Cambridge, Cambridge University Press.

MASON, T. (1995d) 'The origins of the law on the organization of national labour of 20 January 1934', in MASON, T. *Nazism, Fascism and the Working Class*, Cambridge, Cambridge University Press.

MOMMSEN, H. (1988) 'Einleitung', in MOMMSEN, H. and WILLEMS, S. (Eds) *Herrschaftsalltag im Dritten Reich: Studien und Texte*, Düsseldorf, Schwann.

MOMMSEN, H. and WILLEMS, S. (Eds) (1988) *Herrschaftsalltag im Dritten Reich: Studien und Texte*, Düsseldorf, Schwann.

NEUMANN, F. (1984) *Behemoth: Struktur und Praxis des Nationalsozialismus 1933–1944*, Herausgegeben und mit einem Nachwort von G. Schäfer, Frankfurt/M., Fischer.

OTTEN, K. (1989) *Geplante Illusion: Eine Analyse des Faschismus*, Frankfurt/M., Luchterhand.

OTTO, H.-U. and SÜNKER, H. (Eds) (1986) *Soziale Arbeit und Faschismus: Volkspflege und Pädagogik im Nationalsozialismus*, Bielefeld, Böllert — KT Verlag.

OTTO, H.-U. and SÜNKER, H. (Eds) (1989) *Soziale Arbeit und Faschismus*, Frankfurt/M., Suhrkamp.

PEUKERT, D. (1982) *Volksgenossen und Gemeinschaftsfremde: Anpassung, Ausmerze und Aufbegehren unter dem Nationalsozialismus*, Köln, Bund.

PEUKERT, D. (1985) *Grenzen der Sozialdisziplinierung: Aufstieg und Krise der Deutschen Jugendfürsorge 1878 bis 1932*, Köln, Bund.

PEUKERT, D. (1987) *Die Weimarer Republik: Krisenjahre der Klassischen Moderne*, Frankfurt/M., Suhrkamp.

PEUKERT, D. (1988) 'Die Genesis der Endlösung aus dem Geiste der Wissenschaft', in Forum für Philosophie Bad Homburg (Ed), *Zerstörung des Moralischen Selbstbewußtseins: Chance oder Gefährdung?*, Frankfurt/M., Suhrkamp.

PEUKERT, D. (1989) 'Sozialpädagogik', in LANGEWIESCHE, H. and TENORT, H.-E. (Eds) *Handbuch der Deutschen Bildungsgeschichte, Bd. V: 1918–1945, Die Weimarer Republik und die Nationalsozialistische Diktatur*, München, Beck.

PRINZ, M. (1985) 'Sozialpolitik im Wandel der Staatspolitik? — Das Dritte Reich und die Tradition bürgerlicher Sozialreform', in BRUCH, R.v. (Ed) *Weder Kommunismus noch Kapitalismus: Bürgerliche Sozialreform in Deutschland vom Vormärz bis zur Ära Adenauer*, München, Beck.

REICHERT, H. (1935) *Die Neuordnung der Wohlfahrtspflege im Nationalsozialistischen Staate*, Diss. Breslau.

SAAGE, T. (1987) 'Der italienische und der deutsche Faschismus', *Arbeiterbewegung, Faschismus, Neokonservatismus*, Frankfurt/M., Suhrkamp.

SCHEELE, W. (1939) *Gemeinschaft und Völkische Lebensordnung*, Berlin, Junker und Dünnhaupt.

SCHLEICHER, R. (1939) *Die Wandlung der Wohlfahrtspflege durch den Nationalsozialismus*, Diss. Heidelberg.

SCHNURR, ST. (1988) 'Vom Wohlfahrtsstaat zum Erziehungsstaat: Sozialpolitik und soziale Arbeit in der Weimarer Republik und im Nationalsozialismus', *Widersprüche*, **8**, pp. 47–64.

SCHWARTZ, M. (1989) 'Sozialismus und Eugenik: zur fälligen Revision eines Geschichtsbildes', *Internationale Wissenschaftliche Korrespondenz zur Geschichte der Deutschen Arbeiterbewegung*, **25**, pp. 465–89.

SELDTE, F. (1939) *Sozialpolitik im 3. Reich 1933–1938*, München, C.H. Beck'sche Verlagsbuchhandlung.

SIEGEL, T. (1988) 'Rationalisierung statt Klassenkampf: Zur Rolle der Deutschen Arbeitsfront in der nationalsozialistischen Ordnung der Arbeit', in MOMMSEN, H. and WILLEMS, S. (Eds) *Herrschaftsalltag im Dritten Reich: Studien und Texte*, Düsseldorf, Schwann.

SOPADE (1935) *Deutschland-Berichte. Zweiter Jahrgang* (Reprint) (1990), Frankfurt/M., Verlag Petra Nettelbeck.

SPURK, J. (1988) 'Von der Volksgemeinschaft zur Re-Vergemeinschaftung in der Krise des Fordismus: Überlegungen zum Verhältnis von Gemeinschaft und Gesellschaft in der deutschen Geschichte', *Prokla*, **18**, pp. 57–75.

STOLLMANN, R. (1976) 'Faschistische Politik als Gesamtkunstwerk: Tendenzen der Ästhetisierung des politischen Lebens im Nationalsozialismus', in Denkler and Pruemm (Eds) *Die Deutsche Literatur im Dritten Reich*, Stuttgart, Reclam.

SÜNKER, H. (1989a) 'Subjectivity and social work', *Education*, **40**, pp. 95–116.

SÜNKER, H. (1989b) *Bildung, Alltag und Subjektivität*, Weinheim, Deutscher Studienverlag.

SÜNKER, H. (1992) 'The discourse of social work: Normalization verus the autonomy of life praxis', in OTTO, H.U. and FLÖSSER, G. (Eds) *How to Organize Prevention*, Berlin, New York, De Gruyter.

TENNSTEDT, F. (1987) 'Wohltat und Interesse', *Geschichte und Gesellschaft*, **13**, pp. 157–80.

THEUNISSEN, M. (1982) 'Die verdrängte Intersubjektivität in Hegels Philosophie des Rechts', HENRICH, D. and HORSTMANN, R.P. (Eds) *Hegel Philosophie des Rechts: Die Theorie der Rechtsformen und ihre Logik*, Stuttgart, Klett-Cota.

VOGES, M. (1982) 'Klassenkampf in der Betriebsgemeinschaft', *Archiv für Sozialgeschichte*, **21**, pp. 329–83.

VORLÄNDER, H. (1988) *Die NSV. Darstellung und Dokumentation einer Nationalsozialistischen Organisation*, Boppard, Harald Boldt.

WAGNER, E. (1935) *Grundfragen einer Artbewußten Fürsorge*, Berlin, Heymanns.

WAGNER, P. (1988) 'Das Gesetz über die Behandlung Gemeinschaftsfremder: Die Kriminalpolizei und die Vernichtung des Verbrechertums', *Beiträge zur Nationalsozialistischen Gesundheits- und Sozialpolitik*, **6**, Berlin, Rotbuch.

WEHLER, H.-U. (1987) *Deutsche Gesellschaftsgeschichte, Erster Band: Vom Feudalismus des Alten Reiches bis zur Defensiven Modernisierung der Reformära 1700–1815*, München, Beck.

WEINGART, P., KROLL, J. and BAYERTZ, K. (1988) *Rasse, Blut und Gene: Geschichte der Eugenik und Rassenhygiene in Deutschland*, Frankfurt/M., Suhrkamp.

WINKLER, H.A. (1977a) 'Vom Mythos der Volksgemeinschaft', *Archiv für Sozialgeschichte*, **17**, pp. 484–90.

WINKLER, H.A. (1977b) 'Der entbehrliche Stand: Zur Mittelstandspolitik im Dritten Reich', *Archiv für Sozialgeschichte*, **17**, pp. 1–40.

WINKLER, H.A. (1987) *Der Weg in die Katastrophe: Arbeiter und Arbeiterbewegung in der Weimarer Republik 1930–1933*, Berlin/Bonn, Dietz.

DE WITT, TH. (1978) 'The economics and politics of welfare in the Third Reich', *Central European History*, **11**, pp. 256–78.

ZIEBURA, G. (1979) *Frankreich 1789–1870: Entstehung einer Bürgerlichen Gesellschaftsformation*, Frankfurt/M., Campus.

ZIMMERMANN, F.J. (o.J.) (1938/9) *Die NS-Volkswohlfahrt und das Winterhilfswerk des Deutschen Volkes*, Würzburg, Memminger.

3 National-Socialist Youth Policy and the Labour Service: The Work Camp as an Instrument of Social Discipline

Peter Dudek

Introduction

Neither the idea of a compulsory social service nor the emphasis on labour as a goal and means of education were invented by the national socialists. It was far more the case that both had been the subject of intensive discussion in various contexts within educational science since the turn of the century, and they had been justified in sociopolitical, anthropological, and ethical terms. In such disparate fields as vocational training and further training, juvenile detention, and welfare education, the labour school movement or the settlement movement in Germany's eastern regions, physical labour was viewed continuously as educationally valuable, and educators focused their attention here more on questions of individuation and opportunities for socialization than on the status of work as alienated paid labour. Contemporary youth research also viewed employment as a central element of juvenile identity formation, even when their ideal concept of cultural puberty could provide only an inadequate description of the life and working world of the majority of the young. In a working society, which additionally provided only an inadequate sociopolitical response to the mass unemployment toward the end of the 1920s, any kind of employment seemed to be an appropriate way of helping to ameliorate social and political disintegration. Thus, adult educators and social workers viewed the organization of leisure-time, training, and care for unemployed young persons as a broad task and activity field that justified their involvement in the voluntary labour service (*Freiwilliger Arbeitsdienst*, FAD) after 1931, also particularly because the interpretation of unemployment in the Weimar Republic was linked strongly to basic philosophical principles that also did not leave educators unaffected.

Other contexts apart from the question of the educational role of labour and the debate on filling in the 'disastrous gaps in education planning' (Seyfert, 1901) between the general school and the military barracks are involved in the discussion on a general compulsory service. In Germany, this commenced at the turn of the century with the discussion on the introduction of a compulsory community service for women, an obligatory service as a form of citizen's education for women (Dammer, 1988), which, in analogy to military service for men, should be made into a precondition for receiving civil rights. One of the strong supporters of this demand was the bourgeois woman's movement. They viewed it as an opportunity to socialize 'female abilities', namely, to extend their family duties to include social work. However, the passing of the National Assistance Service Act on December 2, 1916 during World War I was far more effective than these debates.[1] Linked to this and in light of the restrictive conditions of the Versailles treaty, the abolition of compulsory military service, the problem of occupational rehabilitation for former soldiers, and, finally, the introduction of a compulsory labour service in Bulgaria in 1920,[2] there arose a discussion on a labour service in the Weimar Republic that involved military-political, economic, and socioeducational arguments. Some aspects were scurrilous, such as the expectation that a labour service would bring about a fundamental renewal of social order; other aspects could be taken more seriously in political terms on the levels of parliament and administration. However, for whatever reasons, the idea of a compulsory work service triggered a search for new forms of life and reproduction in various political milieus beyond the limitations of the labour market; it led to a few work camp experiments within the youth movement and popular education (Dudek, 1985); and ended under the pressure of mass unemployment in the introduction of the FAD following the directives of June 5, 1931 and June 16, 1932.[3] After the summer of 1932, this was available for practically all young persons under the age of 25 for a maximum of forty weeks.

In the following, I shall not present a detailed discussion on either the ideas behind or the organizational history of the labour service (see Dudek, 1988; Köhler, 1967), but initially sketch *compulsory* labour service as a part of national-socialist youth policy. Second, I shall consider the *work camp* (*Lager*) as a location of collective disciplining, and finally present some provisional ideas on the thematic structure of the national-socialist idea of education based on the example of the labour service. Mostly, I shall avoid reference to pure agitation and propaganda documents but refer to relevant doctoral dissertations and practice-related articles from educational journals. I shall also not discuss the current controversy on the status of education and educational science under national socialism that presently seems to be concerned more with statements and the demarcation of fields (Hermann, 1989) rather than with any new research findings. Nonetheless, two comments are necessary in this domain: (a) I shall avoid terms such as 'uneducation', 'perversion', or 're-education'. (b) Previous attempts to ascertain the relation between the FAD and the *Reichsarbeitsdienst* (labour service, RAD) have used the idea of continuity and discontinuity. Authors who emphasize the compulsory character of the RAD and its propaganda function (Köhler, 1967; Lingelbach, 1970) and the activists in the work-camp movement before 1933 tend to hypothesize a disruption here, whereas authors who argue in terms of the theory of fascism (Bartz and Mor, 1979; Rasche, 1968; Schlicker, 1968) view the FAD as a prior form and the basis for the future RAD. I do not wish to make a decisive contribution to these diverging interpretations, but it would seem to me that the alternatives of disruption or continuity are unsatisfactory in terms of educational history and are generally inappropriate for this analysis.

Labour Service as Part of National-Socialist Youth Policy

The introduction of the FAD in 1931 as an instrument of social diffusion by the emergency governments and as a defensive response to the growing number of advocates of a compulsory service was in no way only a right-wing project. Conceived as a short-term labour-market policy measure for the 'mental distraction' (Minister of Labour Stegerwald) of unemployed youth, to be controlled by the employment offices who delegated the individual work measures to providers of the service and providers of work, the entire political spectrum of the Weimar Republic with the exception of the communists were involved in the FAD. It was the object of far-reaching hopes and illusions that went beyond the political situation. For the right-wing associations, the bourgeois youth movement, parts of the Social Democratic Party (SPD), and the trade unions, the labour service was not just a crisis measure of labour-market policy but a lever for redesigning society, be it in the culture-critical sense of a new people's order, in the corporativistic sense of fascism, or from a socialist perspective.[4] Labour, service, and the work camp as a lifestyle for the young were ideas that could achieve a consensus across political fronts in the Weimar Republic. Although they could be interpreted in different ways, their claims to validity were questioned only by minorities.

Konstantin Hierl, who was appointed the 'Fuhrer's representative for the labour service of the NSDAP' in 1930, headed a team that undertook the ideological and organizational preparations for a compulsory labour service for the party well before 1933. In the states of Anhalt, Thuringia, Oldenburg, and Mecklenburg-Schwerin, the concept of a national-socialist compulsory labour service could already be studied in practice in 1932. It was not intended as an instrument to fight unemployment, but as an instrument of collective disciplining in the three stages of compulsory schooling, compulsory work, and compulsory military service. In 1930, in an address given before Hitler, Hierl emphasized the role of the labour service as an 'educational institute' whose purpose was to provide the 'state with an army of workers'.

This army of workers was, according to Hierl:

> ... a means with which the leaders of the state can carry out large-scale projects that serve far-reaching political and cultural goals. This work army is furthermore a means of political education in accordance with the spirit of national socialism; an educational institute in which the brow and the fist of the workers can be welded together. (cited in Hase, 1940, p. 29, translated)

Although the NSDAP rejected the FAD officially, it participated through 'neutral' associations for whom work camps primarily served as a political and paramilitary training. When Hitler finally announced the introduction of a general compulsory labour service on May 1, 1933, the decisive preparations had already been made. The NSDAP possessed detailed organizational plans that Hierl and his colleagues also wanted to turn into reality. The directive of April 28, 1933 (RABl. I, 1933, pp. 124–5)

Table 3.1: Number of Youths in the RAD From 1935 to 1938

Date	Men	Women
December 1935	182,370	10,278
June 1936	204,606	11,739
December 1936	186,733	10,175
June 1937	251,066	14,148
December 1937	165,576	17,946
June 1938	297,543	24,652

Source: Petrick, 1968, p. 158

laid down that only the *Stahlhelm* (Nationalist Association of Ex-Servicemen) and the national-socialist *Reichsverband Deutscher Arbeitsdienstverbände e. V.* were allowed to provide FAD services. Only one day later, a circular signed by Hierl and the National Minister of Labour Seldte sent to all district commissars and district leaders contained the following statement: 'The introduction of the ADP (*Arbeitsdienstpflicht* = compulsory labour service; P.D.) should be so prepared that the first six-month cohort of compulsory service can be drafted by the end of this year.'[5] After the exclusion of the *Stahlhelm*, the *Nationalsozialistische Arbeitsdienst e. V.* was set up on February 2, 1934 as the only provider of services and as a recognized body in public law. In terms of its structure, this was a party organization that was directly responsible to Hitler (Brauer, 1935; Flake, 1935) and linked to the national administration through leading persons who held posts in both bodies (Vogelsang, 1966). It was also given legal disciplinary powers after December 13, 1934.

Nonetheless, Hierl and his colleagues had to make concessions regarding their wide-scale labour service plans (Hierl, 1932, 1934; Stellrecht, 1933, 1934) within the anarchy of competencies that characterized the NS state. The RAD Act of June 25, 1935 introduced a six-month compulsory labour service for 'Aryan' males aged between 18 and 25 years. This 'honorable service to the German *Volk*' should 'rear German youth in the spirit of national socialism to a *Volk* community and to a true concept of work, above all, to a proper respect for manual labour' (RGBl. I, 1935, p. 769, translated). The quantitatively less important labour service for female youth was integrated into the RAD only in 1937 after several organizational restructurings. It was only after the outbreak of World War II that compulsory labour service for female youth was introduced on September 4, 1939. At this time, 36,219 young women were integrated into the RADwj (Iffland, 1941, p. 59).

The discrepancies between the numbers of male and female participants was already evident in the FAD. It reached its peak in November 1932, when it received state funding to the tune of 65 million Reichsmarks and had 285,494 members. However, only about 5 per cent of its members were young women. A glance at the development of the RAD between 1935 and 1938 confirms this imbalance (Table 3.1).

It can be ascertained in this context that the ambitious plans to expand the compulsory labour service in the second half of the 1930s were frustrated by the military and economic interests of the NS regime itself and hampered by the confusion of competencies in the administration.

Although several doctoral dissertations in political science and economics written around 1935 tried to confirm the economic necessity for a compulsory labour service (e.g., Eich, 1936; Humann, 1934; Kraftmeier, 1934; Scheins, 1935), from today's perspective, the economic utility of clearance of moor and wasteland, the land and settlement work, as well as activities in domestic service and agriculture, has to be viewed as rather meager. In addition, even before 1939, the RAD was increasingly involved in projects that had little to do with its original goals. After the outbreak of war, it became increasingly under the control of the army (Absolon, 1958; Benz, 1968, p. 545). The expansion plans of the RADwJ also did not correspond to the labour-market policy situation at the end of the 1930s when industry was reporting an increasing recruitment of female labour. Under the impact of the war, 'labour girls' were mostly recruited into the *Kriegshilfsdienst* (war assistance service, KHD) after October 1941. After the winter of 1942–3, this meant, in practice, assignment to the armaments industry. The conflict between ideology and economics in the female labour service identified by Bajohr (1980) was, from the very onset, also a structural problem of the RAD, because compulsory labour service proved to be an impediment to the purposeful promotion of the rearmament plans of the military in NS education and vocational training policy. As early as 1935, secondary school graduates could already be absolved from labour service if they volunteered for officer training. After October 10, 1936, labour service was reduced to two months for future officers. There were also similar reductions after the winter of 1936–7 for future technical students who could enrol for college even without confirmation that they had completed their labour service following a decree by the national education ministry (Kersting, 1989, pp. 46–50).

At no time, it has to be ascertained, were the interests and the life situation of youth the starting point for national-socialist efforts in the labour service. It was always their instrumentalization for the fictitious interests of the 'German *Volk*'. According to Hierl (1934), 'the unselfish commitment of youth was needed for the *Volk* to rise up again' (p. 13, translated).[6] In any final assessment of the history of the RAD, the low economic utility of its preindustrial labour projects during the 1930s is conspicuous, and the later conflicts between the ideology of work training and the interests of rearmament and war policy are clear.[7] With only a slight degree of exaggeration, one can say that the major contribution of national-socialist labour service policy after 1933 was to improve unemployment statistics, because young agricultural helpers, labour service participants, and relief workers were no longer registered as unemployed. Thus of the 3.5 million persons who had purportedly found a job again by mid-1934, 600,000 were relief workers and 400,000 were youths who had been assigned to agriculture for low pay (Mason, 1977, p. 127).

On the other side, Hierl and his closest colleagues Hellmuth Stellrecht, Fritz Edel, Will Decker, and Hermann Kretzschmann emphasized the educational nature of the RAD in numerous publications. Even in 1942, Wolfgang Scheibe was still able to proclaim, 'The goal of the total registration of the young members of the *Volk* by the national labour service is to train a national-socialist attitude toward the community and toward work' (p. 18 translated). Like the SA and sectors of the Hitler Youth leadership, the planners of the national-socialist labour service exploited the ideological construct of 'German socialism' up to 1934. Just as, for example, Baldur von Schirach reduced the concept of socialism to the symbol of the standard uniform in his 1933–4 speeches (Dudek, 1987), Hierl did exactly the same to the terms 'service' and 'honor of labour'.

Compulsory labour service should create, above all, the great training school for German socialism, that is the German *Volk* community. There is no better means of overcoming the social divisions, class hatred, and class arrogance than when the son of the factory director and the young factory worker, the young academic and the agricultural worker perform the same service in the same uniform and with the same food as a service of honor for the people and fatherland that they share (Hierl, 1934, p. 14, translated).

Although work training in fascism cannot be reduced to the RAD when one considers the basic technical training at general schools and vocational schools or the domestic-science training for girls that also served to form attitudes and character according to the spirit of national socialism (Mager, 1970), compulsory labour service was nonetheless the most extreme form of collective disciplining. Alongside the RAD, further compulsory services as part of NS youth policy partially overlapped and partially competed with the RAD. One can recall, for example, the introduction of the half year of labour for secondary school graduates in 1934 in order to counteract the crisis due to insufficient college capacity, the decree on the duty year for girls of December 15, 1938, the national vocational competition (*Reichsberufswettbewerb*), or the introduction of the 1-year period of agricultural labour in 1934. Most of these extracurricular measures of NS youth policy were characterized by being based on education policy, consisting of simple physical labour, and serving collective disciplining rather than vocational training or further training.

The labour service shared with them the claim to impose a policy of nationalizing youth education to counteract the traditional childrearing institutions of the school and the family, and thus enforce the national-socialist demands for total control over all youth and all phases and areas of life. Like the Hitler Youth, it also possessed its own disciplinary laws, that is, sanctions that should guarantee the trouble-free functioning of the compulsory labour system. If one views the RAD not from the perspective of labour-market-policy strategies, but sees it as *one* means of promoting the NS youth policy of social disciplining that already differs from the FAD in that its clients are no longer just the unemployed but all youth, several questions arise:[8] Which instruments and techniques of persuasion did the educational policy of the RAD possess? How did youth respond to their compulsory service? Did they accept the ideology of service and serving, or did they view their labour service as a compulsory measure that hindered their own career plans? Did the institution of the labour service itself open up career opportunities for work-service leaders with social-educational intentions?[9] Finally, what were the specific effects of NS work training? Research has yet to tackle such questions, and it will also not be possible to provide any final answers here.

In my opinion, the core of national-socialist labour service education was not so much primitive manual labour as an educational means and also not the building site as a 'decisive place of education' (Götting, 1944, p. 19, translated), but it lay in the specific configuration of the *work camp* as a total institution of national-socialist character training. In the history of the bourgeois and proletarian youth movements, the work camp far away from the large cities took on an important function in young group formation. Away from the 'nest' or the 'home', it was the social location in which socialization could be practised under one's own control. While accepted and cultivated as a voluntary way of life in the youth movement, in the system of collective education of the Third Reich, the work camp became *the* decisive instrument for establishing the compulsory community, a means of maintaining and channeling upward job mobility, for separating and excluding opposition and racially discriminated groups. Those who were not worthy, willing, or able to be part of the community in national-socialist terms were drawn into the meshes of a comprehensive work camp system that ranged from re-education camps, punishment camps, assembly centres, work camps, (Peukert, 1981), work education camps (Werner, 1981), prisoner-of-war camps, up to the concentration camps, and this sequence reveals the progressively cumulative radicalization of the NS regime.

The Camp as a Location of Collective Disciplining

Although national socialism did not invent the camp system, it did expand it into an industrially perfected machine of destruction. Alongside these types of camp for re-education, exclusion, and eradication, the camp also had to provide integrating and educational functions in the national-socialist education concept. Both exclusion and integration camps were based on a 'dropping out of the normal spheres of life and work, on a giving oneself up to highly authoritarian and/or highly servile customs' (Krause-Vilmar, 1984, p. 36, translated). Integration camps were considered to be the social location that seemed to promise the greatest chances of success for the 'philosophical schooling' at the 'core of national-socialist education' (Mertens, 1937, p. 4, translated). Whether as schooling camps, military service camps, work camps, sports camps, or youth camps, national-socialist educators and psychologists discovered the camp as a new form of education.[10] And educational science tried to 'orient itself toward the nature and educational value of the camp just as it had previously tried to develop, for example, a theory of the school' (Arp, 1939, p. 29, translated). Educators developed an economics of space and time for camp education, they used their technical knowledge on the techniques of persuasion, and they integrated this into a system of camp education. *In this sense*, the FAD was a precursor of the RAD. It was namely also a field of experimentation for camp education in which educational knowledge was gained below the level of education policy legitimation and handed on in the system of leadership schooling (Tsay, 1940, pp. 111–20).[11] Here, I am thinking less of the concrete contents of political schooling, but of the symbolic and ritual forms of persuasion. In 'education in camps and closed ranks' (Hermannsen, 1938), the national socialists believed that they had found a means that seemed to correspond best to their educational *interventions*.

Closed camps such as those of the RAD can be interpreted as total institutions for educating and controlling their inmates. They are subject to strict rules and aim to foster loyalty and discipline. They are characterized by a far-reaching removal of the distinctions between work, leisure time, and the family. All phases of the day are planned precisely and follow a system of fixed rules. This scenario also includes rituals and stylistic forms such as flag raising, competitions, song, festivities, uniforms, and marching in closed ranks. Transporting the young compulsory recruits into unfamiliar parts of the country and unfamiliar forms of accommodation, the intentional primitiveness of living conditions, as well as the hierarchical and unchangeable organization structures supplemented the wide range of social and psychological techniques of persuasion. Hellmut Petersen wrote about this in a doctoral dissertation on education in the labour service that was supervised by Gustav Deuchler:

> In these camps, influences from outside the labour service and the camp are excluded almost completely. Because of the difficulties raised by large spatial distances, the team has hardly any contact with another environment. These departments are completely independent and have to draw on their own resources. Leader and men are in continuous contact with each other. This establishes the preconditions for the amalgamation of the team into a fixed and narrow comradeship. (Deuchler, 1938, p. 63, translated)

Whereas the idea of the team and service represented the perspective that should bind the behaviour of the individual and the camp community into the collective '*Volk* community', the second goal, comradeship, which regulated the social relationships of the camp members and functioned as a catalyst to community formation, seemed to be at cross purposes to the hierarchic command structure of the camp. According to the educational science of the time, the success of this masculinity-fixed idea of education[12] was based on the person of the leader. In his twofold role as superior with the right to punish and as comrade, he was supposed to establish equality in subordination in the sense of national socialism. For those who did not easily give in to this social disciplining, national-socialist labour service pedagogics had the term of exclusion *kameradschaftsfremd* (hostile to comradeship; Petersen, 1938, p. 53). Those who were particularly hostile to comradeship were secondary school graduates and college students who lacked the necessary attitude toward labour service (Seipp, 1935, pp. 37–50) and all those 'who have something peculiar about them' (Petersen, 1938, p. 53, translated). The comradeship ideology of the NS youth education was not directed toward the individual but toward functionality. It was designed to strengthen group identification in the male-bonding subculture of the labour service; it was elicited through the shared experience of physical labour, in shared festivities and roll calls, the numerous formation exercises, and finally, in the uniforms of the participants. Education into 'political soldiers' was one of the basic goals of the RAD (Kretzschmann, 1935, pp. 382–5); the camp with its combination of isolation, political education, primitive labour, and controlled arrangement of experiences (e.g., Zahn, 1938) was the social location at which national socialism should be experienced. Within the framework of NS youth education, the camp was a means of education that was applied functionally in order to shape political mentalities. The idea of shaping people through camp education was in no way a negative privilege of the national socialists. Techniques and contents of functionable mentality shaping were already available from the experiences of the FAD.[13]

On the other hand, one cannot avoid recognizing that both the initial political situation of the RAD and also the intentions of the educators working in it differed from those of, for example, the FAD measures that have provided such lasting support to contemporary adult education and social work. Also the semantic equation of labour, service, and serving that may have made it easier for some educators to transfer to the RAD cannot cover over the differences between the labour-market-policy emergency measure of the FAD and the political-educational function of the RAD within the framework of NS youth policy. These differences are already reflected in the thematic structure of educational thought after 1933.[14]

The Labour Service as a Topic of Research in Educational Science

In 1925, Ernst Schulz handed in a doctoral dissertation to Max Sering and Eduard Spranger that painstakingly listed the arguments of the supporters and opponents of the labour service and evaluated them in terms of educational theory. Ten years later, this issue had been decided by power politics. Research in political, economic, and educational science turned toward the history, the economics, and the legal structure of the labour service. Although all this work emphasized the educational task of the labour service, even Will Decker[15] had to confirm in 1935 that 'of the 25 scientific works that have been written up to now on the labour service at German universities, only two deal exclusively with its economic side' (p. 6, translated). In this final section, I wish to examine the methodological and theoretical frameworks of some of the scientific studies on the labour service in order to ascertain which motives and which findings encouraged the young scientists of the time to approach the topic of labour service from the perspective of education and education science.

Asking such questions requires the assumption that alongside the rigid national-socialist practice of dismissal in the science system, and alongside the numerous political propaganda publications in the style of the 'heroic realism' (Marcuse) of *Volk* science, there must also have been something like a 'normal' production of scientific knowledge. In an analysis of several dissertations supervised by Ernst Krieck, Micha Brumlik has spoken of the 'new objectivity' and noted in his thoroughly disturbing conclusion that: 'That which I had read there reminded me in every aspect of the essays, master's theses, doctoral dissertations, or also publications that I have had to read over the last 10 years and more' (1980, p. 80, translated). If one relates this thesis to the formal structure of reasoning, to the intentions, methods, and ways of dealing with the scientific literature of the time, then my selection of doctoral dissertations on the FAD and the RAD also confirms this conclusion.[16]

I shall first examine the author's relationship to the topic: Schellenberg is concerned with documenting and analysing the practice of the FAD, emphasizing its socioeducational function, and testing whether it really fulfilled the aspirations for a moral certitude 'that participants in the service find once more, the renewed belief in a deeper meaning and purpose in work and life' (1932, p. 6, translated). Abel tries to 'ascertain and interpret the sociologically and psychologically important shifts in *Gestalt* within the male youths subjected to unemployment' in order to present a 'scientifically based total picture of these unemployed youths' (1935, p. 7, translated). Seipp's study of the half year of labour for secondary school graduates in 1934 already shows that the motive had changed decisively. Guided by the educational theories of Ernst Krieck and Phillip Hördt, he studies 'the issue of the lasting impact of the labour service on future college students and the closely related issue of the necessity of and the limits on the selection for college admission that it permits' (1935, p. VI, translated). Petersen does not just want to assess conditions in the RAD from an education theory perspective, but to 'judge, evaluate, and make recommendations' (1938, p. 9, translated). Kallsperger, in turn, understands her work as a 'contribution to a new German educational science in the service of the rebirth of our *Volk*', and she selects the reality of education in the RAD in order to 'present its effectiveness' (1939, p. 5, translated). The study by the Chinese graduate Tsay also tries to prove how the RAD 'fully and completely successfully' achieves its economic and educational 'goal' (1940, preface, translated). In contrast to this legal-sociological and predominantly descriptive work, the others are empirical studies. Seipp, Petersen, and Kallsperger have personal professional links to the labour service. Abel spent six weeks at an FAD camp in order to break down the social distance between the researcher and his object. All emphasize the basic conviction that only an intimate knowledge of the educational field of the labour service, that is, a kind of organizational knowledge, could guarantee the scientific validity of their statements. They also seem to be in command of the methodological repertoire of the empirical research of the times. They use more or less comprehensive questionnaires (Schellenberg, Abel, Kallsperger, Petersen), draw on written self-reports by labour service participants (Abel, Seipp, Kallsperger), work with statistics, and place themselves in the role of participant observers.

Thus, all these studies use the normal methodological tools of research practice. And in all their announcements on their closeness to the educational field, they simultaneously stress that they are 'free of every dogmatic perspective formulated' (Abel, 1935, p. 28, translated), that they have strengthened the justification for the labour service with 'incorruptible scientific' methods,[17] presented 'a scientific study' (Kallsperger, 1939, p. 7, translated), or worked under 'scientific guidance' (Petersen, 1938, p. 9, translated). Despite such communalities in the methodological self-image of the authors cited here, differences cannot be overlooked. On closer inspection, these are already present in the understanding of science itself: for example, in the aversion toward the products of 'knowledge gained from books' (Petersen, 1938, preface, translated) and the rejection of discursive forms of reasoning, and the insistence on the primacy of politics in the design of educational conditions. These theorists of the labour service finally define the relation between theory and practice as an education policy activism committed to NS ideology. Compared to a contemplative understanding of scientific work, they propose the belief that any 'attempt to provide a scientific sketch without the baptism by fire of experience is a useless attempt. As little as national socialism can be understood by anybody who is not personally prepared to take on the experience of the *Volk* community without placing himself in a special position, so little can the labour service idea be understood by somebody who has not experienced it himself in a camp' (Decker, 1935, p. 6, translated). The politicization of educational relations that manifests here and its commitment to *Volk* and race, the situations and arrangements in which it becomes practice, differ decisively from those before 1933. This is also revealed in the practice of research.

Whereas Abel still focuses on the role of work for a successful identity formation in the young, and unemployed youth are still perceived and taken seriously as subjects, this aspect disappears completely in the RAD literature. Abel and Schellenberg are still able to direct critical questions toward the optimism of the social work caste in the organization of youth unemployment, which their findings admittedly tend to destroy rather than support.[18] While they can continue to recognize the difference between youth unemployment as a 'national educational problem' (Abel) and the individual psychological consequences of unemployment, this aspect is completely missing in the RAD literature. The latter is less concerned with a task-related education that tries to theoretically fuse individual and community education in the traditional sense. It is also no longer interested in the problem of unemployment but in the issue of making organized compulsory labour more effective. The studies cited here no longer ask about the tasks of education as a social assistance but about its impact for the formation of *Volk* comrades.

Theoretically, they draw on Ernst Krieck's concept of a functional education in a specific, national-socialist application. His student Anna Kallsperger formulated this education concept succinctly:

National-socialist education is the totality of all effects of the *Volk* community in the subcommunities of the *Volk*, and the branches, associations, and institutions of the National Socialist German Workers' Party and the national-socialist state, in all tasks, goals, and values exercised on the members of the *Volk* and particularly on the young in order to integrate them into the *Volk* community so that they may fulfil their historical task. The final goal of national-socialist education is thus the *Volk* community of the Reich, and this can be achieved only through the creation of the 'new German person' of Nordic attitude who is duty-bound to the basic laws of the German kind: honor and loyalty (1939, pp. 15–16, translated).

Such a concept that no longer defines education functionally within the framework of a theory of society, but delivers absolute political concepts and reduces subjects to the status of '*Volk* comrades' is forced to refine the techniques of persuasion and to control the conditions governing the effectiveness of education in the above-mentioned sense. It is therefore no surprise that the scientific literature on RAD issues focuses on the effects of camp education. However, it can hardly be claimed that this was carried out realistically: If one assumes that the authors were already convinced of the need for the compulsory labour system through their professional commitment, then one can place more weight on their negative findings than they did themselves.

For example, Seipp records disinterest, skepticism, and rejection of the labour service in the first compulsory enrolment of secondary school graduates in 1934. Most of them viewed the compulsory six months as an unwanted disruption of the beginning of their careers. The 'character formation' during the labour service should therefore dismantle such reservations in the belief 'that the labour service can create the preconditions for these political persons, and this confirms that for students as well, the path over the "working man" is not a detour, but the certain path to integration into the *Volk* community and to recognition of one's tasks as a member of the *Volk*' (1935, p. 38, translated). In the compulsory recruits to Labour District 7 in April 1936, Petersen has to admit that only about one half were members of the NSDAP, and almost 40 per cent showed no interest in politics. In contrast, the strength of the binding power of traditional sports associations remained unchanged, just like the leisure-time orientations of the youths surveyed. Five years after the national socialists came to power, Petersen was forced to confirm 'how distant the times of struggle are for many working men', and he summarizes: 'The men are in need of education in every way: physically and mentally, politically and culturally, particularly with regard to a new concept of labour and to community life. In part, aspects are present that must be developed further and consolidated. This educational task is facilitated and promoted to a strong extent by the willingness and motivation of the working men' (1938, p. 27, translated).

Like Petersen and Kallsperger, Seipp also sees the educational effects of the work service in the re-evaluation of the experience of labour, comradeship, and nature, whose interpretation is directed toward the target of the person committed to political struggle. A national-socialist attitude, this goal of the labour service, was achieved through experience and discipline. It could be attained through situational arrangements of experience and political schooling, through 'continuous community and labour and landscape' (Seipp, 1935, p. 142, translated). But even education in integration camps recognized its limits, namely, 'the mental willingness of the one to be educated' (Seipp, 1935, p. 149, translated). Therefore, in the labour service as well, the education issue was also a 'question of selection and elimination' (Seipp, 1935, p. 149, translated). Here, the limits of education are no longer interpreted as being embedded in societal relationships or even as a structural problem of education, but are assigned to the one who should be educated as limits to educability based on racial or biological deficits.[19] This is why the elimination of those who were 'hostile to the community' and 'hostile to comradeship' was always a part of the thinking in the total education claim that manifested itself in the system of compulsory internment of youth. National-socialist educational scientists provided a theoretical justification for these aspects, and even praised them as characteristic for the new thinking in educational science because, 'national-socialist educational science is nothing other than educational science based on the biological principle with *all its consequences*' (Müller, 1937, p. 148, translated).

Conclusion

One question that still remains unanswered in the history of education is how far the semantics of educational theory in national-socialist labour service concepts was also actually put into practice in education. Was it really only an illusion of the educational scientists of the time encouraged by the public and legal status of the RAD when they believed that they could find scopes for the design of educational relationships here? If this is the case, was this an expression of political blindness, or did such attitudes conceal an understanding of their work that continued to provide social assistance despite the threat that 'through this individual emergency assistance, they would help to keep the wrong system alive' (Weniger, 1959, p. 20, translated)? From the perspective of the youths of the time, it still has to be asked whether and how the permanence of testing, application, and achievement, of political schooling and controlled experiences, the ritualized association of daily work with sociopolitically long-term perspectives was reflected in collective formations of mentality. Future research could try to trace the possibly counterproductive effects of camp education such as hidden forms of resistance, individual and collective refusal, that we are familiar with — at least in part — from the FAD (Dudek, 1988, pp. 225–31).

And finally, how were militaristic and racist elements able to force their way into the educational discussion with hardly any resistance after 1933? Historical research on our discipline has only partial answers to such questions at present, unless one considers that sweeping suspicions of political innocence regarding educational theories or political suspicions regarding individual theorists provide a satisfactory answer. And with regard to the practice of education, could it not be that underneath theoretical developments for '*Volk* and race as the basis and goal of German education' (Berger, 1936), the professional occupational knowledge of educators and their professional routines in the work service or the *Nationalsozialistische Volkswohlfahrt* (People's Welfare) had changed less strongly than the education theory publications on their legitimation would suggest? I am far from knowing answers to these questions. Perhaps historical distance is needed before they can be raised. This may be a threat, as we can see in the so-called 'historians' controversy'. However, it may open up opportunities to destroy false self-assurances in the future of education.

Notes

1 According to the assistance service act (RGBl. I, 1916, pp. 1333–4), all male persons aged between 17 and 60 who were unfit for military service were enlisted for compulsory

labour (Levermann, 1928). Among those protesting against such restrictions were the *Bund Deutscher Frauenvereine* who wanted women to be covered by the act as well. In the very same month, the 'women's work centre' and the 'national committee for women's work during war' were set up under the control of the war office in order to coordinate the expansion of women's work for war purposes.

2 On the introduction of compulsory labour service in the agricultural state of Bulgaria, see Raupach (1932) and Rogosaroff (1937).

3 Decree of June 5, 1931 (RGBl. I, 1931, pp. 279–81); decree of June 16, 1932 (RGBl. I, pp. 352–3).

4 Support for a socialist labour service was strongest in the circles of the SAJ (Sozialistische Arbeiterjugend; P.D.) and socialist students. However, this was a very controversial topic within the SPD and the trade unions.

It was only after the introduction of the FAD that both tempered their criticism of this measure. The *Reichsarbeitsgemeinschaft Soziale Dienste — Hilfswerk der Arbeiterschaft für die erwerbslose Jugend* that they set up on August 10, 1932 grew rapidly into one of the largest service provider associations of the FAD. Only the communists retained their fundamentally oppositional position as a result of their thesis of social fascism, and they viewed the FAD as a further instrument in the increasing subjection of society to fascism (Dudek, 1988, pp. 225–31).

5 Correspondence from April 29, 1933, BA R 77/77.

6 Hierl expressed this similarly during his denazification process in 1949:

I wanted to emphasize the character of the labour service as a service of honor to the *Volk*. . . . Everyday business in the labour service took a soldierly form. If you have to keep law and order among 200 frisky 18- to 19-year-olds, some of whom are also dissolute and rough boys, in a comparatively restricted space and to train them to carry out their duties conscientiously, to live together as comrades, and to be considerate of others, to get good work out of them, then a strong male discipline is indispensable. Education toward this is always bound to the maintenance of certain forms. (BA Nachlaß Hierl, Nr. 11, translated)

7 Hence, in 1949, Hierl conceded that the RAD had to 'enter the service of the war effort' after 1939:

Part of the labour service was already used as construction troops behind the army front at the beginning of the war. War developments in 1943 led to a further part having to be used for air defense in the anti-aircraft artillery. And, finally, in the last years of the war, the constraints of the war situation meant that despite a reduction of service to two months, the labour service had to take on tasks that were really the responsibility of the reserve army, namely, basic soldier's training with weapons as well. (BA Nachlaß Hierl, Nr. 11, translated)

8 Satisfactory studies on the male RAD are not yet available. For the RADwj, compare Morgan (1978), Bajohr (1980), and Miller (1980).

9 For the RADwJ, Bajohr has analysed the image of the new woman's profession of labour-service leader. Hermann Nohl has reported that he recommended the labour service to his female school students as an occupational field in which they would still be able to find opportunities to engage in their own educational planning. According to Elisabeth Siegel (1982, p. 263, translated), many of them found leading jobs in this 'oasis among the national-socialist educational institutions'.

10 For the RAD, Lingelbach (1970, pp. 136–46) has been the first to analyse the camp as a means of education. The passages on camp education in Ehrhardt (1968) continue to make instructive reading.

11 Kretzschmann wrote about the ideals of national-socialist labour service leaders as follows:

> The ideal labour-service leader is bound to the front and to the *Volk*. He is not a one-sided specialist. The worker and the farmer join together in him. The internal and external soldierly attitude is a precondition that is taken for granted, and in cultural terms, he must have the ability to shape things in the way toward which the healthy youth movement strives. For him, education means 'presenting a living model', and remaining young inside. For this is the only way in which he can engender enthusiasm in the young. (1935, p. 384, translated)

Apart from the strong emphasis on the soldierly, it is easy to detect similarities to non-national-socialist educational leader ideals (Dudek, 1988, pp. 200–31).

12 Petersen, for example, can only imagine comradeship 'as the relationship from man to man'. 'Comradeship is not softness, but simple and straight, dry and hard masculinity' (1938, p. 39, translated). In this context, compare also the dissertation from Gaupp (1936) that was also influenced by Krieck's functional education theory.

13 Impressive confirmation of this thesis can be found in, for example, Raupach (1934).

14 Whereas the educators involved in the FAD placed value on reducing the negative consequences of youth unemployment in order to contribute to reducing social decay, the education strategists of the RAD were interested in developing educational methods that would make 'service in all its totality into an experience of community'.

Formation exercises, physical education, political education, cleaning and mending sessions, service training, roll calls, singing, knocking off work, treks, this is all a shaping of experience of community. Loyalty, obedience, and comradeship are the words that stand over this shaping of experience. They let the individual be aware that the community is more important than his person, and thus develop personalities who are capable of the highest personal achievement for the sake of the greater community! (Decker, 1937, p. 280, translated).

15 Wilhelm Decker (1899–1945) was a *Gauredner* and *Reichsredner* (district and national representative) of the NSDAP, member of the German parliament, inspector for education and training in the national leadership of the RAD, and an honorary professor of educational science at the Political University of Berlin.

16 In the following, I refer to the work of Heinrich Abel (1935) on the situation of unemployed male youths, supervised by Friedrich Schneider at Cologne; Ernst Schellenberg's (1932) work on the FAD that was handed in to Walter Norden and Emil Lederer at Berlin; Paul Slipp's (1935) doctoral dissertation on the six-month labour service supervised by Gerhard Pfahler at Gießen; the work of Petersen (1938) encouraged by Gustav Deuchler at Hamburg; Anna Kallsperger's (1939) doctoral dissertation handed in to Ernst Krieck at Heidelberg; and the work of Tsay (1940) that was accepted by Jens Jessen at Berlin. With the exception of the last-mentioned study, all the others were produced with the framework of educational science, although they differed greatly in their theoretical foundations.

17 According to Will Decker in the preface to Seipp's work (1935, p. 1).

18 Abel, for example, comes to a rather unoptimistic conclusion: 'In all the efforts at social work named, it was generally only a specific class of young unemployed who were accessed, and these were those young persons who were least at risk compared to the total numbers involved' (1935, p. 183, translated).

19 For NS educational scientists, this 'law of racial homogeneity' (Hehlmann, 1939, p. 14) was the decisive difference compared to the 'old' educational science before 1933. The drawing of such borders particularly dismissed the concept of educability.

References

ABEL, H. (1935) *Die Gestalt der männlichen arbeitslosen Jugend: Eine jugendkundliche Untersuchung über Grundlagen und Grenzen sozialpädagogischer Betreuung der Arbeitslosen Jugend*, Köln, Pilgram.

ABSOLON, R. (1958) *Der Einsatz des Reichsarbeitsdienstes im Kriege: Die Dienstverhältnisse der Angehörigen des RAD im Wehrmachtseinsatz*, Kornelimünster.

ARP, W. (1939) 'Erziehung im Lager', *Nationalsozialistisches Bildungswesen*, 4, pp. 29–43.

BAJOHR, ST. (1980) 'Weiblicher Arbeitsdienst im Dritten Reich: Ein Konflikt zwischen Ideologie und Ökonomie', *Vierteljahreshefte für Zeitgeschichte*, 28, pp. 331–57.

BARTZ, J. and MOR, D. (1979) 'Der Weg in die Jugendzwangsarbeit: Maßnahmen gegen die Jugendarbeitslosigkeit zwischen 1925 und 1935', in LENHARDT, G. (Ed) *Der Hilflose Sozialstaat: Jugendarbeitslosigkeit und Politik*, Frankfurt/M, Suhrkamp.

BENZ, W. (1968) 'Vom Freiwilligen Arbeitsdienst zur Arbeitsdienstpflicht', *Vierteljahreshefte für Zeitgeschichte*, 16, pp. 317–46.

BERGER, F. (1936) *Volk und Rasse als Grundlage und Ziel deutscher Erziehung*, Stuttgart, Kohlhammer.

BRAUER, H. (1935) *Der Arbeitsdienst in seiner historischen Entwicklung und gegenwärtigen Rechtlichen Gestalt*, Hamburg, Schimhus.

BRUMLIK, M. (1986) 'NS-Pädagogik in Forschung und Lehr Dissertationen und Lehrveranstaltungen an der Universität Heidelberg 1934–1943: Ein Bericht über das Wirken von Ernst Krieck', in OTTO, H.U. and SÜNKER, H. (Ed) *Soziale Arbeit und Faschismus*, Bielefeld, Böllert.

DAMMER, S. (1988) *Mütterlichkeit und Frauendienstpflicht: Versuche der Vergesellschaftung 'weiblicher Fähigkeiten' durch eine Dienstverpflichtung (Deutschland 1890–1918)*, Weinheim, Deutscher Studien-Verlag.

DECKER, W. (1935) *Die politische Aufgabe des Arbeitsdienstes*, Berlin, Junker und Dünnhaupt.

DECKER, W. (1937) 'Methoden der Erziehung im deutschen Arbeitsdienst', *Internationale Zeitschrift für Erziehung*, 6, pp. 280–1.

DUDEK, P. (1985) 'Freiwilliger Arbeitsdienst und Arbeitslager: Jugendliche in der Weimarer Republik zwischen pädagogischer Theorie und Sozialdisziplinierung', *Neue Praxis*, 15, pp. 261–87.

DUDEK, P. (1987) 'Die Rolle der "jungen Generation" und ihr Bedeutungswandel in der nationalsozialistischen Ideologie', *Bildung und Erziehung*, 40, pp. 183–99.

DUDEK, P. (1988) *Erziehung durch Arbeit: Arbeitslagerbewegung und Freiwilliger Arbeitsdienst 1920–1935*, Opladen, Westdeutscher Verlag.

EHRHARDT, J. (1968) 'Erziehungsdenken und Erziehungspraxis im Nationalsozialismus', Berlin (Unpublished).

EICH, A. (1936) *Die volkswirtschaftliche Aufgabe des Reichsarbeitsdienstes*, Forchheim, Mauser.

FISCHER, K.J. (1936) *Organisierte Arbeit als Staatsdienst*, Heidelberg, Verlagsanstalt.

FLAKE, K. (1935) *Das Verwaltungsrecht des Deutschen Arbeitsdienstes*, Herne, Knaden.

GAUPP, A. (1936) *Vorarbeiten zur Pädagogik der Kameradschaft*, Frankfurt/O, Paul Beholtz.

GÖTTING, L. (1944) *Die Arbeit als Erziehungsmittel im Reichsarbeitsdienst*, Berlin, Franz Eher.

HASE, G. (1940) *Der Werdegang des Arbeitsdienstes: Von der Erwerbslosenhilfe zum Reichsarbeitsdienst*, Berlin, Günther Heinig.

HEHLMANN, W. (1939) 'Erziehung als Wesensformung: Gedanken zum Neubau der Erziehungswissenschaft', *NS-Bildungswesen*, 4, pp. 13–21.

HERRMANN, U. (1989) 'Geschichtsdeutung als Disziplinpolitik?: Anmerkungen zur Kontroverse über das Verhältnis von Pädagogik und Nationalsozialismus', *Die Deutsche Schule*, **81**, pp. 366–73.

HERMANNSEN, W. (1938) 'Erziehung in Lager und Kolonne ist grundlegende Kulturarbeit', *Weltanschauung und Schule*, **2**, pp. 271–80.

HIERL, K. (1932) *Sinn und Gestaltung der Arbeitsdienstpflicht*, München, Franz Eher.

HIERL, K. (1934) *Arbeitsdienst ist Dienst am Volk*, Leipzig, Verlagsgesellschaft.

HUMANN, P. (1934) 'Die wirtschaftliche Seite des Arbeitsdienstes', Hamburg (Unpublished).

IFFLAND, TH. (1941) 'Organisation und Gliederung des Reichsarbeitsdienstes für die weibliche Jugend', *Jahrbuch des Reichsarbeitsdienstes 1941*, pp. 59–61.

KALLSPERGER, A. (1939) *Nationalsozialistische Erziehung im Reichsarbeitsdienst für die weibliche Jugend*, Leipzig, Oskar Leiner.

KERSTING, F.-W. (1989) *Militär und Jugend im NS-Staat: Rüstungs- und Schulpolitik der Wehrmacht*, Wiesbaden, Deutscher Universitäts-Verlag.

KÖHLER, H. (1967) *Arbeitsdienst in Deutschland: Pläne und Verwirklichungsformen bis zur Einführung der Arbeitsdienstpflicht 1935*, Berlin, Duncker and Humblot.

KRAFTMEIER, G. (1934) *Die Wirtschaftliche Bedeutung einer Deutschen Arbeitsdienstpflicht*, Greifswald, Julius Abel.

KRAUSE-VILMAR, D. (1984) 'Das Lager als Lebensform des Nationalsozialismus: Anmerkungen und Fragen', *Pädagogische Rundschau*, **38**, pp. 29–38.

KRETZSCHMANN, H. (1935) 'Der Arbeitsdienst als Erziehungsschule zum Nationalsozialismus', in HILLER, F. (Ed) *Deutsche Erziehung im neuen Staat*, Langensalza/Berlin/Leipzig, Beltz.

LEVERMANN, H. (1928) *Vom Hilfsdienstgesetz über die Technische Nothilfe zur Arbeitsdienstpflicht*, Kulmbach, Industrie- und Verlagsdruckerei.

LINGELBACH, K. CH. (1970) *Erziehung und Erziehungstheorien im nationalsozialistischen Deutschland*, Weinheim/Basel, Beltz.

LITT, TH. (1934) 'Die Stellung der Geisteswissenschaften im nationalsozialistischen Staate', *Die Erziehung*, **9**, pp. 12–33.

MAGER, B. (1970) 'Arbeitserziehung im Faschismus', in ALT, R. (Ed) *Geschichte der Arbeitserziehung in Deutschland*, **2**, Berlin, Volk und Wissen.

MASON, T. (1977) *Sozialpolitik im Dritten Reich: Arbeiterklasse und Volksgemeinschaft*, Opladen, Westdeutscher Verlag.

MERTENS, A. (1937) *Schulungslager und Lagererziehung*, Dortmund, Crüwell.

MILLER, G. (1980) 'Erziehung durch den Reichsarbeitsdienst für die weibliche Jugend (RADwJ): Ein Beitrag zur Aufklärung nationalsozialistischer Erziehungsideologie', in HEINEMANN, M. (Ed) *Erziehung und Schulung im Dritten Reich*, **2**, Stuttgart, Klett.

MORGAN, D. (1978) 'Weiblicher Arbeitsdienst in Deutschland', Mainz (Unpublished).

MÜLLER, K.E. (1937) 'Der Wandel im pädagogischen Denken', *NS-Bildungswesen*, **2**, pp. 139–53.

PETERSEN, H. (1938) *Die Erziehung der Deutschen Jungmannschaft im Reichsarbeitsdienst*, Hamburg, Junker and Dünnhaupt.

PETRICK, F. (1968) *Zur sozialen Lage der Arbeiterjugend in Deutschland 1933–1939*, Berlin.

PEUKERT, D. (1981) 'Arbeitslager und Jugend-KZ: Die Behandlung "Gemeinschaftsfremder" im Dritten Reich', in PEUKERT, D. and REULECKE, J. (Ed) *Die Reihen fast geschlossen*, Wuppertal, Hammer.

RASCHE, E. (1968) 'Die Entwicklung des Freiwilligen Arbeitsdienstes in den Jahren der Weltwirtschaftskrise und der Kampf des Kommunistischen Jugendverbandes Deutschlands gegen den FAD 1930–1933', Dresden (Unpublished).

RAUPACH, H. (1932) *Arbeitsdienst in Bulgarien*, Berlin/Leipzig, Walter de Gruyter.

RAUPACH, H. (1934) 'Freizeitgestaltung im Arbeitsdienst', in GRAEFE, B. (Ed) *Leitfaden für den Arbeitsdienst*, Berlin, Bernard and Graefe.

ROGOSAROFF, I. (1937) 'Der bulgarische Arbeitsdienst als Erziehungsmittel', *Internationale Zeitschrift für Erziehung*, **6**, pp. 242–54.

SEIPP, P. (1935) 'Formung und Auslese im Reichsarbeitsdienst: Das Ergebnis des Diensthalbjahres 1934', Gießen (Unpublished).

SEYFERT, R. (1901) *Zur Erziehung der Jünglinge aus dem Volke: Vorschläge zur Ausfüllung einer verhängnisvolle Lücke im Erziehungsplane*, Leipzig, Ernst Wunderlich.

SCHEIBE, W. (1942) *Aufgabe und Aufbau des Reichsarbeitsdienstes*, Leipzig, W. Kohlhammer.

SCHEINS, F. (1935) *Die volkswirtschaftliche Bedeutung der Arbeitsdienstpflicht*, Köln, Georg Zimmermann.

SCHELLENBERG, E. (1932) *Der Freiwillige Arbeitsdienst auf Grund seiner bisherigen Erfahrungen*, Berlin, Franz Vahlen.

SCHLICKER, W. (1968) 'Freiwilliger Arbeitsdienst und Arbeitsdienstpflicht 1918–1933: Die Rolle der militaristischen und faschistischen Kräfte in den Arbeitsdienstbestrebungen der Weimarer Republik', Potsdam (Unpublished).

SCHULZ, E. (1925) 'Die Arbeitsdienstpflicht', Berlin (Unpublished).

SIEGEL, E. (1982) 'Selbstdarstellung', in PONGRATZ, L. (Ed) *Pädagogik in Selbstdarstellungen*, **4**, Hamburg, Junius.

STELLRECHT, H. (1933) *Der Deutsche Arbeitsdienst: Aufgaben, Organisation, Aufbau*, Berlin, Mittler and Sohn.

STELLRECHT, H. (1934) *Arbeitsdienst und Nationalsozialismus*, Berlin, Mittler and Sohn.

TENORTH H.-E. (1986) 'Erziehung und Erziehungswissenschaft von 1930–1945: Über Kontroversen ihrer Analyse', *Zeitschrift für Pädagogik*, **35**, pp. 261–80.

TSAY, J.-S. (1940) 'Der Reichsarbeitsdienst: Geschichte, Aufgabe, Organisation und Verwaltung des deutschen Arbeitsdienstes einschließlich des Arbeitsdienstes für die weibliche Jugend', Berlin (Unpublished).

VOGELSANG, TH. (1966) 'Zur Entwicklung des Arbeitsdienstes', in *Gutachten des Instituts für Zeitgeschichte*, **2**, Stuttgart, Metzler.

WENIGER, E. (1959) 'Herman Nohl und die sozialpädagogische Bewegung', *Zeitschrift für Pädagogik*, **1**, Beiheft, pp. 5–20.

WERNER, W. (1981) 'Die Arbeitserziehungslager als Mittel nationalsozialistischer "Sozialpolitik" gegen deutsche Arbeiter', in DLUGOBORSKI, W. (Ed) *Zweiter Weltkrieg und sozialer Wandel: Achsenmächte und besetzte Länder*, Göttingen, Vandenhoeck and Ruprecht.

ZAHN, K.P. (1938) 'Feiergestaltung im Reichsarbeitsdienst', *Weltanschauung und Schule*, **2**, pp. 169–77.

4 Totalizing of Experience: Educational Camps[1]

Jürgen Schiedeck and Martin Stahlmann

Mass has to become liquid if it is to be malleable.
E. Krieck, *Nationalpolitische Erziehung*

Introduction

During the twelve years of national socialist rule, almost all age groups and social classes of the *Reich* passed through a multitude of camps with different functions but the same kind of structure. Hardly anybody was able to avoid this 'educational' intervention of the system.[2]

The camp was not invented by the national socialists. As a form of education, it had already played an important role in the youth movement. However, whereas in the latter, it was a conscious attempt to distinguish oneself from the bourgeois lifestyle of the adult world; under national socialism, it became a way of life in itself.

This chapter aims to report on the structure and function of this prototypical national socialist way of life and type of education in its various forms. We base this report on two assumptions.

Firstly the purpose of each camp, regardless of its form and content, was to 'educate'. Here, we agree with Kupffer (1984) that fascist education has to be understood as a cipher.

> Education, in the form of a historical-philosophical and political anticipation of salvation, was made into a substitute for the political revolution that did not occur; it functioned as a cipher for the turning away from politics and the turning toward the *totalitarian assessment of the entire person* [my emphasis]. This had about as much to do with 'education' as Hitler's political beliefs had to do with 'politics'. (Kupffer, 1984, p. 79, translated)

Secondly the camp is finally a form of expression of national socialism itself. The camp principle reflects the national socialist conception of 'normal' life as a situation of chronic struggle. In the self-concept of national socialism, the '*Volk* community' was a social formation located beyond bourgeois society that, like troops in battle, was in a continuous state of emergency.

In this sense, the camp had an almost prototypical character for national socialist education — for example, with reference to the underlying 'blood-and-soil' ideology — and permitted a consistent implementation of national socialist (educational) goals.

We first want to draw the clearest possible picture of this central sector of national socialist education. Within the limited space of this chapter, this has to take the form of a rather general overview, although many individual aspects of 'camp education' in fascism would be worth looking at by themselves (selection, militarization, etc.). Second, we wish to clarify how elementary principles of national socialist 'educational theory' were transformed into an educational reality in the camp structure, and third, we want to work out the manipulative and power-stabilizing mechanisms of this form of education.

We shall limit our analysis to the camps that had something to do with education in the broadest sense. The issue of prison, concentration, and extermination camps — the most brutal instruments of national socialist rule — will not be addressed directly, although they always remain present in the background when dealing with such a topic (see, Kogon, 1988; *Konzentrationslager Dokument* F 321, 1989; Krause-Vilmar, 1984).

Furthermore, we have to limit ourselves by saying that we are not describing 'how things really were', because many publications on the topic covered in this analysis[3] were propaganda that was not intended to inform but primarily to 'persuade', so that the depiction of 'reality' was mostly ideologized. Naturally, this does not mean that statements on camp life and daily life in camps are completely impossible. Under the constraints mentioned above and after a critical analysis of the texts and descriptions, it is nonetheless possible to reconstruct a picture of the various national socialist camps. In addition, unequivocal and firm statements are possible on the forms and types, the self-concept, and the 'theory' of camps, as well as their role within the national socialist education system.

The Camp As a Form of Organization

This section will first work out the standard basic structure found in nearly all camps regardless of their special (content-related and biographical) orientation, and follow this up by discussing the breadth of content and the biographical range of the camps.

Standard Basic Structure

We consider that the central aspects, particularly from the perspective of national socialist educational ideology, were: the location of the camps, (ritual) daily routines, internal structure, and the wearing of uniforms. These will now be dealt with briefly.

Basically, permanent camps can be differentiated from mobile tent and hut camps. The former had a fixed *location* — a 'home', for example, a country mansion or a converted factory — and were occupied by changing groups following a set turn-over. Changing locations were programmed for the mobile camps. These were generally directed, on the one hand, toward their clients; on the other hand, toward the internal goals of the camp. For example, the exchange camps (*Austauschlager*) of the national socialist teacher association (*Nationalsozialistischer Lehrerbund*, NSLB) were set up in the 'border zones' so that participants could gain an impression of the 'humiliation of the Versailles Treaty' and the supposed suffering of those living there ('border zone struggle').

The camps of the Hitler youth organizations for boys (*Hitlerjugend*, HJ) and girls (*Bund Deutscher Mädel*, BDM) were generally held close to the local district. These were mostly tented camps that had to be set up according to exactly prescribed alignments (see *Kulturamt der Reichsjugendführung* [Ed.], 1937; Ramm, 1934; *Reichsjugendführung* [Ed.], 1934).

In each case, the location and type of camp was previously selected carefully by the camp leader and/or organizers in line with the (actual) purpose of the meeting. Mostly, an effort was made to set up camps in the open country outside the cities and urban centres.

The *daily routine* was almost identical in every camp. Its major components such as morning reveille with the password of the day, raising and lowering the flag, sounding the tattoo, and the like were simultaneously ritual activities. The important aspect of this for the camp organizers was to strengthen the feeling among the participants that the same ritual was taking place at the same time in all camps. This was viewed as an attainment of '*Volk* community'. Camps also had a lot in common when it came to the teaching topics, regardless of a camp's special orientation. For example, topics almost everywhere included the '*Führer*', the 'movement', 'national socialist philosophy', and the Versailles Treaty. Sports (of a paramilitary nature) also played a major role as a self-evident part of the daily routine (except in pure work camps). Wearing a *uniform* and weapons practice were also obligatory. 'The weapon is the companion of every soldierly achievement, it belongs to the camp equipment like the uniform. Shooting practice increases self-esteem and body awareness; therefore shooting should not be underrepresented in the camp' (Mertens, 1937, p. 32, translated). Uniforms also served another purpose: They should cover up the social differences that existed in civil life and create the illusion of a 'true community'. The 'comradely *Du* (familiar form of address)' also contributed to this. As a camp participant reported:

> All class differences have disappeared. Titles and official ranks are put aside. We now recognize only one form of address: comrade and *Du*! This is where you know the true comrade, completely regardless of whether outside in the field, on the 25-kilometer pack march . . . it is always a question of sticking together in real, true, helpful, and honest comradeship. (*Nationalsozialistische Erziehung*, 1935, p. 257, translated)

The *internal structure* of the camp was characterized by strict hierarchies completely in line with the principle of 'leader and followers'. This principle only appears to contradict the leveling out of social differences mentioned above, as the following quote reveals:

> Marching in step and keeping in line are the foundations on which the camp is based, and, for this reason, the running of camps cannot be imagined without them. The truly free person approves of this constraint through intrinsic conviction and follows it willingly. (Mertens, 1937, p. 15, translated)

The top of the camp hierarchy was occupied by a specially selected camp leader who had demanding responsibilities. For example, a camp leader in the German Labour Front (*Deutsche Arbeitsfront*, DAF) had to meet the following qualifications:

> (1) Individual membership in the DAF, when possible, also in the NSDAP; (2) political reliability, to be confirmed through a clean certificate from the personnel office of the party; (3) proof of Aryan descent through submitting an ancestry card or proof of pedigree; (4) presentation of a correctly completed work book. (Birkenholz, 1938a, p. 470, translated)

Because there were so many camps, the 'camp leader' (*Lagerführer*, see Birkenholz, 1939) and the 'agricultural-year mistress' (*Landjahrerzieherin*, see Jürgens, 1942; Sopp, 1940) were established as new professions. The profession of *Landjahrerzieherin* was conceived by the national socialists as a 'return to the original women's profession' after women had 'encroached' increasingly into 'unnatural professions for their gender' (Jürgens, 1942, p. 6, translated). Such new professions were predominantly located in social welfare and camp education (for more detail on this, see Schiedeck, 1989).

Breadth of Content and Biographical Range

The following list describing the various types of camp should illustrate the totality of the coverage of the population and the breadth of content addressed. The two following quotes underline not only the variety of types of camp but also the assumption that almost every German had to attend at least one camp between 1933 and 1945.

> A network of camps covers our country from the sea to the high mountains, from the heaths and forests of the East to the industrial areas in the West. Camps for party functionaries; for SA, SS, and HJ; for lawyers, artists, physicians, civil servants, managers; for men and for women; for the young and the very old. (Mertens, 1937, p. 3, translated)

> There are camps in tents and in houses, camps for thirty and for several hundred, even 1,000 participants; there are camps that concentrate on physical labour and others that concentrate on mental training; camps that

hardly last one week and permanent camps whose members change every six weeks or every six months; camps with a full-time permanent staff and others that cope with a minimum of fixed organization. This is joined by the great multitude of purposes for the camps; even within the enormous organization of the labour service, the diversity of work programmes gives the camps different characters. These are joined by training camps, sports camps of every kind — an incalculable variety of special communities . . . and when the sun goes down, camp teams fall in for evening colors all over Germany. (Günther, 1934, p. 809, translated)

Our description of the types of camp takes a biographical perspective, that is, we differentiate camps into those for school children, adolescents, college students, and workers or the unemployed.[4] There is no compelling reason for such a differentiation, and it serves only heuristic purposes. As a precise description of every type of camp would fill an entire book, we shall present only what we consider to be the major types of camp;[5] those that we view as being less relevant will only be mentioned in passing.

Youth / School Children

Leisure-time camps for adolescents and children. Leisure time, hiking, and nature played an important role, particularly during the early years of national socialism. By drawing on the *Wandervogel* and other youth movements, it was possible to fall back on familiar forms of education and thus counter eventual mistrust. In order to recruit as many young persons as possible for such camps, large-scale publicity campaigns were organized. An example of such a campaign is given by a summer camp in the region of Saxony in 1935.

The action was initiated everywhere simultaneously on 15 April, 1935. Coloured posters were distributed in very large numbers (to public offices, businesses, advertising hoardings); publicity evenings, camps, and marches were organized throughout Saxony.

> In addition, all available showcases and notice boards in schools were turned over completely to the topic of leisure-time pursuits after April 15. Slides were used to advertise in the movie theaters. However, the press had the main task: Regular headlines, reports on journeys and camps, as well as photographs placed our goals in the foreground . . . Together with the local chapter of the HJ, the junior section (*Jungvolk*), and the BDM . . . roll calls were held that urgently reminded all members of our demands. Not least, it is necessary to mention the advertising work in schools, in which *special teaching lessons* [my emphasis] were used on the history and the tasks of the HJ . . . Alongside the press, radio was also called in . . . Plays, interviews, and other publicity broadcasts offered the necessary explanations and frameworks. Particular attention should be focused here on the propaganda for young workers. (HJ Sommerlager, 1936, p. 12, translated)

Finally, in the summer of 1935, three hundred fourteen-day camps were held with a total of 60,000 Saxon boys. Their main topic was 'border zone training'. 'The Saxon HJ stands prepared, hard and pure in its rows and in its work, to set itself as a bulwark against all foreign influences that are subversive to Germanness' (HJ Sommerlager, 1936, p. 13, translated).

Other camps with a so-called leisure-time character were not just concerned with leisure time and/or rest and recuperation, 'because we do not organize leisure-time camp [in the HJ] in the sense of charitable rest homes, but demand participants to be eager to engage in sports and philosophical training' (Schlinke, 1938, p. 501, translated). In this way, youth was committed to the desired course through many different forms of leisure-time camps:

Leisure-time Camps

1 Rest camps or leisure-time camps (see Gauger [Ed.], 1936; *NSV*, 1, 1934; Schlinke, 1938).
2 Field camps or mountain camps run by the HJ (see Bayerl, 1935, p. 9; Heil, 1937; Kaufmann, 1937; *Nationalsozialistische Erziehung*, 1935, p. 259; *Reichszeitung der deutschen Erzieher*, 9, 1935, p. 21).
3 'Germanic' camps in the East (in contrast to camps also attended by foreign youth) (see *Das Junge Deutschland*, 1943, p. 59).

Community camps for school children. These types of camp were organized alongside school lessons. Their task was:

> . . . not to bring school children closer to national socialist thought through instructions in class and books, but *to place it at the center of experience* [my emphasis]. . . . In such camps, the concern is *to reach all school children through Volk-like education* [my emphasis]. (Ramm, 1934, p. 1013, translated)[6]

'Selection Camps' (Ausleselager) for the Formation of a School Elite

'Selection camps' played a particularly important role for the national socialists. On the one side, they were used to weed out and finally to eradicate 'unworthy life'; on the other side — and this is the form to be discussed here — under the heading 'selection of the gifted', school students, adolescents, and college students were registered, assessed, and selected in camps. 'Inspection and selection camps' in this sense were expanded after 1941 following a decree by the National Education Ministry (RdErl. d. RmfWEV of 9.9.1941) and organized into a preselection phase and an actual selection phase (lasting about ten days). The purpose of these camps was not to assess professional ability, but 'attitude toward the world and character traits' (Reichsausleselager, 1941, p. 202, translated). Hence, the concern was to create an elite for the 'new order' in line with the regime's racial policy and philosophy:

... so that the selection camps will maintain the character of being the form adjusted to the differentiation of human personality and human community in which both the protectors of the racial substance and the carriers of culture are selected and deployed to promote the life of the *Volk* community. Thus, the selection camp is not just brought into line organically with the personality and its life forms, but is adjusted and directed toward the greater context in which the individual and the professions live: toward the *Volk*, whose continued existence and cultural strength are to be preserved. (Lottmann, 1942, p. 134, translated)

Knoop (1942) formulated the goal and function of inspection camps for the selection of school students for teacher training colleges: 'First, life in the camp community allows us to recognize the true form and true value of a human being, and the total immersion avoids any one-sidedness in the evaluation' (p. 38, translated; see, also, Blume, 1942).

Further types of selection camp were:

1　National training camps and training camps (organized in district areas and local districts) used for 'leadership selection' or the national socialist training of the next generation of party members.

2　National leadership camps for HJ leaders (e.g., the 2nd *Reichsführerlager* of the HJ at Weimar from May 20 to 30, 1937).

3　Youth resettlement camps: Girls aged between 14 and 21 were assigned to resettlement camps for vocational selection. In 1942, a total of 50,000 young persons were collected into such camps for a six-month 'leader selection' (see *Das Junge Deutschland*, 1943, p. 57).

4　In order to carry out 'characterological personality research', a selection camp was set up in 1937 for 'children in care, students from schools for backward children, adolescents under the supervision of social workers, juvenile delinquents, and the like' (Künkele, 1938, p. 38, translated). Over a period of three weeks, the young persons should first be trained and assessed in order to finally select the 'worthy elements' (Künkele, 1938, p. 38, translated).

Military Service Camps and Premilitary Training Camps

Although similar camps already existed beforehand, proper premilitary training camps for male youth were set up only after the war began. Following a decree by the *'Führer'*, a corresponding directive issued by the National Education Ministry including implementation guidelines was published on May 25, 1942 (see *DWEV*, 1942, pp. 209–10). The 'courses', in part lasting several weeks, were led by members of the HJ leadership 'who have proved themselves in the leadership of soldiers in the army or the Waffen-SS' (Hein, 1943, p. 69, translated). Alongside recruiting young persons for the Waffen-SS, the curriculum provided paramilitary training. Camp graduates received war training certificates and the achievement badge of the

HJ (see Greisler, 1943). The goal was to 'perfect the existing purposeful development of soldierly talents and knowledge' (Hein, 1943, p. 69, translated; see, also,
Das Junge Deutschland, 1943, p. 58).

'Remand Camps' for Youth

This form of camp had an explicit disciplinary function as well as an indoctrinating
one. Based on the usual division into 'hereditarily healthy and hereditarily sick
human material', camps were set up that should enrol those who were considered
to still be potentially 'educable' (in this case, children in care). Those who were
assessed as being 'unable to participate in the community' or 'suffering from hereditary disease' had to anticipate transfer to a concentration camp (see Werner,
1944, p. 102).

Typical examples of such camps were the police juvenile protection camps
(*Polizeiliche Jugendschutzlager*) in Moringen (for boys, set up in 1940) and Uckermark (for girls, set up in 1942; see Werner, 1944, p. 101) that were designed to
supplement special education. In the Moringen camp, 'educators' were recruited from
the Waffen-SS; the guards, from the SS-*Totenkopf* divisions. 'Criminal-biological'
research was also carried out. The main educational method was work (partly in
armaments factories; see *Nachrichtendienst des Deutschen Vereins für Öffentliche
und Private Fürsorge* (*NDV*) 1940, pp. 174–5; *NDV*, 2, 1941, pp. 45–6; *NDV*, 9,
1941, pp. 218–19; Werner, 1941, 1944).

Although officially called remand camps, both Moringen and Uckermark were
actually concentration camps, with Moringen being responsible for the death of at
least fifty-nine youths (for a detailed account, see Guse, Kohrs and Vahsen, 1986;
Liebel and Bott, 1980).

University/College Students

Preparation Camp for Future College Students

What became compulsory in 1936 had a long tradition within the national socialist
student organization (NSDSB; see Mähner, 1935). After being founded in 1926, the
NSDSB initially worked mostly on training its own members. After the *gleichschaltung* (coordination) of academic life, it then became 'responsible' for all college
students. Under the 'law of the team', young students should be 'formed' in the camp
so that they 'approach their academic studies with a national socialist basic attitude
and do not let themselves be confused by any theory regardless of how scientific
it may seem to be' (Mähner, 1935, p. 95, translated).

In April 1936, such a preparation camp was held for 110 college students at
the city of Lähn (now Wleń in Poland). Some of the topics addressed were: 'the
university in the border zone' and 'national socialism as the mental vanquisher of
the middle ages' (see *Die Volkschule*, 1936/37, p. 205). Other types of camp mentioned for the academic field were:

1   Scientific work camps run by the *Reichsstudentenführung* (see Günther, 1934; Volk im Werden, 1937, p. 210).

2   Examination camps: Training camps set up parallel to college courses both during the semester and during the vacations (see *DWEV*, 1938, pp. 181, 300, 415).

3   Student preparation camps (see Hebell, 1936/7).

4   University training camps: The Rittmarshausen training camp for future students close to the city of Göttingen is well-documented (see Schulungslager Rittmarshausen, 1935).

5   Hiking camps for sports students (e.g., at the end of July in 1938 for the attendance of the gymnastic and sports festival at Breslau). The statement that the students were to be accommodated in tents or in 'closed quarters' (see *DWEV*, 1938, p. 300) reveals that this was a camp.

Trainee Lawyer Camps

From 1936 onward, law students were ordered to attend the community camp 'Hanns Kerl' by the Ministry of Justice (see *Deutsche Justiz*, Ausg. A, Nr. 11/1935, p. 388; Friedrich, 1936). This camp followed the goal of 'bringing trainee lawyers from all different districts of Germany closer together in order to train them for a period of two months exclusively in *issues and ideas that concern our national socialist Volk and its leadership* (Freisler, 1936, p. 90).[7] Thus, 600 to 700 persons per camp were trained in not only national socialist philosophy but also national socialist legislation. Alongside the Nuremberg Laws, other topics were the law to prevent hereditary disease, Roman law, and German law (see Friedrich, 1936, p. 759). These camps were an obligatory part of training, that is, a candidate could not sit for examinations without providing confirmation of attendance of such a camp (see Ministry of Justice of March 9, 1935 in *Deutsche Justiz*, Ausg. A, Nr. 11/1935, p. 388).

Young Workers and Apprentices

Theoretical training, practical job preparation, and/or further training were the central tasks of courses for this target group. Individually, these were held in the following camps:

1   Pre-apprenticeship camps for unemployed youths as a job preparation measure (see *Deutsche Zeitschrift für Wohlfahrtspflege*, 1934, 35, p. 233).

2   Vocational training camps: Additional one-week vocational training camps giving theoretical training and practical work experience held for groups of approximately thirty youths during summer (see Strecke, 1940).

3   Vocational selection camps. After the beginning of 1941, these served as a substitute for the National Vocational Competition (*Reichsberufswettkampf*) in selecting and training particularly trustworthy apprentices and

young workers (see *Das Junge Deutschland*, 1/2, 1943, pp. 55–56; Müller, 1942; Nölting, 1941; Wiese, 1942).

Adult Employees

National Camps for Civil Servants

Candidates for higher office aged between 35 and 40 (and rated as fit enough to do camp service) were assigned to a three-week 'special philosophical training' (see *DWEV*, 1938, p. 415). There were also (a) university lecturer camps (see Schulungs-slager Rittmarshausen, 1935); and (b) newspaper reporter camps (see *Deutsche Presse*, 11, 1936, pp. 124–5).

Community Camps for Teachers

These included the following:
1   National-socialist teacher organization (NSLB) exchange camps: These camps focused training on the 'border zone issue'. Teachers were sent to, for example, Saxony or Silesia during the school vacations in order to take fourteen-day courses on the prehistory, history, and racial history of the particular region (see *Reichszeitung der Deutschen Erzieher*, 12, 1937; *Schleswig-Holsteinische Schulzeitung*, 3, 1937) aimed at 'knowledge of the *Volk* on a *Volk* history basis' (Pieper, 1937, p. 293, translated). This was considered to be a way of teaching 'the spirit of the front' and 'sol-dierly attitudes': 'Without his [the participant] noticing it . . . the vacation exchange camp has also contributed to bringing him even closer to the absolute front line as a soldier of Adolf Hitler and a national socialist educator' (Pieper, 1937, p. 293, translated). Another purpose was to bring teachers from different districts closer together and that under clear polit-ical conditions. 'The fighter in the border zones should not feel abandoned' (Knoop, 1937, p. 40, translated). The great importance assigned to this aspect of training is revealed very clearly in the following quotations:

> Most camps carry proud labels that provide direct information on the core of the mental training work in our exchange camp: Sons of the border zones — Members of the master race; Creative *Volk*; *Volk* in struggle; We ride toward the Eastern lands. (*Schleswig-Holsteinische Schulzeitung*, 3, 1937, p. 36, translated)

Or following the same line: 'Every room carries an apt name: Eupen, Posen, Danzig, Bromberg, Apenrade, Meran remind the participants every day and every hour of the shame of Versailles' (*Nationalsozialistische Erziehung*, 1935, p. 257, translated).

2   Music camps/Choral camps: These camps organized by the Central Institute for Training and Teaching (*Zentralinstitut für Erziehung und Unterricht*) should 'lead' music teachers 'back to the buried sources of the true German concept of music' (Hentschel, 1936/7, p. 677, translated; see, also, *Die Deutsche Volksschule*, 1935/6, p. 251).

3   Training camps for teachers and preschool personnel: These approximately seven- to ten-day camps were also organized in part by the *Zentralinstitut* together with the NSLB and other organizations. For example, in June 1935, a seven-day prehistory training camp was organized together with the National Prehistorical Association (*Reichsbund für deutsche Vorgeschichte*) (see *Die Volksschule*, 1935/6, pp. 178, 211, 250, 375, 845).

4   District training camps for preschool personnel (see *Schleswig-Holsteinische Schulzeitung*, 13, 1937, pp. 182–xxx).

5   Field sports camps/Winter sports camps (see *Die Volksschule*, 1935/6, p. 175; 1936/7, p. 206; *DWEV*, 1935, p. 180).

Work Camps for (Unemployed) Adults

Here, it is necessary to discriminate between work camps (e.g., national labour service) and those that were really prison or concentration camps. We wish to limit ourselves to the former. The voluntary labour service (*Freiwilliger Arbeitsdienst*, FAD) and public work camps before 1933 already made strong educational claims. Alongside work, they focused on 'education to community, work, and a national ethos' (NDV, 4/5, 1933, p. 597).[8] The national labour service (*Reichsarbeitsdienst*, RAD) work camps and the labour service camps took over from the FAD camps after they were abolished in 1933. In this year, there were already eighty-six such camps in Schleswig-Holstein alone housing approximately 4,000 mostly young inmates (see *Schleswig-Holsteinische Schulzeitung*, 1933, p. 413).

National Highway Camps and Comparable Camps

Both to fight high unemployment and also implement their massive building plans, the national socialists began to organize thousands of workers in work camps after the mid-1930s. Examples are the work camps for the 'national highways' and the 'West Wall'. In 1938, for example, 500,000 men were accommodated in 'national highway camps' (see Birkenholz, 1938a; Weik, 1936), each containing an average of 216 men housed in twelve huts with eighteen men to each hut (see Birkenholz, 1938b). Care of the workers, even after working hours, was the responsibility of the German Labour Front (*Deutsche Arbeitsfront*, DAF). However, the camps did not just follow goals oriented toward increasing productivity, but also had more far-reaching intentions of educational relevance: 'Above all, he [the worker] should gain a clear understanding of the correct form of community life through the national socialist philosophy' (Gerlach, 1940, p. 33, translated). And following the same lines:

Alongside the material worth of labor, the ideal worth should also find expression. The cultural organization and care of leisure time through the district officers and the camp leaders working together with the national socialist community of *Kraft durch Freude* [strength through joy]. (Birkenholz, 1938a, p. 474, translated; see, also, Indefrey, 1936)

Further forms of the work camp that should be mentioned here are:

1   Work camps for young persons in care (see *Deutsche Zeitschrift für Wohlfahrtspflege*, 1934/5, p. 273; Küper, 1933).
2   BDM retraining camps as part of the land-service year and the women's labour service. Their goal was to mobilize female labour for agriculture (see Kunzelmann, 1934, 1935a, 1935b).
3   Relief organization camps for unemployed welfare recipients set up by the higher echelons of the SA command (see NDV, 5, 1934, p. 143).
4   Harvest camps, land service camps, land-year camps (lasting six months) (see Dietrich, 1934; Hermannsen, 1936; Jürgens, 1942; Leppien and Leppien, 1989; Wulckow, 1938).
5   Exercise camps/Special camps organized by the State Social Insurance Board (*Landesversicherungsanstalt*) for 'handicapped' youths in preparation for the labour service. The main purpose of this measure was to reduce social insurance costs (see *Deutsche Zeitschrift für Wohlfahrtspflege*, 1934/5, p. 232; Hoske, 1934).
6.   Camps for injured war veterans: The goals and character of these camps were described as: 'What a feeling to be able to stand in ranks and columns again and obey an order . . . or even to visit a unit of the army of the Third Reich together' (Schellenberg, 1937, p. 492, translated, reporting on a camp in the summer of 1937).
7   Training camps for German forestry (see Müller-Thomas, 1937).

After this short and more descriptive account of the main structural features and forms of camp education, the following section will show how central principles of national socialist educational theory flowed into attempts to give the complex phenomenon of the 'camp' a theoretical foundation. This will confirm the hypothesis proposed at the beginning of the chapter that the camp is the prototype of national socialist education, that is, its educational goals and means are not implemented in such a consistent and compressed form at any other location.

Contemporary Attempts at a Theoretical Underpinning of the Camp

In this context, we understand a 'theory of the camp' in terms of more general discussions dealing on a basic level with the goal and impact of this form of education as well as its theoretical roots. Our concern is to work out the special character as well as the specific relevance and adequacy of this form of education for the national socialist state.

The first thing emphasized by contemporary authors who attempted to develop such a theoretical foundation of the camp as a form of education was that it was 'appropriate to the German type of person', by which they meant that the camp 'is embedded deeply within our Nordic blood inheritance' (Pudelko, 1935a, p. 112, translated), and thus 'the most suitable, reliable, and natural expression for the development of the German person' (Mertens, 1937, p. 3, translated).

This clearly reveals the racist ideology, which also played a major role in camp education. The binding and unifying 'power' of a 'true *Volk*-like wholeness' is considered to be its 'racial substance' (Hehlmann, 1939, p. 13), its 'racial soul' (Rosenberg, 1936, p. 3), or the 'mysterious rhythm of inherited blood' (Sturm, 1942, p. 118).

Although historical roots are seen in the army camps of the Spartans and the Romans as well as the camp as a nomadic life-form (see Arp, 1939; Bayerl, 1935), the actual precursor of the national socialist camp is taken to be the 'Germanic pioneer camp' (*Unternehmungslager*, Arp, 1939, p. 30). Pudelko (1935a) also refers to the 'bands of settlers' who underwent their identity formation and developed their orientations in the camp, and comes to the subsequent conclusion that the camp as a form of education is as old 'as the desire for political power among Indo-Germanic-Nordic peoples' (p. 112, translated).

Another strong influence was the experience that 'life at the front' during World War I left behind in the 'German soldier'. This was the first occasion during which he had experienced 'true comradeship', unconditional responsibility for his colleagues, and thus 'true community'.

> The camp that I mean is called: *The battlefields of the great war*. Truly, *they were the camp of a generation* . . . The 'trenches' in front, the so-called 'reserves' directly behind the front, the 'rest camp'; each and every one welded everybody together into a close and strong community. (Bayerl, 1935, p. 7, translated)

The specific characteristics of these historical precursors, which express themselves in their soldierly character, can now be found once more, according to these authors, in the camps of the 'Third Reich'. Accordingly, the national socialist camp is ruled by the spirit of leadership, of comradeship, of struggle, and of able-bodiedness; daily life in the camp is marked by the 'primitiveness of its warrior-like life-style' (Stapel, 1934, p. 364, translated; see, also, Arp, 1939, p. 31).

Soldierly bearing in the strictest sense was also characteristic for the 'premilitary training camps' and the 'military sports' that were a component of nearly all camps, but also in the broader and more general sense for pure training camps ('philosophical struggle') and the camps in the RAD ('Soldiers of labour in the work battle'). The soldierly aspects of the camp found their external expression in the paramilitary organizational structure, the wearing of uniforms, and weapons training. Naturally, this way of organizing camps served as a premilitary training of the participants, but in addition, and in essence, the intention was political. Camp education was political-philosophical education, and its task was perceived as the achievement of an inner attitude corresponding to a strict external form (see Hermannsen, 1936, pp. 2–3; Mertens, 1937, p. 7). This should not be achieved through a rational teaching of the philosophical principles of national socialism, but through direct and immediate experience. The idea was to make it possible to experience 'real-life national socialism'. 'The community camp is a pitiless grinding stone and touchstone, a finely meshed sieve in which the philosophy of national socialism should be lived rather than taught' (Maasen, 1934, p. 440, translated; see, also, Ramm, 1934, p. 1013).

Camp leaders were assigned an important role in managing this task. As the camp hierarchy was structured strictly according to the leader-followers principle, they had to be the source of guiding and decisive commands.

Camp leaders had to be the guarantors of an absolutely pure 'national socialist attitude' in the camp, but they also had to possess the human abilities of 'being able to be father, brother, comrade, superior, and priest' (Wulckow, 1938, p. 225, translated), and they had to understand how to shape the decisive character of the camp. They had to achieve this solely through the strength of their authority and personality, because 'true leaders' were not leaders through their office or authority, but through their 'being'. Being a leader was thus understood as being something ordained by nature. Hence, Sturm (1942) is only being consistent with this when he declares completely succinctly: 'He who does not wish to be a leader with his whole being should become a follower' (p. 127, translated). This then acknowledges once more the 'natural order' of the camp.

However, the efforts to appeal to all sides of persons through the camp did not just focus on the human factor 'leader' alone. The camp was also designed to have an educational impact as a whole. Nothing should be left to chance; everything had to be planned down to the smallest detail. One central role was assigned here to the external design of the camp:

> The camp is not something superficial, but expresses the attitudes of the persons who have created it and all their abilities: soldierly discipline — courage — honesty — cheerfulness — love of the soil and the land — economic and agricultural understanding — a sense of order — a sense of beauty and life-style. (Schlaghecke, 1937, p. 10, translated; see, also, Mertens, 1937, p. 26)

This started with the choice of location and the arrangement of tents or huts, whereby attention was paid to ensuring that the camp fitted into the landscape as organically as possible and, so to speak, merged together with it into one unit. In this way, the camp 'can lead its inmates into inner bonds with the powers and strengths of the landscape' (Maasen, 1934, p. 441, translated), and 'make the landscape into a source of ideal experience' (Schlaghecke, 1937, p. 9, translated; see, also, Jantzen, 1935a). A similar formative impact was also assigned to spatial design, so that, in some ways, the camp was viewed as an aesthetic total context (on the aesthetic character of national socialist education, see Kupffer, 1982).

Alongside the conscious design of the material side of the camp, components of indirect education were just as important if not more important: the staging and ritualization of all activities in the camp. The regular rhythm of daily routines with its ritual activities from raising the flag and morning reveille to lowering the flag and sounding the tattoo were designed to achieve a lasting internal stimulation and formation of the participants. Everything should by synchronized with everything else and form an 'entirety'. This view becomes very clear in the following quotation:

> Raising the flag in the mornings and lowering the flag in the evenings were always the most mysterious and festive moments in the day. Soon we also noticed how the maxim of the day and our song in the morning always corresponded to what we then discussed in the training or during the social evening. In this way, a day always fitted completely together. (Gauger [Ed.], 1936, p. 58, translated)

The highlights of this kind of inner arousal were the camp celebrations and festivities. These celebrations with their quasi-liturgical construction (appeal, proclamation, avowal) should weld the participants together into a confessional community that should spread beyond the camp and finally serve the 'becoming a *Volk*' (*Volkwerdung*; see Seibold, 1938; Vondung, 1971). The quasi-religious character of this staging was expressed not only in the order of events (music, chorus, words of avowal) but also in the design of the external framework of the 'ceremonial sites' set up in nearly all camps. The national socialists were completely aware of the emotionalizing impact of these functions and applied it purposefully. Celebration was viewed explicitly as a 'form of education' (Seibold, 1938), and as a 'basic form of *Volk*-like education' (Hoerdt, 1937) with a far-reaching impact extending into the realms of the mystical.

> Because the celebration leads the individual into the secret current that wells up out of the basis of life as a whole, because the individuals sense their mysterious solidarity in the celebration, the education of the Greater German Reich takes advantage of this conscientiously and according to plan, in order to lead the members of the *Volk*, young and old, together on the days when we commemorate our heros and the fate of our *Volk* to a shared hearing of the voices that speak to us from the depths of the blood and from the web of fate. (Sturm, 1942, p. 131, translated)

According to national socialist anthropology, the human — and particular the 'Nordic type' one — is primarily an emotional and action-oriented and less a rationally controlled and intellectual being. Accordingly, educational means focus particularly on the prerational and emotional layers of the human psyche. Education should evolve primarily through 'experience' and this, above all, through the 'experience of community'.

What is important in education is nonetheless purely the *experience* [my emphasis] that does not encounter the human being through fate but can be brought about through education. And here it is not so much the individual experience, but the mass experience in and through *community* [my emphasis] that is important for education. (Wallowitz, no date, pp. 78–9; see, also, Stellrecht, 1942)

However, 'community' in this sense is not a real social category that grows out of shared activity, out of interactions, but is defined naturally and organically. In this understanding, a precondition of community is that 'those in an educational community belong to the same species'. Because '. . . only when this precondition of belonging to the same species is met, can an internal orientation in the same direction arise and the educational community becomes the community of belief' (Hehlmann, 1941, p. 445, translated).

Thus, national socialist education is never concerned with the individual for the individual's sake, but always with the 'valuable single person' (Benze, 1943) in his or her function as a bearer of the '*Volk* community' and as a guarantor of its 'recovery' and its 'growth'. 'According to this, national socialist education is the formation of the personality in the sense of the activation of those powers that are to be found in the community organism and find their fulfillment in the nation' (Beck, 1933, p. 20, translated).

On the other hand, however, human beings can only develop completely on the basis of their 'membership in the group' (*Gleichhaftigkeit*): 'The individual is never an autonomous and self-sufficient being but is fitted into a total organism as a member, and this membership is the precondition for the individual to attain personal growth, fulfillment, and maturity' (Krieck, 1933, p. 1, translated, see, also, 1935–7, p. 1). In this way, national socialist education presents itself as education into the community through the community.

However, the educational effect of a camp is not just viewed as the sum of each individual educational effect, but is explained through the impact of the camp 'as a whole'. Nonetheless, this is presented as no longer being capable of being grasped in a rational way, but only metaphysically as the 'spirit' (Günther, 1934) or 'atmosphere' (Stapel, 1934, p. 364) of the camp. It is these effects that seize the mood, the psyche, the experience of the individual participant and tend to form him or her in a lasting way. 'In the meeting with elementary powers that enable us to experience strong and simple sensations once more, lies the great impact of the world of the camp' (Günther, 1934, p. 811, translated). This is where the actual secret of the camp, its almost magical impact is seen.

What has happened deep inside them — day after day under the flying flag of the Hitler Youth Movement, in serious creativity and in cheerful, re-laxed hours with their comrades — how they have fetched this into them-selves — the cool sea breeze, the sound of the sea, the fragrance of the ripening earth, the wood with the dark conifers or the slender beech trees — they cannot say. But they will show it in the office, in the factory, at

home, at school, all the many working days throughout one complete long
winter up until the next summer camp through cheerful, self-evident fulfillment of duty. (Gauger [Ed.], 1936, p. 11, translated)

It was this that was expected to produce the desired total influence, the unconditional 'formation' and 'shaping' of the 'entire person'. Thus, the goal is not only
pure ideological indoctrination but an even more far-reaching 'dressing' of the
individual.

Education in this sense had to understand how 'to seize persons internally at
the deepest point of their being . . . and completely remodel them' (Groß, 1934,
p. 27, translated). However, this would only be possible 'when we do not use the
power of reason . . . but when we let all the power of an incredible but real and
intrinsically true suggestion take effect' (Groß, 1934, p. 27, translated).

The consciously irrational character of national socialist education is also very
apparent in the writings of Krieck — a major representative of national socialist
'educational theory'. He considered it necessary to turn to the 'underworld of the
soul' (1932, p. 37) in education, and stressed in this the importance of the 'national
socialist art of mass arousal and mass movement' (p. 38) that he assigned a model
function for national socialist education, because this was the only way in which
education could really have a community-forming effect.

At the same time, during the states of ecstatically increased arousal, not
only do the senses become more awake, fantasy more far-reaching, the
soul more fluid, but the many in an assembled group melt into a psychic
unit, to unity of feeling, to community: Mass becomes malleable when
mentally aroused. (Krieck, 1932, p. 39, translated)

In summary, we can state that the camp was stylized into an ontological,
metahistorical, and archaic form of education, life, and sociability in the national
socialist ideology in which 'racial', '*Volk*-like', and 'species-appropriate' essential
characteristics of 'pure Germanness' became reality in a quasi-natural way. The
'instinctual and racially determined aspiration' was addressed in the camp, made to
resonate, and reactivated. Therefore, nothing actually new was created, it was only
the 'pure, real, and true' that had been buried by the 'genetically foreign' and 'racially alien' influences of 'liberalism' that fought its way free again. In this way, the
camp appears as a magical total context.

The Function of the Camp within the National Socialist
System of Rule

Up to now, we have tried to clarify the role that national socialism assigned to the
camp as a custom-made form of education to fulfil its goals of mastery, and the
extent to which it applied this instrument. In this final section, we want to provide
a more detailed examination of how the national socialist camp system contributed

to the stabilization of its political power. We shall discriminate here between purposes and the means that were actually applied in the camps. The purposes can be summarized under the headings *mobilization, militarization,* and *discipline.*

Mobilization

National socialism understood itself as a 'movement', and, in light of political practice, this term should certainly be taken literally. The national socialists wanted to rouse the masses, the '*Volk*'; tear it free from the monotony and normality of daily life; provide it with a new, unified goal; and set it in motion toward this goal. The camp played a decisive role in this plan. A striking feature was the 'activistic content' through which it strove toward an 'education through the act' (Arp, 1939, p. 38, translated). Through this, the national socialists created for themselves a means by which they could legally reach a large portion of the population and manipulate them under the 'ciphers' (Kupffer, 1984) of work, education, and training. The camp inmates were torn from their habitual frames of social reference and pressed into a completely organized network that kept them continuously short of breath and on the move. There was no relaxation, they were seized completely, and their attention was taken fully. In this sense, the camp functioned as a kind of political and social 'continuous-flow water heater' that tried to raise the necessary 'mental running temperature' to the level required for the goals of national socialism and then to keep it there.

Militarization

Closely linked to this first goal — and not clearly separable from it — is the second goal, *militarization.* It can be understood as a more aggressive, special form of mobilization. The soldierly character of the camp described above and the shaping of all camp life into a 'struggle' followed the goal of effecting a gigantic 'mobilization' and creating the fiction of a 'permanent state of war'.

> In the camp, one is at one's closest to the enemy. One has moved from the bourgeois-civilian front into the most forward combat zone, this is why the life of the team of the *Volk* pulsates at its strongest here . . . Each day is exactly like the previous one, a day of 'struggle', and this turns the camp into both an explosively loaded and a concentrated male group, just like those fighting teams that mastered the organized battle as shock troops in the Great War and imposed their will on the masses in the brawls and street battles marking the political struggles in the postwar period. . . . The *life* in the camp must therefore be the same as a battle training. (Heinz, 1935, pp. 113–14, translated)

In addition, systematic profiles of the enemy were built up, and a ubiquitous threat was suggested from 'alien races', 'world Judaism', or 'Bolshevism'. The camp inmates should weld themselves together into a 'shock troop' to counter these threats. Thus, the camp played an important role in the militarization of society: directly, through premilitary training; indirectly, by creating the psychological willingness to participate in or tolerate war-like actions.

Discipline

The goal of a clearly exclusive and punishing *disciplining* of camp inmates is obvious and will therefore not be dealt with in more detail. What is more interesting is to point out that *all* national socialist camps, even the apparently harmless leisure-time camps and accommodation camps such as the national highway construction camps, had an intrinsic disciplinary character through their structure, that is, through the absolute planning of camp life and the complete coverage of the inmates' time, because the camp symbolized the power and overall presence of the national socialist hegemony. The inmates were registered, controlled, and assessed completely. There was no privacy, no individuality; everything personal was suppressed and had to submit to 'voluntary' allegiance. Hence, the impact of the camp was disciplining in that, on the one hand, it had the character of a 'total institution' (Goffmann) through its closure and its isolated location; and, on the other hand, it exercised 'structural violence' (Galtung) through its organization. To modify a phrase coined by Bernfeld (1973), one can say that the camp rears — as an institution.

However, ideologically and through the use of appropriate means, an attempt was made to veil this repressive character and reinterpret it positively. The imposition of psychological and social *Gleichschaltung* — the 'taking away of citizenship and the giving of comradeship' (see Arp, 1939) — was proclaimed by the national socialists as a higher form of social life and as confirmation of the progressive 'renewal of community' and the intensive 'transformation into a *Volk*', thus, as a victory over 'liberalism'. In concrete terms, they tried to do this through a rigorous imposition of *equality* among the participants. The uniform, the 'comradely *Du*', and the same simple lifestyle were intended to suggest a '*Volk* community in miniature' in which all social differences and class contrasts were considered to be abolished and the 'mutuality of the species' came completely to the fore. This superficial and only external equality should facilitate the melting into a 'true community'. This community-forming process should then be further accelerated and intensified by a general *emotionalization*. The ritual daily routines, marching in columns, music and celebrations should engulf the participants emotionally, 'soften them up' on a prerational level, and make them more accessible to the influences of national socialism. The aim was to produce a kind of 'psychological greenhouse effect' that would intensify 'being engulfed by national socialist beliefs' while simultaneously switching off the 'cold intellect'.

A final contribution was the use of *heroizing*, that is, the raising up of the camp participants to 'heroes in the fateful struggle of the German *Volk*'. Pride and self-esteem should be enhanced through dramatic appeals to the participants as 'bearers of the German race' and 'keepers of the Nordic blood'. In this way, the devaluation on an individual level experienced through equalization and the factual subordination as a 'member of the team' were compensated by an exaggerated idolization on a collective level.

To summarize, this chapter has tried to cast light on an aspect of national socialist education that we consider to be particularly crucial. It may well be that the real status of camp education within the fascist system of government can only be guessed at from today's perspective. Nonetheless, it was part of an ideology that Marcuse had already seen through in 1934: 'At the end of the path . . . lies the point at which the illusionary function of the ideology transforms into a disillusioned one: Transfiguration and concealment are replaced by open brutality' (p. 181, translated).

Notes

1 We wish to thank Prof. Heinrich Kupffer (Berlin) for his helpful comments and Marion Engmann for her careful corrections to the German manuscript.
2 The following statistics provide some insight into how far German youth was drawn into such measures. As it is very difficult to obtain reliable figures (see Heine, 1988; Leppien and Leppien 1989), the following numbers have to be viewed as illustrative.

   For HJ camps, we have the following figures for the period from 1934 to 1937. From 1934 to 1936, 4,216 camps were organized. In 1935 and 1936, there were 3,180 smaller camps (fifty to 300 participants) and 477 medium-sized camps (300 to 1,000 participants). The total number of participants quadrupled from 1934 to a peak of 561,764 in 1936.

   Number of participants related to size of camps:
   Small camps: 1936 = 287,636 participants
   Medium-sized
   camps: 1935 = 101,379
                       1936 = 173,444
   End of July   1937 = 159,180
   Large camps: 1937 = 151,480

   This means that from 1935 up to the end of 1937 a total of 973,803 boys passed through the camps of the HJ.

   The following figures are available for the *Bund Deutscher Mädel* (BDM): 1937 = 452 camps with a total of 96,699 participants (see Kaufmann, 1937, pp. 361–2).

   Special camps: 1942. In 1942, there were 3,808 special camps attended by 287,891 boys. Of these, 702 camps (= 42,531 participants) were for the war effort; 1,576 camps (= 136,755 participants) were for rest and recuperation; and 1,539 camps (= 108,645 participants) were for training and preparation for important war tasks (taken from *Das Junge Deutschland*, 3, 1943).

   Children's evacuation camps. According to Heine (1988), approximately 600,000 children were evacuated to camps for children in 1942. For the entire field of national socialist welfare (NSV), Heine continues: '500,000 children purportedly were evacuated to the countryside through the NSV in 1942' (p. 18, translated).

   Agricultural Year Camps (Landjahrlager). Here as well, information is only vague. Leppien (1989) reports: 'In any case, approximately 300,000 girls and boys went through the 8-month intensive land-year education between 1943 and 1945. About 3,000 male and female camp leaders "formed" them and were themselves decisively shaped by the land year' (p. 11, translated).

Land service. 'In the land service alone, 30,000 boys and girls and 1,853 male and camp leaders are organized. The premilitary training camps are attended by complete age cohorts. Hundreds of thousands of boys and girls receive a well-prepared welcome in the children's evacuation camps. In 1938, only approximately 400,000 young persons attended about 1,800 camps. Today [1943], without taking residential youth homes into account, a total of *at least 1.5 million young persons are subjected to strict educational work in the Hitler Youth Movement over several weeks in 7,000 to 8,000 camps every year* (Würschinger, 1943).

3   Our presentation is based mostly on an inspection of available contemporary journals (1933–45) dealing with general education issues, school education, or welfare and social policy. Journals from outside these fields were only referred to when concrete references were given. Finally, publications and reports of the NSDAP or other national socialist organizations dealing with camps were consulted when these could still be located.

4   Camps were generally segregated for boys and men or girls and women. This was justified by referring to the different 'natures' of the genders. For example, boys were made for the 'soldierly'. With reference to the land-year camps, this meant: 'For the 14-year-old boy, the camp, its soldierly forms, and living together with comrades of the same age is a completely natural life form'. Girls, in contrast, should be prepared for their 'natural' role as women and mothers. However, the differences in the *form* of the camps were only gradual in nature: 'The specific characteristics of the girls' camps are determined mostly by a different work focus compared to the boys' land year. For the girls, work in house and kitchen, stable and garden, and in childcare is clearly the most important part of their natural preparation for their careers as housewives and mothers in both the camp and on the peasant's farm' (Hermannsen, 1940, p. 70, translated; for the land year, see Leppien and Leppien, 1989, p. 24).

5   It can be assumed that one and the same form of camp was sometimes given different titles. On the one hand, this underlines the fact that the camps often had the same basic structure, whereas, on the other hand, it shows how several goals could also be followed at the same time within one camp. For example, (paramilitary) sports and training in national socialist philosophy were compulsory in all camps.

6   The camp concept also encroached on the institution of the school. From the very outset, relations between schools and the HJ or, in other words, between teachers and 'youth leaders', were tense. B. von Schirach inveighed against teachers in many speeches and emphasized their loss of authority as the consequence of the wakening 'new self-understanding' of 'German youth'. He considered that youth were increasingly able to discriminate between an 'authority as teacher assigned by officialdom' and the 'innate authority of the leader' (Schirach, 1934, p. 171, translated). The educator of the future would therefore be the 'youth leader' as 'a priest of the national socialist faith and an officer of the national socialist service' (Schirach, 1938, p. 125, translated).

With reference to the antagonism between 'teaching' and 'leading' constructed by the HJ, a dichotomy of school and camp was also confirmed in which the school appeared as something artificial, unnatural, and distant from life, whereas the camp, in contrast, embodied the 'real and true'. 'If school provides the weapons for the life struggle, then the camp is the precondition for this struggle. If school is static and unmoving, the camp is dynamic and mobile. If school discipline is military, then the order of the camp is based on soldierly attitudes. If school cultivates knowledge, then the camp cultivates feeling and belief. If school is aimed toward reasoning, then the camp wants the entire person. If somewhere in school there is a great lack of reality, then the camp is a reality that cannot be bureaucratized' (Jung, 1936, p. 38, translated).

Teachers tried to counter this decadent character of the school in the eyes of the national socialists by starting to integrate elements of camp education. For example, the school's country retreat was turned into a camp or a 'paramilitary sports camp' (see Gravenhorst, 1935; Kanzler, 1936), 'national political courses' for higher secondary school students were run as camps in youth hostels (see Nationalpolitische Lehrgänge für Schüler, 1935), and a new type of school, the 'camp school' appeared through the evacuation of children to the countryside (see Effinger, 1942; Freyer, 1942; KLV, 1981; Springenschmid, 1941) in which teachers became 'camp leaders' (see Dabel, 1942). This was not just viewed as a temporary measure to evacuate school children from the cities and 'areas threatened by air attack', but as the development of a radical new form of school more in line with the 'character' of national socialism that would overcome the 'weaknesses' of the traditional school described above. 'What is more important is that this has created an educational institution in which the school and the HJ stand together, that therefore brings us closer than before to achieving the national socialist unity of education. What is also essential is that this has given school teaching a completely new face, because the teacher is no longer the one-sided provider of knowledge but educator, camp leader, colleague, and paternal friend of the youth . . . All this is not merely things that have arisen through the necessity of war that will disappear once more after the war. It is far more the case that the entire German education system will profit from them' (Springenschmid, 1941, p. 135, translated).

In addition, an integration of school and 'camp' was brought about in the national socialist elite schools, both party-internal and public, that were all designed as residential boarding schools (see, e.g., Orlow, 1965; Scholtz, 1967, 1973; Überhorst [Ed.], 1969).

7 This was Roland Freisler (1938–45, killed in an air raid). As president of the so-called 'People's Court' (1942–5) and the most radical advocate of national socialist penal principles, he embodied the terror of national socialist justice. From 1934 to 1938, he was a state secretary in the Ministry of Justice.

8 Work camps, and even a regular work camp movement proceeding from the youth movement had already existed since the mid-1920s (see Dudek, 1988; Feidel-Mertz, 1977; Keil, 1932; Kugler, 1933; Littmann, 1932). Originally as camps for college students alone, later as '*Volk* camps' composed of equal proportions of young workers, young farmers, and college students, they followed the goal of providing political education to the young. Socially useful physical community work was an important element. The organizers derived the educational character of the camp from the principles of *self-organization* and *self-determination*. Work camps were accordingly, 'Places for practicing an organized communal life for young persons who are willing to take on responsibility and organize their own laws. Every external constraint falsifies the camp that can only legitimize the societal value of its strict form through the voluntary compliance of all participants. The camp administers itself; the leadership has to be carried by the trust of the whole' (Keil, 1932, p. 35, translated).

In addition, the educational effect of the camp was considered to derive from the controversial discussion of different philosophical and political points of view. 'The mental tension of the camp arises precisely from the hard confrontation of interests that cannot just remain a mere program, but has to assert its reality and seriousness through the attitudes and achievements of the groups representing them before the eyes of all, and prove its political and educational power in chivalrous confrontation. Whereas, in this way, the variety and strengths of contrasts give the camp its value, any one-sidedness through impatience and browbeating in individual groups of participants or through the one-sided influence of the leadership threatens its existence' (Keil, 1932, p. 36, translated).

This democratic basic attitude thus shared nothing but its name with the authoritarian, disciplinary, and totalitarian character of the national socialist work camp.

References

ARP, W. (1939) 'Erziehung im Lager', *Nationalsozialistisches Bildungswesen*, **1**, pp. 29–43.

AUSLESELAGER DES NSLB (1937) *Reichszeitung der Deutschen Erzieher*, **12**, pp. 468–503.

BAEUMLER, A. (1942) *Bildung und Gemeinschaft*, Berlin.

BARNHÖFER, H. (1942) 'Erziehungs- und Erlebnisformen in der KVL', *Der Deutsche Erzieher*, **10**, pp. 284–5.

BATTENBERG, L. (1938) 'HJ-Übungslager für Körperbehinderte und Entwicklungsgehemmte', *Das Junge Deutschland*, **4**, pp. 155–73.

BAYERL, L. (1935) 'Die erzieherische Bedeutung des Lagergedankens', *Der Volksschulwart*, **1**, pp. 3–16.

BECK, F. (1933) *Geistige Grundlagen der Erziehung*, Osterwieck.

BENZE, R. (1943) *Erziehung im Großdeutschen Reich: Eine Überschau über ihre Ziele, Wege und Einrichtungen*, Frankfurt/M.

BERNFELD, S. (1973) *Sisyphos oder die Grenzen der Erziehung*, Frankfurt/M.

BIRKENHOLZ, C. (1938a) 'Die Betreuung der Bauarbeiter in Gemeinschaftslagern', *Monatshefte für NS-Sozialpolitik*, pp. 469–74.

BIRKENHOLZ, C. (1938b) 'Die Betreuung der Reichsautobahnarbeiter', *Monatshefte für NS-Sozialpolitik*, pp. 15–18.

BIRKENHOLZ, C. (1939) 'Der Beruf des Lagerführers', *Reichsarbeitsblatt*, **24**, pp. II 293–II 297.

BLUME, W. (1942) 'Das Musterlager', *Das Junge Deutschland*, **12**, pp. 331–3.

DABEL, G. (1942) 'Lehrer als Lagerleiter', *Das Junge Deutschland*, pp. 41–3.

DIETRICH, A. (1934) 'Vom Geist der Lagererziehung', *Die Volksschule*, **3**, pp. 71–7.

DUDEK, P. (1988) *Erziehung durch Arbeit: Arbeitslagerbewegung und Freiwilliger Arbeitsdienst 1920–1935*, Opladen.

DUMKE, A. (1943) 'Vom Kattegatt zum Knivsberg (Ein KLV-Lager fährt durch Dänemark)', *Die Deutsche Volksschule*, **2**, pp. 41–4.

EFFINGER, A. (1942) 'Die Schule im Lager', *Das Junge Deutschland*, pp. 233–6.

FEIDEL-NERTZ, H. (1977) 'Ein Stück gemeinsamen Lebens. Bemerkungen zur Arbeitslagerbewegung in der Weimarer Republik und dem folgenden Text. Das Arbeitslager', in BERGMANN, K. and FRANK, G. (Ed) *Bildungsarbeit mit Erwachsenen: Handbuch für Selbstbestimmtes Lernen*, pp. 37–60.

FEIERGESTALTUNG (1937) 'Ein Bericht vom Reichsschulungslager des NLSB', *Nationalsozialistische Erziehung*, p. 213.

FIEDLER, M. (1938) 'Aus dem Jungmädellager', *Deutsches Jugendland*, **5**, pp. 94–5.

FISCHER, H.G. (1942) 'Auslese und Begabung', *Das Junge Deutschland*, **8**, pp. 201–6.

FREISLER, R. (1936) 'Deutsches Rechtsleben 1935 und 1936: Ein Rückblick und ein Ausblick', *Deutsche Justiz*, Ausgabe A, **11**, pp. 90–7.

FREYER, O. (1942) 'Das KLV-Lager als neue Erziehungsform', *Der Deutsche Erzieher*, **9**, pp. 255–8.

FRIEDRICH (1936) 'Das Gemeinschaftslager Hanns Kerrl', *Deutsche Justiz*, **20**, pp. 759–61.

GALINSKI, D., HERBERT, U. and LACHAUER, U. (Ed) (1982) *Nazis und Nachbarn: Schüler erforschen den Alltag im Nationalsozialismus*, Reinbek.

GAMM, H.J. (1962) *Der braune Kult*, Hamburg.

GAMM, H.J. (1964) *Führung und Verführung*, München.

GAUGER, G. (Ed) (1936) *Mädel im Freizeitlager: Berichte aus pommerschen Sommerlagern*, Potsdam.

GERLACH, E. (1940) 'Die Deutsche Arbeitsfront als Hauptträgerin in der Lagerbetreuung', *Monatshefte für NS-Sozialpolitik*, pp. 32–3.

GRAVENHORST, F. (1935) 'Das Schullandheim als Lager', *Nationalsozialistische Erziehung*, **20**, pp. 157–8.

GREISLER, F. (1943) 'Was leisten die Wehrertüchtigungslager?: Erfahrungen eines Lagerführers', *Das Junge Deutschland*, **3**, pp. 71–3.

GROß, W. (1934) *Rassepolitische Erziehung*, Berlin.

GRÜNEBERG, H. (1935) 'Erziehung und Landschaft', *Die Deutsche Schule*, pp. 460–4.

GÜNTHER, A.E. (1934) 'Das Lager', *Deutsches Volkstum*, pp. 809–13.

GUSE, M., KOHRS, A. and VAHSEN, F. (1986) 'Das Jugendlager Moringen: Ein Jugendkonzentrationslager', in OTTO, H.-U. and SÜNKER, H. (Ed) *Soziale Arbeit und Faschismus*, Bielefeld, pp. 321–44.

HEBELL, S. (1936/7) 'Mannschaft als Voraussetzung nationalsozialistischer Lehrererziehung', *Die Volksschule*, pp. 205–7.

HEHLMANN, W. (1939) 'Erziehung als Wesensformung', *Nationalsozialistisches Bildungswesen*, **1**, pp. 13–21.

HEHLMANN, W. (1941) *Pädagogisches Wörterbuch*, Stuttgart.

HEIL, R. (1937) 'Die Zeltlager der Hitler-Jugend', *Gesundheit und Erziehung*, **4**, pp. 97–100.

HEIN, G. (1943) 'Was leisten die Wehrertüchtigungslager?: Bericht eines Inspekteurs', *Das Junge Deutschland*, **3**, pp. 68–71.

HEINE, F. (1988) *Die Nationalsozialistische Volkswohlfahrt*, Bonn.

HEINZ, L. (1935) 'Lagerführer und Lagerführung', *Deutsche Volkserziehung*, **4**, pp. 113–17.

HENTSCHEL, R. (1936/7) 'Musik und Spiel', *Die Volksschule*, pp. 677–8.

HERMANNSEN, W. (1936) 'Weshalb Lagererziehung?', *Landjahr Schulungsbriefe*, **6**, pp. 2–4.

HERMANNSEN, W. (1940) 'Die Lagererziehung', *Landjahr-Schulungsbriefe*, **3/4**, pp. 68–71.

HOERDT, PH. (1932) *Ernst Krieck: Volk als Schicksal und Aufgabe*, Heidelberg.

HOERDT, PH. (1937) *Grundformen volkhafter Bildung*, Frankfurt/M.

HOFFSCHLÄGER, M. (1936) '. . . Wendiger und neu aufgeschlossen. So war es im ersten Frauenlager des NSLB', *Nationalsozialistische Erziehung*, **2**, p. 22.

HOSKE, H. (1934) 'Sonderlager im Arbeitsdienst als bevölkerungspolitische Notwendigkeit', *Gesundheit und Erziehung*, **7**, pp. 273–81.

INDEFREY, F. (1936) 'Kraft durch Freude in den Reichsautobahnlagern', *Die Straße*, **1**, pp. 21–3.

JANTZEN, W. (1935a) 'Standort eines Lagers', *Deutsche Volkserziehung*, **4**, pp. 124–5.

JANTZEN, W. (1935b) 'Der Lagerleiter als Quartiermeister', *Deutsche Volkserziehung*, **4**, pp. 126–7.

JUNG, C.H. (1936) 'Schule und Lager', *Neue Bahnen*, **2**, pp. 37–40.

JÜRGENS, A. (1942) 'Die Mädelschaftsführerin im Landjahrlager', *Landjahr Schulungsbriefe*, **10**, pp. 197–9.

KANZLER, R. (1936) 'Das Schullandheim als Wehrsportlager', *Das Schullandheim*, **3**, pp. 39–40.

KAUFMANN, G. (1937) 'Die deutsche Jugend im Zeltlager', *Das Junge Deutschland*, pp. 360–6.

KEIL, G. (1932) *Vormarsch der Arbeitslagerbewegung*, Berlin/Leipzig.

KLV (1982) *Die Erweiterte Kinder-Land-Verschickung: KLV-Lager 1940–1945*, Eine Dokumentation, zusammengestellt und bearbeitet von Gerhard Dabel im Auftrag der Dokumentations-Gemeinschaft KLV e.V., Freiburg.

KNOOP, K. (1937) 'Schulung im Austauschlager Wartha in Schlesien, Juli 1936', *Schleswig-Holsteinische Schulzeitung*, pp. 40–2.

KNOOP, K. (1942) 'Bericht über das Musterungslager an der Lehrerbildungsanstalt Ratzeburg', *Mitteilungsblatt des NSLB, Gau Schleswig-Holstein, Beilage zu Der Deutsche Erzieher*, **1**, p. 38.

KOGON, E. (1988) *Der SS-Staat: Das System der Deutschen Konzentrationslager*, München.

KOLB, G.B. (1936) 'Unser Schulungslager als Gemeinschaft in seinem Leben und seiner Schau', *Reichszeitung der deutschen Erzieher*, **2**, pp. 17–19.

KONZENTRATIONSLAGER (1989) Dokument FF321 für den Internationalen Militärgerichtshof Nürnberg. Hg. vom Frannzösischen Büro des Informationsdienstes für Kriegsverbrecher. Durchgesehen, erläutert und mit einem Nachwort versehen von P. Neitzke und M. Weinmann, Frankfurt/M.

KRANNHALS, P. (1933) 'Das organische, ganzheitliche Denken und die völkische Erziehung', *Die Deutsche Schule*, pp. 593–603.

KRAUSE-VILMAR, D. (1984) 'Das Lager als Lebensform des Nationalsozialismus', *Pädagogische Rundschau*, pp. 29–38.

KRIECK, E. (1932) *Nationalpolitische Erziehung*, Leipzig.

KRIECK, E. (1933) *Nationalsozialistische Erziehung*, Osterwieck.

KRIECK, E. (1936) *Völkisch-politische Anthropologie. Erster Teil: Die Wirklichkeit*, Leipzig.

KRIECK, E. (1935–7) 'Nationalsozialistische Erziehung', in LAMMERS, H.H. (Ed) *Die Verwaltungsakademie: Ein Handbuch für den Beamten im Nationalsozialistischen Staat*, **1**, I/8, Berlin.

KUGLER, H. (1933) 'Die erzieherische Aufgabe im Arbeitsdienst', *Pädagogisches Zentralblatt*, **1**, pp. 9–22.

KULTURAMT DER REICHSJUGENDFÜHRUNG (Ed) (1937) *Freude, Zucht, Glaube: Handbuch für die kulturelle Arbeit im Lager*, Potsdam.

KÜNKELE, PH. (1938) 'Gemeinschaftslager als Stätte der charakterologischen Persönlichkeitsforschung, erörtert am Beispiel eines Ausleselagers', *Zeitschrift für Pädagogische Psychologie*, pp. 37–46.

KUNZELMANN, G. (1934) 'Mädelumschulungslager', *Das Junge Deutschland*, **12**, pp. 362–5.

KUNZELMANN, G. (1935a) 'Fortschritte der Mädelumschulungsarbeit', *Das Junge Deutschland*, pp. 172–3.

KUNZELMANN, G. (1935b) 'Umschulungslager, Landhilfe und Frauenarbeitsdienst', *Das Junge Deutschland*, pp. 411–3.

KÜPER, M. (1933) 'Arbeitslager und Fürsorgeerziehung', *Soziale Praxis*, **49**, pp. 1437–40.

KUPFFER, H. (1982) 'Zur gesellschaftlichen Bedeutung und Kritik ästhetisch-orientierter Pädagogiken', *Bildung und Erziehung*, **2**, pp. 194–207.

KUPFFER, H. (1984) *Der Faschismus und das Menschenbild der deutschen Pädagogik*, Frankfurt/M.

DIE LAGERERZIEHUNG (1940) *Landjahr-Schulungsbriefe*, **3/4**, pp. 68–71.

LEICHSENRING, K. (1938) 'Vom Wesen der Gemeinschaft', *Nationalsozialistisches Bildungswesen*, pp. 641–9.

LEPPIEN, A. and LEPPIEN, J.P. (1989) *Mädel-Landjahr in Schleswig-Holstein*, Neumünster.

LIEBEL, N. and BOTT, H. (1980) 'Schutzlager als Vorbild der geschlossenen Unterbringung?, *Pädextra Sozialarbeit*, **4**, pp. 36–41.

LITTMANN, A. (1932) 'Die pädagogische Bedeutung der Arbeitslagerbewegung', *Blätter des Deutschen Roten Kreuzes*, **6**, pp. 330–7.

LOTTERMOSER, H. (1938) 'Leistungssteigerung durch HJ-Lager', *Das Junge Deutschland*, **4**, pp. 168–73.

LOTTMANN, W. (1942) 'Das Ausleselager als Auslesemethode', *Zeitschrift für pädagogische Psychologie*, pp. 129–34.

MAASEN, N. (1934) 'Das Schulungslager', *Die Mittelschule*, **39**, pp. 440–1.

MÄHNER, G. (1935) 'Die politische Erziehungsarbeit in den Schulungslagern des NSD-Studentenbundes', *Volk im Werden*, pp. 93–9.

MARCUSE, H. (1934) 'Der Kampf gegen den Liberalismus in der totalitären Staatsauffassung', *Zeitschrift für Sozialforschung*, pp. 161–195. (reprint München, 1980)

MERTENS, A. (1937) *Schulungslager und Lagererziehung*, Dortmund/Breslau.

MÜLLER, A. (1942) 'Ausleselager', *Das Junge Deutschland*, **8**, pp. 193–201.

MÜLLER-THOMAS (1937) 'Schulungslager für deutsche Waldarbeit', *Deutsche Forstbeamtenzeitung*, **2**, pp. 35–6.

NATIONALPOLITISCHE LEHRGÄNGE FÜR SCHÜLER (1935) Eine Denkschrift des Oberpräsidenten der Rheinprovinz. Frankfurt/M.

NÖLTING, W. (1941) 'Begabungsauslese durch Ausleselager', *Wirtschaftsblatt der Industrie- und Handelskammer zu Berlin*, **38**, pp. 727–9.

ORLOW, D. (1965) 'Die Adolf-Hitler-Schulen', *Vierteljahrshefte für Zeitgeschichte*, **3**, pp. 272–84.

OTTO, H.-U. and SÜNKER, H. (Ed) (1986) *Soziale Arbeit und Faschismus*, Bielefeld.

PIEPER, G. (1937) 'Austauschlager: Ihr Sinn und ihre Gestaltung', *Nationalsozialistische Erziehung*, p. 293.

PUDELKO, A. (1935a) 'Das Lager als Erziehungsform', *Deutsche Volkserziehung*, **4**, pp. 111–13.

PUDELKO, A. (1935b) 'Ordnung und Gesetz des Lagers', *Deutsche Volkserziehung*, **4**, pp. 118–23.

RAMM, K. (1934) 'Die Lagergemeinschaft', *Pädagogische Warte*, pp. 1013–17.

REICHSAUSLESELAGER EIN NEUER WEG ZUR BEGABTENFÖRDERUNG (1941) *Monatsheft für NS-Sozialpolitik*, pp. 201–4.

REICHSAUTOBAHNLAGER (1937) *Die Straße*, **9**, pp. 242–8.

REICHSJUGENDFÜHRUNG (Ed) (1934) *Pimpf im Dienst: Ein Handbuch für das Deutsche Jungvolk in der HJ*, Potsdam.

REICHSJUGENDFÜHRUNG (Ed) (n.d.) *Reichsjugendlager der HJ in Weimar 20. bis 30. Mai 1937*, Berlin.

REICHSLEITUNG DER NSDAP HAUPTAMT FÜR ERZIEHER (Ed) (1937) *Fest- und Feiergestaltung im NSLB*, **4**, *Musikpflege im Lager*, München.

ROHRBACH, M. (1936) 'Mit Schülerinnen im nationalpolitischen Schulungslager', *Nationalsozialistische Mädchenerziehung*, **2**, pp. 32–7.

ROSENBERG, A. (1936) 'Nationalsozialistische Erziehung', *Wille und Macht*, **4**, pp. 1–6.

ROSSBERG, M. (1941) 'Erziehungsstaat und Schule', *Nationalsozialistisches Bildungswesen*, **4**.

SACHS, C. (1982) 'Die Geschichte des RAD-Lagers, Graf Eberhard im Bart, in Geislingen/ Steige', in GALINSKI, D., HERBERT, U. and LACHAUER, U. (Ed) *Nazis und Nachbarn: Schüler erforschen den Alltag im Nationalsozialismus*, Reinbek.

SCHELLENBERG, G. (1937) 'Eine Zwischenbilanz der Lagerschulung', *Nationalsozialistische Erziehung*, pp. 491–2.

SCHIEDECK, J. (1989) 'Mütterschulung im Nationalsozialismus', *Theorie und Praxis der sozialen Arbeit*, **9**, pp. 344–53.

SCHIRACH, B.V. (1934) *Die Hitler-Jugend*, Berlin.

SCHIRACH, B.V. (1938) *Revolution der Erziehung*, Berlin.

SCHLAGHECKE, W. (1937) Das Heim im Reichsarbeitsdienist, Frankfurt/M. (no publisher).

SCHLINKE, H. (1938) 'Gesundheitsertüchtigung in den Freizeitlagern 1935', *Das Junge Deutschland*, pp. 501–5.

SCHLÜNDER, E. (1936) 'Die körperliche Schulung im Deutschen Jungvolk', *Wille und Macht*, 7, pp. 2–5.

SCHOLTZ, H. (1967) 'Die NS-Ordensburgen', *Vierteljahrshefte für Zeitgeschichte*, 3, pp. 269–98.

SCHOLTZ, H. (1973) *Nationalsozialistische Ausleseschulen*, Göttingen.

(DAS) SCHULUNGSLAGER RITTMARSHAUSEN (1935) SEIN SINN UND SEINE AUFGABE, Göttingen.

SCHWARZ, H. (1936) *Zur philosophischen Grundlegung des Nationalsozialismus*, Berlin.

SEIBOLD, K. (1938) 'Die Feier als völkische Lebens- und Erziehungsform', *Nationalsozialistisches Bildungswesen*, pp. 591–622.

SOMMERLAGER, H.J. (1936) Gebiet 16 Sachsen HJ, Dresden.

SOPP, F. (1940) Vom Wesen der Führerin, dargestellt an der Arbeit der Lagerführerin im Reichsarbeitsdienst', *Frauenkultur*, 9, pp. 6–7.

SPRINGENSCHMID, K. (1941) 'Die Lagerschule', *Die Schule im Volke*, 7, pp. 129–35.

STAPEL, W. (1934) 'Die alten und die neuen Erziehungsformen', *Deutsches Volkstum*, pp. 359–65.

STELLRECHT, H. (1942) 'Erziehung durch Erleben', *Weltanschauung und Schule*, 3, pp. 45–50.

STRECKE, E. (1940) 'Das Berufsschulungslager', *Das Junge Deutschland*.

STURM, K.F. (1942) *Deutsche Erziehung im Werden*, Osterwieck.

ÜBERHORST, H. (Ed) (1969) *Elite für die Diktatur: Die Nationalpolitischen Erziehungsanstalten 1933–1945*, Düsseldorf.

VOGEL, K. (1936) 'Lager Gütergotz in Schnappschüssen gesehen', *Deutsche Presse*, 1, pp. 126–7.

VONDUNG, K. (1971) *Magie und Manipulation: Ideologischer Kult und politische Religion*, Göttingen.

WALLOWITZ, W. (no date) *Deutsche Nationalerziehung*, Leipzig.

WEIK, F. (1936) 'Reichsautobahnlager', *Die Straße*, 1, pp. 18–19.

WERNER, P. (1944) 'Die polizeilichen Jugendschutzlager', *Die Deutsche Jugendhilfe*, 11/12, pp. 101–5.

WIESE, H. (1942) 'Die Ausleselager im Arbeitseinsatz', *Das Junge Deutschland*, pp. 22–6.

WULCKOW, H. (1938) 'Erzieherische Erfahrungen eines Lagerführers', *Landjahrschulungsbriefe*, 8/9, pp. 22–3.

WÜRSCHINGER, O. (1943) 'Von der Zeltburg zum Feldlager', *Das Junge Deutschland*, 3.

5 Youth Welfare, Social Crisis and Political Reaction: Correctional Education in the Final Phase of the Weimar Republic

Elizabeth Harvey

This chapter examines the impact of the political and economic crisis of the final years of the Weimar Republic on youth welfare in general and correctional education in particular.[1] Between 1929 and 1933, mass unemployment and poverty, coupled with public spending cuts, placed an unprecedented strain on public youth welfare provision and exacerbated an already existing crisis in correctional education. At the same time, the shift to the Right in Weimar politics created a climate increasingly hostile to the youth welfare reforms sought by left-wing liberals and Social Democrats. Conservative welfare politicians and professionals seized the initiative and pressed for a fundamental reorientation of correctional education on the basis of targeting educational resources according to criteria of probable 'success'. The proposals of the Right were only partially realized before 1933, some being implemented more fully only after the National Socialist takeover; nevertheless, the basis for some of the crucial shifts in youth welfare policy under the Nazi regime was laid in the final phase of the Republic.[2]

'A Whole Generation Is Being Driven to Delinquency': Youth Unemployment and Its Consequences

Youth unemployment was the central issue in the final years of the Republic for those concerned with youth welfare.[3] In July 1932, there were 632,224 unemployed below the age of 21, 76 per cent of whom were aged between 18 and 21 (Richter, 1933). The 14–18-year-olds were less hard hit than the 18–21-year-olds for two reasons. Firstly, they constituted a pool of cheap labour: employers took on school-leavers as apprentices at the age of 14 or 15 and, typically, fired them at the end of their apprenticeship when they were 17 or 18. Secondly, school-leavers entering the labour market in the years between 1929 and 1934 belonged to the smaller cohorts born during the First World War.[4] The 18–21-year-olds were in a much worse position. The higher wages laid down for them by collective agreements were a disincentive to employ them, and young male workers sometimes found themselves the target of works councils' efforts to preserve jobs for the fathers of families at the expense of younger, single men (Geary, 1987).

Once out of a job, the young unemployed in the Depression years faced the prospect of a long and arduous search for work and difficulties in claiming unemployment benefit in the meantime. The 1927 Law on Labour Exchanges and Unemployment Insurance (*Gesetz über Arbeitsvermittlung und Arbeitslosenversicherung*) included young workers under 21 in its regulations, so that if they had been in insured employment for the required period they were entitled to unemployment benefit (*Arbeitslosenunterstützung*), with the additional stipulation, however, that they could be required to perform obligatory labour (*Pflichtarbeit*) in return for their benefit.[5] This entitlement was eroded systematically by the Brüning government. The emergency decree of 5 June 1931 in particular represented a drastic worsening of the position of the young unemployed: it removed the entitlement of young people under 21 to unemployment benefit if they lived at home and were deemed by the local labour office to be in a position to be supported by their family. For those excluded from unemployment benefit proper, there remained the possibility of welfare assistance, at the discretion of the local welfare office. In practice this form of assistance was often denied to young people and — like unemployment benefit — could be made conditional on the participation of the young person concerned in a public works scheme (Harvey, 1993; Homburg, 1987).

Contemporary observers were quick to point out the links between youth unemployment and growing social disorder. They painted a stark picture of growing numbers of young unemployed men 'on the road' in search of work and gathering in hostels for down-and-outs; of unemployed youths being recruited into organized crime and political violence, and the unemployed of both sexes sliding into moral degeneracy (Ehrhardt, 1929/30, 1930; Muser, 1933). While such portrayals linking youth unemployment, political violence and social anarchy could be exaggerated, they were not without some plausibility. Young unemployed men were a prominent element in the radical anti-republican paramilitary organizations which clashed on the streets in the final years and months of the Republic (Fischer, 1983; Rosenhaft, 1983). Juvenile crime rose during the Depression, even though it did not rise as dramatically as might have been expected; and a subculture of youth gangs, some of them criminal, flourished in the big cities.[6]

Conflicting political outlooks coloured contemporary analyses of the problem of youth unemployment and the solutions proposed to deal with it. The conservative Right predictably stressed the need for strengthening the forces of authority within the family and society. Those in the educational reform camp, typically with liberal or Social Democratic political sympathies, tried to maintain their vision of a modern, therapeutically-informed approach to youth welfare. At the same time, the educational reform lobby was forced to come to terms with the fact that existing youth welfare provision was unable to cope with the demands placed upon it as a result of mass youth unemployment.

Public Youth Welfare on the Defensive

Youth welfare institutions formed a crucial part of the programmes and policies pursued by the governments of Weimar Germany to promote the education, welfare and social integration of children and young people. In its narrower sense of *Jugendfürsorge* as opposed to *Jugendpflege* (the latter term being used for 'youth work' in the sense of youth clubs, recreational activities, etc.), youth welfare had developed as a specialized branch of public welfare in Germany alongside the evolving system of juvenile justice from around the end of the nineteenth century. The public provision of youth welfare was codified at national level in 1922 in the National Youth Welfare Law (*Reichsjugendwohlfahrtsgesetz*), which among other things laid down a statutory minimum of tasks to be carried out by local youth welfare departments (*Jugendämter*).[7]

Youth welfare was concerned with individual cases of potential or actual educational neglect among minors. It set out to be both preventive — for instance one of the tasks laid down for youth welfare departments was the public guardianship of illegitimate children — as well as therapeutic, in cases where a child's socialization through the normal institutions of family and school appeared to have failed. In such cases, where the physical or moral health of a child was deemed to be at risk, the state was to intervene as the guarantor of every German child's statutory 'right to education to physical, spiritual and social fitness' (National Youth Welfare Law, 1922, paragraph 1). The pioneers of public welfare had not only fought for this right to be enshrined in law: they had also insisted that qualified social workers and adequate institutions be provided so that state intervention in cases of children and adolescents 'at risk' would be swift and effective. Such intervention might take the form of care in a foster family, probation (*Schutzaufsicht*) or referral to correctional education (see below).

The system of public youth welfare was scarcely consolidated when it was confronted with the problems caused by the Depression. Unemployment and poverty turned young people 'at risk' into a mass phenomenon. The National Youth Welfare Law, passed at a time of low youth unemployment, had not included provision for the young unemployed in its list of core tasks for local youth welfare departments. Nevertheless, youth welfare departments in big cities took it upon themselves to improvise — as far as they could within the limits set by their budgets — schemes which would draw in and cater for the young unemployed (Wauer, 1931; Magnus, 1927). However, as the tasks confronting youth welfare departments grew their resources dwindled. As Brüning's budget-balancing efforts at national level shifted the burden of supporting the unemployed onto local authority welfare departments, other branches of local welfare expenditure were cut back correspondingly. These cuts put a squeeze on all those youth welfare measures which were over and above the statutory minimum prescribed by the National Youth Welfare Law — including welfare for the unemployed (Kall, 1931).

As the fiscal constraints grew, public youth welfare institutions also found themselves under ideological attack from right-wingers who used eugenic arguments to 'prove' the wastefulness of public welfare. Since it was self-evidently targeted at the 'inferior' section of the population, so went the argument, public welfare acted counter-selectively; regrettable enough in 'normal' times, such a misdirection of public resources in times of economic crisis had to be stopped (Wessel, 1931). Applied to the case of youth welfare, this thinking led to the demand that resources be spent on the deviant and delinquent only where the benefits 'for the nation as a whole' could clearly justify the costs. This sort of Social Darwinist-inspired thinking was not new, but in the course of the Depression it came to be voiced more loudly and openly in government circles and in the specialist welfare press (Weindling, 1989).

Defending public youth welfare in this climate was an uphill task, though its advocates duly protested against the financial cuts and drew up 'emergency programmes' for youth welfare in the crisis (RdI, 1932). However, resistance to the cuts in youth welfare was hampered by the fact that youth welfare circles were not united among themselves. Some (though admittedly not all) spokesmen of private welfare organizations expressed the hope that the scaling down of public youth welfare provision might benefit them: they welcomed what appeared to be an opportunity to revise the hard-fought compromise of the National Youth Welfare Law between the public and private providers of welfare to the former's advantage. The private welfare organizations were encouraged in such hopes by the fact that the SPD, which had pushed hardest for the expansion of public welfare provision, had lost the political initiative. 'Private welfare is now coming back into its own, after having been pronounced dead ten years ago and despite efforts by the public authorities to kill it off', proclaimed a representative of the German Red Cross at a congress in September 1930 (Kessler, 1930, p. 576).

Disagreements were also evident among those who sought to maintain the public youth welfare system. Radical left-wing views appeared to be growing among the rank and file of social workers in response to the political threat from the Right.[8] Prominent liberal and Social Democratic reformers noted this development with alarm (Wachenheim, 1931a). However, they themselves remained on the defensive, confronted constantly with the problem of how far to resist and how far to compromise with the cuts and with right-wing plans for restructuring youth welfare. This dilemma posed itself particularly acutely for those concerned with the issue of correctional education.

Correctional Education: The Retreat from Reform?

Taking a juvenile into correctional education was the most drastic measure that the state youth welfare system could resort to. Juveniles under 20 years of age considered to be endangered by their social environment (National Youth Welfare Law, paragraph 63, section 1.1) or already delinquent (paragraph 63, section 1.2) could on the basis of a court order be removed from their homes and placed either with a foster family or employer, or, as in nearly half of all cases, in a reformatory.

Correctional education was the most controversial aspect of public youth welfare provision. Its critics pointed out that it meant an effective deprivation of liberty, the duration of which was not determined in advance (in contrast to a prison sentence) and which often lasted for several years. They attacked its clumsy referral and review procedures and its discriminatory class character. Middle-class parents, it was alleged — not without reason — usually had the means to prevent their children being taken into public care.[9] The most serious allegations concerned the reformatories, the majority of which were still run (with the aid of state subsidies) by confessional welfare agencies. Here, argued the critics, outdated educational methods continued to be practised by institutions whose aim was to save souls and produce God-fearing subjects who knew their place in life. Overall, liberal and left-wing critics argued that correctional education in its current form was not only inhumane but above all ineffectual as a way of educating children and adolescents to be citizens and productive members of a modern society.

An educational reform campaign to carry out a complete overhaul of correctional education emerged after the First World War and gathered momentum in the Republic's early years.[10] Among the main forces behind this campaign, which was inspired by the work of educational pioneers such as Karl Wilker, were the Social Democratic welfare organization Arbeiterwohlfahrt (founded 1919) and the Gilde Soziale Arbeit (founded 1925), the latter being a grouping of social workers and educationalists who shared a background in the youth movement.[11] The reforms proposed included the expansion of state as opposed to private reformatory provision, the strengthening of the legal rights of juveniles referred to correctional education, and the transfer of the administration of correctional education in Prussia from regional to local control. As far as conditions inside the reformatories were concerned, the campaigners called for tougher inspections of privately-run reformatories, the banning of corporal punishment, the introduction of a degree of self-government for inmates, the appointment of better-qualified staff and the improvement of vocational training.[12]

While the reform campaign made a certain amount of headway in the course of the 1920s in publicizing its criticisms and demands, it was only after a series of reformatory scandals that the campaigners were able effectively to bring pressure to bear on the institutions and public authorities which had hitherto resisted change.[13] Faced with growing public disquiet over reformatory conditions, in 1931 the Prussian welfare ministry issued revised guidelines on correctional education, and the Conference on Correctional Education (*Allgemeiner Fürsorgeerziehungstag* or AFET) published a declaration which amounted to a critique of past errors.[14] However, it would be wrong to over-estimate the impact made by the educational reform campaign even by this stage. Model reformatories where progressive educational principles were consistently practised were few in number. The wave of scandals had led to some remedial action by the authorities, but it also had the effect of making juvenile courts and youth welfare departments reluctant to refer youngsters to correctional education except as a last resort, which led in turn to a growing concentration of 'difficult cases', usually older adolescents, in correctional education.[15] At the same time, disciplinary problems in the reformatories grew as inmates became increasingly aware of their rights, or rather their lack of them. Opposition to the reformatory regime was sometimes encouraged and assisted by the Communist campaign against correctional education, which intensified towards the end of the 1920s (Brandt, 1929; Schellenberg, 1931).

A crisis thus already existed in correctional education before the economic crisis made itself felt, but the existing problems were exacerbated by the effects of the Depression. It had been axiomatic for Social Democrats, liberals and conservative educationalists alike that the key to the social reintegration of delinquent juveniles was instilling into them a strong work ethic and preparing them for jobs outside the institution. Mass unemployment made this educational strategy increasingly illusory. Jobs as domestic servants or agricultural workers were the most that could be obtained for ex-reformatory inmates, and even these were getting harder to find.[16] For the conservative camp in correctional education, this trend merely confirmed their view that old ways were the best ways. For the reformers who had campaigned for facilities to train inmates — girls as well as boys — for skilled trades, it was a dilemma. Some insisted that the goals of the reform campaign be revised in line with changing circumstances. Thus, for instance, Hans Achinger, speaking at a meeting of the Gilde Soziale Arbeit in July 1932, pleaded for an abandonment of 'unrealistic' demands. Training juveniles in correctional education for skilled trades was, he argued, a misdirection of resources at a time when 'thousands of normal youngsters are glad to escape from perpetual unemployment into the most primitive work on the land' (Achinger, 1932).

That young people in reformatories had it too good in comparison with adolescents outside was a criticism repeated frequently by those who advocated a reduction of welfare for the 'undeserving'. The Prussian welfare ministry may have been responding to such allegations when in February 1931 it instructed correctional education authorities in Prussia to ensure that the standard of living in the institutions was held to a level appropriate for the austere times.[17] By that stage, however, excessive opulence is unlikely to have been a feature of reformatories either in Prussia or anywhere else. During the Depression years many reformatories were closed down altogether: an estimated 10–15 per cent of all the reformatories run by the confessional welfare organizations closed between 1928 and 1932.[18] Those remaining in operation cut back on staffing and facilities.

Reductions in reformatory standards were a blow to the educational reformers, whose slogan had been 'better no reformatories than bad reformatories' (Bondy, 1930/1). Rudolf Schlosser, director of the reformatory in Bräunsdorf, warned against allowing the standard of living in the reformatories to sink to that endured by the most impoverished sections of the proletariat: it should, he argued, represent a standard to which inmates could and should aspire in later life.[19] However, not all the educational reformers shared this view; some, like Hans Achinger, whose views on vocational education have already been mentioned above, considered cuts in reformatory facilities necessary and justifiable (Achinger, 1932).

Deteriorating material conditions in the reformatories exacerbated the existing educational difficulties created by the fall in referrals of the younger and more tractable 'material' and the discontent of the adolescent inmates. Revolts, escapes and violent reactions by staff against inmates continued, doing further damage to the already tarnished image of correctional education (Francke, 1932). The unrest fuelled a call for tougher discipline: hardly had the liberal reformers begun to make an impact on the attitudes of the establishment than the backlash against liberalization began.[20] Indeed, by the autumn of 1932 some educational reformers themselves appeared ready to make some concessions on the issue of discipline. Previously, liberal reformers had responded unanimously to calls for 'back to the birch' with the argument that disorder and indiscipline among reformatory inmates was not so much a consequence of the new liberal educational methods as of their misguided application (Bondy, 1931). Now, however, some prominent voices from within the liberal reform camp could be heard questioning the wisdom of excessively liberal disciplinary methods and complaining that the pendulum had swung too far in the liberal direction. Justus Ehrhardt, a senior social worker in the Berlin youth welfare office and member of the Gilde Soziale Arbeit, wrote in October 1932 in a major youth welfare journal that 'there will have to be an end to the over-emphasis on banning punishments. This has now reached a stage where on account of someone's ear being boxed whole commissions are set in motion, questions are asked in parliament, thick files are accumulated . . .' (Ehrhardt, 1932/3, p. 229). On 26 October 1932, Curt Bondy, professor of educational science in Gottingen and director of the Eisenach youth prison, spoke at a public meeting called by educational and welfare organizations 'against the reaction in education'. Bondy rejected the right-wing calls for a simple return to authoritarian methods. He emphasized, however, the need for discipline and obedience to the demands of the social group as key principles of modern social education. He warned against the degeneration of an educational style which was in his view too heavily oriented to the 'sentimentality' and individualism of the youth movement and which no longer corresponded to the needs of the times. These remarks were interpreted by left-wing critics in the audience as a tactical withdrawal from previous liberal positions in an attempt to present the line of least resistance to the growing forces of the Right. These critics declared that the adoption of Bondy's position would bring the educational reform movement itself into the camp of reaction.[21]

The 'Limits of Educability' and the Reorientation of Correctional Education, 1931/2

The strength of the 'reaction in education' became evident as the debates on reformatories shifted from discussing educational methods towards the fundamental issue of defining the tasks and target group of correctional education. This debate reflected the search for a new policy which would both reduce costs and solve the educational problems in the reformatories.

The increasing financial pressure on correctional education produced in 1931/2 a growing lobby of administrators and reformatory directors who sought to cope with spending cuts by altering the categories of juveniles for whom correctional education could be ordered. In this predominantly Prussian lobby, which within the context of welfare politics constituted the conservative correctional education 'establishment', there were two driving forces. One was the organization of Prussian regional authorities (*Verband der Preußischen Provinzen*); the other was a group of reformatory directors and correctional education administrators who comprised the still dominant conservative wing of the AFET. It sought to cut costs while improving the 'success rates' of correctional education, maintaining the viability of existing public and private reformatories, upholding the principle of confessional education and preserving the regionally-based structure of correctional education administration.[22]

In the summer of 1931, the head of the regional authority in the Rhineland presented to the Prussian state government a plan for legislative change.[23] The general aim of this plan was to concentrate the resources of correctional education on younger children and adolescents 'at risk' instead of on those who were actually delinquent. Its advocates argued that catching and 'treating' potentially asocial juveniles at an early stage would prove in the long run to be an economy measure. The crisis in correctional education, in their eyes, was not so much due to the institutions but to the unsuitable and defective 'material' with which the system was called upon to deal.

Such a reorientation of correctional education required, firstly, an increase in the number of younger and 'lighter' cases referred. The National Youth Welfare Law of 1922 contained a clause (paragraph 63, section 1) which was generally read as giving priority to fostering or other care at local authority expense over 'preventive' referrals to correctional education.[24] The new plans for correctional education drawn up in 1931/2 were based on the regulations enabling 'preventive referrals' which had applied in Prussia under the ruling of 1915 but had been superseded by the National Youth Welfare Law. The advocates of 'preventive' referrals sought to restore the 1915 regulations in Prussia and extend them to the rest of the Reich.

The controversy over a change of referral practice was fiercest in Prussia, where rivalries between local authority youth welfare departments and regional correctional education authorities were most intense.[25] Liberal and Social Democratic reformers and administrators had welcomed and encouraged the decline in referrals of younger children to correctional education as long as the local youth welfare departments had been in a position to provide alternative methods of care on the local level. They condemned the right-wingers' demands for amendments to the law to enable earlier referral as a ploy on the part of the confessional organizations and the regional correctional education authorities to consolidate their power at the expense of the local youth welfare authorities.[26] However, local youth welfare authorities were not in a strong position to challenge the correctional education lobby: under the impact of Brüning's financial cuts, the local youth welfare services could not in practice provide the care they advocated as an alternative to correctional education (Friedländer, 1931). Despite the reluctance of the Prussian state government to support the change,[27] the advocates of 'preventive referral' got their way: the Reich Ministry of the Interior inserted clauses designed to enable 'preventive referral' into the first draft of an emergency decree on correctional education in November 1931.[28]

The other aspect of the Prussian correctional education lobby's plans to change its target group was to exclude and debar from it the more troublesome categories of juveniles: the older age groups and the 'ineducables' (*Unerziehbare*). This entailed, firstly, the reduction of the average age of juveniles in correctional education. This was to be achieved through lowering the upper age limit for referral (hitherto 18 years, but up to 20 years where the prospects of educational success were deemed to be good) and for release (hitherto 21 years). Secondly, 'ineducables' were to be excluded from correctional education. This would entail both the release of such juveniles who were already in correctional education, and a stricter selection at the referral stage according to the likelihood of educational success. The definition of what constituted 'ineducability' was deliberately left vague: 'ineducables' included not only those characterized as having 'hereditary mental or emotional abnormalities', but also those juveniles who were simply rebellious. The exclusion of the ineducables, it was argued, would end a 'misuse' and an 'inflation' of correctional education; it would restore order to reformatory life and improve the reformatories' public image. In addition, according to this view, it would save valuable resources squandered at a time of national economic crisis on juveniles unresponsive to and undeserving of such care and attention.[29]

Unlike the demand for an increase in 'preventive referral', the issue of the older and more 'difficult' juveniles in correctional education was not a specifically Prussian concern. Nor was the issue a new one: throughout the Weimar period, youth welfare experts had been discussing whether there were 'limits of educability' and, if so, how they could be defined. It was a question made more complicated in the Depression by the intertwining of two basically distinct approaches to the problem of educational difficulty.

On the one hand, an essentially pedagogical debate on the limits of education was in progress. This was partly a product of the far-reaching ambitions and ideals of the educational reformers: education, in their view, should not merely drill the youngster into outer conformity, but bring about profound and inward change in the young person's attitudes and behaviour. This was to be achieved in a pedagogical atmosphere of freedom and comradeship between educator and educated. If a young person's development was irreversible, if the influences of their milieu had already shaped them so far as to make them resistant to all educational efforts, went the argument, then education had found its limits. It was in the context of this debate that Bertha Paulssen, a senior administrator in the Hamburg youth welfare department and prominent representative of the campaign to modernize and liberalize reformatory education for girls, wrote in November 1931 that youth welfare institutions should cut their losses where certain categories of adolescents were concerned. Despite its racist overtones, her argument stressed above all the cultural and environmental limits of educability:

> I am thinking here particularly of artistes, dancers, girls from gypsy families, girls of mixed race and others. These girls are generally very experienced. Their development is complete; respectable middle-class life with its rules is something quite alien to them, and they have no possibility of integrating themselves into an existence based on such precepts.[30]

It was regrettable, she concluded, that existing laws did not allow for the release of such persons from correctional education.

Not all representatives of liberal reforming opinion shared Bertha Paulssen's views. Some educational reformers agreed with her that limiting the numbers of juveniles in correctional education was preferable to cutting standards for all, and that it would be sensible to limit numbers where educational success appeared least likely. Others rejected the idea of excluding the allegedly 'tough cases'; they pointed out that labelling adolescents as 'ineducable' would prove a temptation for reformatories to shirk their responsibilities.

The dangers of educationalists deciding, on whatever grounds, that certain youngsters would prove perpetually resistant to educational efforts were all the greater in the Depression given the growing prevalence of a more sinister discourse about 'ineducability' based on biologistic premises. The rise of the 'science of delinquency'[31] had brought with it attempts to diagnose and treat more successfully those juveniles seen as hard or impossible to educate. The racial hygienists' contribution was to focus on the degree to which juveniles' educability was affected by their genetic makeup. A prominent exponent of this approach was Werner Villinger, a colleague of Bertha Paulssen in the Hamburg youth welfare office. In his reports for the juvenile court, he consistently sought to highlight the hereditary dimension to the psychological defects and intellectual inadequacies he diagnosed. In 1931, he declared that correctional education in Hamburg was 'most severely burdened by constitutionally abnormal children and juveniles, most of whom display intellectual weakness and psychopathic tendencies, often in combination'.[32] Villinger, it was true, emphasized that 'abnormal' children were not *necessarily* ineducable; he, after all, was interested in promoting psychiatric expertise as the key to treating even unpromising cases. However, such subtleties could easily get lost when a biologistic approach was taken up by others more interested in ridding the Weimar welfare state of its 'burdens'. A particularly forthright position was formulated by Helmuth Schreiner in 1931 in the journal of the Innere Mission, the Protestant welfare organization: it was hubris, he argued, to assume that everyone was educable. Limits were set by nature; no educational efforts could redeem anything from 'ruined hereditary material' (*einer zerstörten Erbmasse*). Any solution to the current problems of correctional education, he argued, had to be based on an awareness of the biological limits of educability.[33]

Notions of biological inferiority and of genetically determined conditions of being 'difficult to educate' or 'ineducable' fitted well into the climate in the Depression of targeting education and welfare resources more effectively on the 'valuable'. Meanwhile, with proposals for legislative change still under discussion, the exclusion of the older age groups and of allegedly 'ineducable' juveniles from correctional education was already beginning in practice: it was reported that the authorities concerned were either holding back from referring difficult cases, or authorizing the release of particularly recalcitrant inmates.[34]

Still more controversial than the proposal to remove the more difficult categories of juvenile from correctional education was the issue of what should be done with such youngsters if they were released. A number of suggestions were made regarding what should be done with the 'ineducables' who were expelled or debarred from correctional education. Only a minority of youth welfare experts regarded with equanimity the prospect of simply releasing the 'ineducables' back into society.

Many supported proposals for alternative forms of detention which were intended to be cheaper and tougher than correctional education.

One proposed alternative to the reformatory for the 'ineducables' was the work-house (*Arbeitshaus*). This was suggested by the organization of Prussian regional authorities to the Reich Ministry of the Interior in November 1931. The Prussian regional authorities argued that it was necessary to stop 'ineducables' deliberately misbehaving to effect their release and that a 'greater evil' should threaten those expelled from correctional education on grounds of ineducability.[35] In November 1931, drawing up the first draft of the emergency decree on correctional education, the Reich Ministry of the Interior proposed that paragraph 73 of the National Youth Welfare Law be amended to allow juveniles aged between 18 and 21 who had 'demonstrated an obstinate resistance, not attributable to a pathological constitution, to the educational measures of correctional education' to be referred to the workhouse.[36]

An outcry from educational reformers greeted this plan. The workhouse was an institution which in the Weimar period hitherto had been reserved for the detention of adult 'asocials' who were referred there by the police after convictions for vagrancy, pimping, drunkenness, prostitution, etc. The proposal to send juveniles there was denounced as a return to an educational Dark Age (Wachenheim, 1931b). The liberal reformers succeeded in December 1931 in getting the clause on the workhouse removed from the government draft, and the Ministry of the Interior omitted any mention of special provision for released 'ineducables' from the second draft of the emergency decree, dated January 1932. In response, the right-wing correctional education lobby threw itself into a campaign for the introduction of the long-debated 'protective detention' (*Bewahrung*), specifically to cope with juveniles excluded from correctional education who would 'put themselves and society at risk' if they were left to their own devices.

Protective detention appeared to be a simple way for the welfare services to deal with a number of 'problem' categories of people. In theory, it was to protect those regarded as weak-willed and eugenically unfit 'from themselves' as well as protecting society from their anti-social behaviour.[37] The demand for a law on protective detention was not simply a product of a right-wing backlash in the final years of the Republic. On the contrary, it had been discussed since the beginning of the Weimar Republic by welfare specialists ranging in political affiliation from the Right to the Social Democratic Left, and had been proposed in Reichstag resolutions backed by the Social Democrats between 1925 and 1927. In 1927, the Reich Ministry of the Interior drafted a law which envisaged protective detention for persons over 18 years who were or were in danger of becoming *verwahrlost*, and who had either been placed under public care and authority (*entmündigt*) on the grounds of 'mental weakness', or who were alcoholic, or who had been convicted for begging, vagrancy or prostitution.[38] The decisive obstacle to the realization of these plans had been the problem of financing them. Now, with the economy and public finances in crisis, undeterred by the fate of all previous attempts to introduce protective detention, the correctional education lobby tried once more. In January 1932, the AFET demanded the immediate introduction of a law on protective detention, in order to close the loophole opening up as a result of the cuts in correctional education.[39] With regard to alternative and stricter forms of detention for youngsters released from correctional education, practice again anticipated legislative change. Legal forms presented few obstacles to enterprising administrators in the Prussian province of the Rhineland, where the regional youth welfare authority introduced such detention for older girls in the summer of 1932 (Neuhaus, 1932).

Meanwhile, the efforts of the Prussian correctional education establishment to obtain the legal changes they sought were bearing little fruit. After consultations with the governments of the *Länder* in the spring of 1932, the Brüning government made no further moves to issue the planned emergency decree. In the summer of 1932, however, Papen's Minister of the Interior, Freiherr von Gayl, took up the plans once more.[40] A long silence on the part of the ministry ensued; then, on 4 November 1932, the Papen government suddenly issued an emergency decree revising the regulations regarding correctional education, taking specialist youth welfare circles by surprise.[41]

The details of the emergency decree fulfilled the wishes of the conservative correctional education establishment with regard to the exclusion of 'difficult' juveniles. While the upper age limit for referral in normal cases continued, as in the National Youth Welfare Law, to be the juvenile's eighteenth birthday, the upper age limit for referral in exceptional cases was reduced from the twentieth birthday to the nineteenth birthday. In the law of 1922, the upper age limit for release had been the young person's twenty-first birthday: now, the upper age limit for release in all but exceptional cases was to be the nineteenth birthday. In special cases, the authorities could apply for an extension of correctional education up till the young person's twenty-first birthday. The release of 'ineducables' was legalized, and the referral to correctional education was made conditional in every case on the prospect of educational success.

In one important respect, however, the decree did not satisfy the Prussian correctional education lobby. No provisions were made for alternative forms of detention for the older and/or 'ineducable' juveniles who would be released from correctional education as a result of the decree. The paradox that at the height of the political and social crisis the state was voluntarily relinquishing an important means of control over a group of particularly troublesome adolescents was not lost on critics. The youth welfare director in Lübeck had already pointed out the possible consequences for law and order of a restriction of correctional education: 'with public order in its present state, and the so-called *Halbstarken* playing such a prominent role, a retreat by the state in its function as educator will seem like the bankruptcy of state authority'.[42]

Insofar as the decree of 4 November 1932 restricted the categories of juveniles eligible for referral to correctional education, it could be seen as a measure which, while being designed to fulfil a number of goals, was largely motivated by financial considerations. However, financial factors played a minor role with regard to other provisions of the decree. These provisions extended the powers and responsibilities of the correctional authorities at the expense of the local youth welfare departments, in order to bring about an increase of 'preventive' referrals to correctional education of younger juveniles 'at risk'.[43] This was clearly not an economy measure; indeed, it seemed that the resulting costs of extra referrals might well outweigh the savings made by excluding the older adolescents.

The effects of the emergency decree were less dramatic in practice than widely predicted or feared; in particular, the chaos expected to result from releasing the older inmates of the reformatories did not ensue. This was for two reasons. Firstly, not all the 19- and 20-year-olds in correctional education were released immediately: a supplementary decree issued on 28 November 1932 in response to reformatory directors' protests enabled correctional education authorities to postpone the release of these age groups until March 1933. About a fifth of 19- and 20-year-olds in correctional education had their release postponed in this way.[44] Secondly, a large number of those who were released from correctional education as a result of the decree turned out not to have been in reformatories anyway. They were either living with their employers or foster families, were on parole at home or had escaped and were untraceable. In the course of the financial year 1932/3 the number of juveniles in reformatories fell by 20.7 per cent, while the number of juveniles in foster families and with employers fell by 37 per cent. For the latter group of juveniles, the release from correctional education was more or less a formality. In such cases, the efforts to rid correctional education of its older cases were more a matter of rationalization than of setting a new course for youth welfare policy.

What actually happened to the 19- and 20-year-olds who were released from reformatories must remain a matter for speculation. Their numbers were estimated to be 7000 in Prussia, 250 in Württemberg, only 25 in Hamburg.[45] A Prussian report mentioned that 'the voluntary labour service and the nationalist organizations have given some of them a temporary home' (Zengerling, 1933/4, p. 127).

Though so much had been talked about the problem of the 'ineducables' before the emergency decree was issued, the number of youngsters actually released from correctional education on the grounds of 'ineducability' rather than age was very small: one estimate put it at between 6 and 7 per cent of those released (Hundinger, 1933, p. 133). It was pointed out that many 'ineducables' were released on grounds of age anyway. On the other hand, the lack of alternative detention facilities may have inhibited large-scale expulsions. By the end of the financial year 1932/3, 218 juveniles in the Reich, of whom 192 were from Prussia, had been released on the grounds of 'significant mental or emotional abnormality' and 67 on the grounds of 'character'. Of those released, it was reported that the majority had already been in mental hospitals and asylums. Here again, the ending of correctional education was of more significance for the correctional education authorities than for the juveniles concerned, who simply remained where they were with merely the legal basis having changed.[46]

Regarding the pattern of new referrals, the decree had within the first few months the expected effect of increasing the proportion of referrals of younger children on the grounds of 'prevention'. Between April and the end of November 1932, 203 juveniles were referred to correctional education in Prussia on the grounds of 'risk' and 2866 on the grounds of delinquency. Between 1 December 1932 and 31 March 1933, 207 were referred on the grounds of 'risk', and 1313 on the grounds of delinquency. Referrals of older juveniles to correctional education fell: however, here the decree merely confirmed a trend already evident in 1931/2.

The 'Dictatorship of Poverty' and New Trends in Youth Welfare Policy at the End of the Weimar Republic

The correctional education system released a few thousand adolescents at the end of 1932 on to the streets and left local welfare services to deal with them. This merely added to the dilemma of the local authority youth welfare facilities, which were already unable to cope with the tens of thousands out of work and 'at risk'. In one sense, what a later commentator called the 'declaration of bankruptcy' by the reformatories with regard to their more recalcitrant inmates (Braunschweig, 1939, p. 285) was of limited significance compared with the scale of the overall problem of adolescent destitution and delinquency. Justus Ehrhardt pointed out in a pessimistic article of October 1932 that correctional education had become an increasingly arbitrary measure anyway, 'a sort of lottery, where you don't know whether you will lose or win, get referred or not' (Ehrhardt, 1932/3, p. 228).

The problems confronting youth welfare workers in the Depression who tried to educate and influence young people 'at risk' by means of probation were spelled out by a leading Social Democratic spokesman on youth welfare issues in January 1932.[47] He pointed out that unemployment not only made it impossible to find a job for a youngster on probation: it also created tensions in families, which placed a young person in a situation of additional risk. Nor were youth organizations able to fill the gap. Other commentators pointed out the impact of staffing cuts: many probation cases which were still officially on the books were in practice simply abandoned (Oswalt, 1932). Justus Ehrhardt summed up the sense of powerlessness felt by social workers dealing with unemployed youngsters 'at risk':

> When a youngster proves to the social worker down to the last penny that he cannot survive on his benefit and that he has to get the rest of what he needs from begging, stealing or prostituting himself, even the most positive attitude on the part of the social worker is useless.[48]

In the final phase of the Republic, liberal and Social Democratic educational reformers began to cast around for new solutions to the mass problem of young people 'at risk'. The voluntary labour service (*Freiwilliger Arbeitsdienst*), for instance, initiated by the Brüning government and expanded under Papen, gained widespread — albeit qualified — support in youth welfare circles. Despite their qualms, for instance about the degree of involvement in the programme by radical right-wing organizations, it seemed to many involved in youth welfare and education that the defects of the voluntary labour service programme were outweighed by its potential as an instrument of mass education.[49] At the same time, it was clear that the much-publicized measures introduced by the governments of Brüning, Papen and Schleicher were palliatives rather than real solutions to the social problems created by the Depression.

In late 1932, social workers were reported to be suffering from 'a fatal feeling of resignation' in face of the tasks confronting them and the inadequacy of the means available to enable them to intervene. At a meeting of the Gilde Soziale Arbeit in October 1932, the Berlin juvenile court judge Herbert Francke was reported as having given an accurate summary of the situation: 'he demonstrated how dependent we are today on the state of the economy and spoke of the dictatorship of poverty, which finds in youth welfare the point of least resistance'.[50]

The morale of the left-wing and liberal reformers was further undermined in the last weeks before the National Socialist takeover by the erosion of their institutional base in youth welfare and education. The pioneering reformatory in Frankfurt am Main, the Westendheim, was closed at the end of December 1932 because of the sharp decline in the number of inmates. Herbert Francke was transferred away from the juvenile courts in November 1932; Curt Bondy was dismissed from his post as director of the youth prison in Eisenach in December 1932. These were presentiments of the more comprehensive purge that was to come.[51]

1933 and After: Trends in Youth Welfare Under National Socialism

An analysis of youth welfare in Nazi Germany would go far beyond the limits of this essay: the following remarks merely highlight some of the trends in youth welfare following the Nazi takeover.

The influence of liberal and Social Democratic educational reformers on youth welfare policy was, as has already been mentioned, being eroded before 1933; following the Nazi takeover, the ministries and departments concerned with youth welfare were quickly purged of politically and 'racially' suspect personnel. Thus purged, the youth welfare institutions of the Weimar era were retained, adapted and harnessed to Nazi goals. Youth welfare policy had now to be oriented towards the interests of the *Volksgemeinschaft* rather than the interests of the individual child; accordingly, youth welfare departments were to apply to the children and young people coming under their jurisdiction a rigorous policy of selection, defining them according to their level of 'racial value' or 'hereditary quality' and treating them accordingly.

This agenda of selection and exclusion had a number of implications for correctional education after 1933. Neglected, deprived and delinquent children and adolescents who were referred to correctional education might be assigned, as 'lighter cases', to the newly-set up homes run by the NSV (*Nationalsozialistische Volkswohlfahrt*); or, if judged of 'inferior' quality, to the homes run by the confessional welfare organizations. There, inmates ran the risk of being selected for sterilization; if judged 'ineducable', they might be assigned to 'protective detention', which although not introduced formally was introduced in practice. Overall, this development was a blow to the confessional welfare organizations, who had initially greeted the new regime in the hope that it would restore the influence they felt the Weimar welfare system had denied them. Instead, they were relegated to the role of providers of care for the supposedly 'less valuable' members of the community, while the NSV set about building up its welfare empire.[52]

Meanwhile, the context in which youth welfare institutions were operating was changing profoundly. Politicians and professionals concerned with youth welfare during the Depression had seen the need, but lacked the resources, to tackle the problem of youth unemployment and what appeared to be a rising tide of juvenile delinquency and neglect. From 1933 onwards, measures to remove the young unemployed from the streets onto a variety of work schemes were quickly expanded and new schemes improvised.[53] For the mass of children and young people from ten years upwards, the various branches of the Hitler Youth created a new 'educational' institution which sought to control and channel adolescent leisure into activities useful to the regime.[54] And for those who broke the law or flouted Nazi norms, sanctions and penalties proliferated: from 1940 onwards, alongside the system of juvenile justice, emerged the new institution of *Jugendschutzlager* (concentration camp for juveniles).[55]

This sketch cannot do justice to the complexity of developments in youth welfare after 1933: apart from anything else, it ignores the extent of institutional friction, organizational chaos and deliberate non-compliance which could slow down or hinder the implementation of Nazi policies, issues which other essays in this collection explore in more depth. What it has tried to show is how while in some respects Nazi youth welfare policies signalled a new departure, the regime at the same time was able to build upon developments which took place before 1933. The Depression years had been a catalyst for the emergence of a welfare agenda that sought to target welfare provision on the 'deserving' and 'fit' at the expense of the 'undeserving'/'unfit', with an increasing emphasis on the supposedly hereditary factors determining 'asocial' behaviour and 'ineducability'. This agenda, which influenced but did not fully transform welfare policy in the final phase of the Republic, was taken up and implemented systematically by youth welfare institutions under the Nazi regime.

Notes

1   While based on the original contribution to *Sozialarbeit und Faschismus*, this chapter is a revised version which draws on Chapters 7 and 8 of the author's (1993) *Youth and the Welfare State in Weimar Germany*, Oxford, Oxford University Press. The material from those chapters appears with the kind permission of Oxford University Press.

2   On youth welfare in the final phase of the Weimar Republic, see C. Hasenclever (1978) *Jugendhilfe und Jugendgesetzgebung seit 1900*, Göttingen, Vandenhoeck & Ruprecht; R. Baron, '"Ballastexistenzen": Sparmaßnahmen in der Krise; Fürsorgeerziehung im Übergang zum Dritten Reich', in G. Vobruba (1983) (Ed) *'Wir sitzen alle in einem Boot': Gemeinschaftsrhetorik in der Krise*, Frankfurt/M. and New York, Campus; D. J.K. Peukert (1986) *Grenzen der Sozialdisziplinierung: Aufstieg und Krise der deutschen Jugendfürsorge 1878–1932*, Köln, Bund-Verlag; M. Gräse (1995) *Der blockierte Wohlfahrtsstaat: Unterschichtjugend und Jugendfürsorge in der Weimarer Republik*, Göttingen, Vandenhoeck & Ruprecht.

3 On youth unemployment and policies towards unemployed youth in Weimar Germany, see D.J.K. Peukert (1987) *Jugend zwischen Krieg und Krise: Lebenswelten von Arbeiterjungen in der Weimarer Republik*, Köln, Bund-Verlag, pp. 167–88; id., 'The lost generation: Youth unemployment at the end of the Weimar Republic', in R.J. Evans and D. Geary (1987) (Eds) *The German Unemployed: Experiences and Consequences of Mass Unemployment from the Weimar Republic to the Third Reich*, London, Croom Helm, pp. 172–93; P.D. Stachura (1989) *The Weimar Republic and the Younger Proletariat: An Economic and Social Analysis*, London, Macmillan; E. Harvey, *Youth and the Welfare State*, pp. 103–51. The quotation 'A whole generation is being driven to delinquency' is taken from: 'Der Inhalt der Hungerverordnung', *Rote Fahne*, 7 June 1931.

4 In 1925, 14–18-year-olds totalled 5.246 million (= 8.4 per cent of the population; in 1933, 14–18-year-olds totalled 2.933 million (= 4.5 per cent of the population). *Statistisches Jahrbuch für das deutsche Reich* 1935, p. 13.

5 K.C. Führer (1990) *Arbeitslosigkeit und die Entstehung der Arbeitslosenversicherung 1902–1927*, Berlin, pp. 342–5. Apprentices were not obliged to pay unemployment insurance contributions until six months before the apprenticeship contract was due to expire.

6 On juvenile crime during the Depression, see E. Harvey, *Youth and the Welfare State*, pp. 189–90; on gangs, O. Voss and H. Schön (1930) 'Cliquen jugendlicher Verwahrloster als sozialpädagogisches Problem', in C. Mennicke (Ed) *Erfahrungen der Jungen*, Potsdam, pp. 69–89.

7 On the National Youth Welfare Law, see C. Hasenclever, *Jugendhilfe und Jugendgesetzgebung*, pp. 48–77; E. Harvey, *Youth and the Welfare State*, pp. 165–73.

8 'Gilde und Politik', *RG*, **21** (November 1931).

9 Dr. Wagner-Roemnitz (1918–19) 'Fürsorgeerziehung und Arbeiterschaft', *SP*, **28**, 52, pp. 953–5; E. Schellenberg (1931) 'FE und Proletariat', *Proletarische Sozialpolitik*, **4**, 1, pp. 21–3. On the social background of those referred to correctional education, see Peukert, *Sozialdisziplinierung*, pp. 338–9, 355; Gräse, *Der blockierte Wohlfahrtsstaat*, p. 93.

10 On the ideas of the educational reformers, see D.J.K. Peukert, *Sozialdisziplinierung*, pp. 199–206.

11 Among Karl Wilker's writings were 'Erziehungsheim Lindenhof: Ein Stück Tat gewordene Jugendbewegung', *Internationale Erziehungsrundschau* 11, 1920, pp. 91–104 and *Fürsorgeerziehung als Lebensschulung: Ein Aufruf zur Tat*, Berlin, 1921. On the youth welfare work of the Arbeiterwohlfahrt, see E. Harvey (1987) *Youth Welfare and Social Democracy in Weimar Germany: The Work of Walter Friedländer*, New Alyth, Lochee Publications, and id., 'Sozialdemokratische Jugendhilfereform in der Praxis: Walter Friedländer und das Bezirksjugendamt Prenzlauer Berg in der Weimarer Republik', *Theorie und Praxis der sozialen Arbeit* 36, 6 (1985), pp. 218–29. On the Gilde Soziale Arbeit, see *Fünfzig Jahre Gilde Soziale Arbeit 1925–75*, 1975.

12 'Richtlinien des Hauptausschusses für Arbeiterwohlfahrt zur Umgestaltung der FE mit Erläuterungen', *AW*, **4**, 10, 1929, pp. 289–320; J. Ehrhardt (1930) 'Die Gilde "Soziale Arbeit" und der AFET', *Der Zwiespruch* **12**, 44, p. 523; id. (1930) 'Die Krise der Anstaltserziehung', *Der Zwiespruch* **12**, 15, pp. 169–70.

13 On the scandals, see D.J.K. Peukert, *Sozialdisziplinierung*, pp. 243–4; E. Harvey, *Youth and the Welfare State*, pp. 236, 240; C. Kuhlmann (1989) *Erbkrank oder erziehbar? Jugendhilfe als Vorsorge und Aussonderung in der Fürsorgeerziehung in Westfalen von 1933–1945*, Weinheim and Munich, Juventa, pp. 32–3, 37; M. Gräse, *Der blockierte Wohlfahrtsstaat*, pp. 102–6.

14 'Runderlaß des Preußischen Ministeriums für Volkswohlfahrt vom 20. 6. 1931 betr. Fürsorgeerziehung', *Volkswohlfahrt*, **12**, 1931, col. 620; 'Erklärung des Allgemeinen Fürsorgeerziehungstages', *ZBl*, **23**, 6, 1931/2, p. 193.

15 As a proportion of total referrals to correctional education in Prussia, children under 14 years constituted 43.5 per cent in 1926/7, but only 22.8 per cent in 1931/2. For Prussian correctional education statistics for these years, see *Volkswohlfahrt*, **13**, 1932, pp. 162–86, 694–723; *Zeitschrift des Preußischen Statistischen Landesamtes*, **72**, 1934, pp. 413–30.

16 'Auszug aus dem Jahresbericht über die FE Minderjähriger in der Provinz Hannover für die Zeit April 1931–März 1932', *Volkswohlfahrt*, **13**, 1932, cols. 941–5. On the poor job prospects of ex-reformatory inmates, see M. Gräse, *Der blockierte Wohlfahrtsstaat*, pp. 119–29.

17 Preußisches Ministerium für Volkswohlfahrt an die Oberpräsidenten, betr. Fürsorgeerziehungskosten, 26 February 1931, BA Koblenz, R36, 1976.

18 Rudolf Schlosser's estimate, in Bericht über die Sitzung des Fachausschusses 1 des AFET, 9/10 December 1932, StAH, Jugendbehörde I, 232, vol. 1.

19 Schlosser, in 'Bericht über die Sitzung des Fachausschusses 1 des AFET', see note above.

20 Erklärung des Landesdirektors der Provinz Brandenburg zu den Vorgängen in der Provinzialanstalt Strausberg am 16./17. Februar 1932', quoted in H. Webler, 'Neue Anstaltsprozesse', *ZBl*, **24**, 2, 1932/3, pp. 58–9.

21 'Gegen die pädagogische Reaktion', *ZBl*, **24**, 9, 1932/3, pp. 343–4; 'Pädagogische Bewegung oder pädagogische Reaktion', *RG*, 1 January 1933, 1 February 1933; H. Jacoby (1980) *Von des Kaisers Schule zu Hitlers Zuchthaus*, Frankfurt am Main, pp. 169–70.

22 For a discussion of the somewhat dubious 'success statistics' produced by the Prussian confessional education authorities, see D.J.K. Peukert, *Sozialdisziplinierung*, pp. 346, 358.

23 'Abbruch der vorbeugenden Erziehungsfürsorge?', *WRP*, **7**, 15, 1931, pp. 239–40.

24 Dr. Memelsdorff, 'Denkschrift über die Abgrenzung zwischen Fürsorgepflicht und Fürsorgeerziehung', 8 May 1928, BA Koblenz, R36, 1997. This interpretation of the law was confirmed by a decision by the Reichsgericht in April 1929. This decision displeased those with a vested interest in confessional reformatory education: whereas the principle of placing a child according to its confession was laid down for correctional education (National Youth Welfare Law, paragraph 69), it was not prescribed for fostering at local authority expense under paragraph 63, section 1. On this issue, see G. von Mann (1930) 'Um die Zukunft unserer Anstalten', *Jugendwohl*, **19**, pp. 2–4.

25 Landeshauptmann der Provinz Sachsen an den deutschen Städtetag, 18 May 1931, BA Koblenz, R36, 1996.

26 H. Francke an Paul Blumenthal, 5 November 1931; W. Hertz, 'Vorbericht für die Sitzung des Wohlfahrtsausschusses des Deutschen Städtetags', 13 November 1931, StAH, Jugendbehörde I, 232, vol. 1.

27 Preußisches Ministerium für Volkswohlfahrt an den RMdI, 23 August 1931, ZStA Merseburg, Rep. 120, BB XV 61 (now transferred to Geheimes Staatsarchiv Preußischer Kulturbesitz, Berlin-Dahlem); Preußisches Ministerium für Volkswohlfahrt an den RMdI, Februar 1932, BA Koblenz, R36, 2005.

28 Entwurf des RMdI einer Notverordnung zur Fürsorgeerziehung, November 1932, StAH, Jugendbehörde I, 232, vol. 1.

29 'Abbruch der vorbeugenden Erziehungsfürsorge?', *WRP*, **7**, 15, 1931, pp. 239–40.

30 Bertha Paulssen (Landesjugendamt Hamburg) an Gertrud Bäumer (RMdI), 11 November 1931. StAH, Jugendbehörde I, 232, vol. 1.

31 The term is used by D.J.K. Peukert, *Sozialdisziplinierung*, p. 151.
32 Dienstbesprechung des Jugendamtes, 17 December 1931, StAH, Jugendbehörde I, 3, vol. 1.
33 H. Schreiner (1931) 'Der Kampf um die Fürsorgeerziehung', *Innere Mission im Evangelischen Deutschland*, **26**, pp. 194–9, here p. 198, cited by D.J.K. Peukert, *Sozialdisziplinierung*, p. 250.
34 For examples of this see E. Harvey, *Youth and the Welfare State*, pp. 254–5.
35 Verband der preußischen Provinzen an den RMdI, 23 November 1931, BA Koblenz, R36, 1983.
36 Entwurf des RMdI einer Notverordnung zur Fürsorgeerziehung, November 1932, StAH, Jugendbehörde I, 232, vol. 1.
37 On protective detention, see D.J.K. Peukert, *Sozialdisziplinierung*, pp. 263–301.
38 Niederschrift über die Verhandlungen der Kommission zur Beratung eines Entwurfs zu einem Bewahrungsgesetz, 13 January 1927, BA Potsdam, 15.01, 1373; RMdI an die Landesregierungen betr. Bewahrungsgesetz, 26 January 1928, StAH, Medizinalkollegium, II U 3.
39 AFET, Rundschreiben vom 25. Jan. 1932, StAH, Jugendbehörde I, 232, vol. 1.
40 RMdI an den Staatssekretär in der Reichskanzlei, 29 July 1932, BA Potsdam, 30.01, 1518.
41 Verordnung des Reichspräsidenten über Jugendwohlfahrt vom 4. November 1932, *RGBl* 1932, I, no. 74, p. 522.
42 Behörde für Arbeit und Wohlfahrt Lübeck an den Lübecker Senat, 29 September 1931, StAH, Jugendbehörde I, 232, vol. 1.
43 Verordnung des Reichspräsidenten über Jugendwohlfahrt, 4 November 1932, *RGBl*, 1932, I, p. 522: deletion of paragraph 55, amendment of paragraph 63 of RJWG.
44 RMdI an den Staatssekretär in der Reichskanzlei, 22 November 1932, BA Koblenz, R43 II, 785; VO des Reichspräsidenten über Fürsorgeerziehung vom 28. November 1932, *RGBl*, 1932, I, Nr. 77, p. 531; Loebich, 'Neuerungen in der Fürsorgeerziehung', *BWW*, **86**, 1, 1933, pp. 5–8.
45 Estimates for Prussia: Konferenz der Landesvertreter im RMdI, 15 November 1932, StAH, Jugendbehörde I, 232, vol. 1; for Württemberg: Loebich, 'Neuerungen in der FE'; for Hamburg: Wilhelm Hertz, 'Die Notverordnung des Reichspräsidenten über Jugendwohlfahrt', *Jugend-und Volkswohl*, **8**, 4, 1932.
46 F. Zengerling, 'Fürsorgeerziehung in Preußen', p. 126.
47 W. Friedländer, in Niederschrift über die Besprechung eines Notprogramms für Kinder- und Jugendfürsorge im Preußischen Ministerium für Volkswohlfahrt, 29 January 1932, BA Koblenz R36, 1460.
48 J. Ehrhardt, 'Gefahren in der Jugendfürsorge', p. 226.
49 On the voluntary labour service generally, see H. Köhler (1967) *Arbeitsdienst in Deutschland: Pläne und Verwirklichungsformen bis zur Einführung der Arbeitsdienstpflicht im Jahre 1935*, Berlin; P. Dudek (1988) *Erziehung durch Arbeit: Arbeitslagerbewegung und Freiwilliger Arbeitsdienst 1920–1935*, Opladen, Westdeutscher Verlag; D. Morgan (1978) *Weiblicher Arbeitsdienst in Deutschland*, Darmstadt. On the response of youth welfare reformers and educationalists to the voluntary labour service: K. Ruth (1931/2) 'Der Freiwillige Arbeitsdienst Jugendlicher', *ZBl*, **23**, 7, pp. 240–4; 'Bericht über die Schulungswoche in Friedrichsroda 1932', *RG*, **23** July 1932, pp. 15–16; W. Friedländer (1932), 'Fachkonferenz für die Ausgestaltung des FAD für Frauen', *AW*, **7**, 22, pp. 699–701.
50 E. Behnke (1932) reporting on Gilde meeting of 27 October 1932, *RG*, **25**, 1 December.

51 'Versetzung von Landgerichtsdirektor Francke', *RG*, November 1932; 'Curt Bondy gekündigt: Ein Erfolg der Reaktion', *RG*, December 1932; Jacoby, *Von Kaisers Schule zu Hitlers Zuchthaus*, pp. 169–70.

52 On correctional education in Nazi Germany, see C. Kuhlmann, *Erbkrank oder erziehbar?*.

53 Such schemes, which served a number of functions, one of which was to remove young people temporarily from the labour market, included the voluntary labour service (compulsory for men from 1935); 'Farm Aid' (*Landhilfe*); the 'Farm Year' (*Landjahr*) (from 1934); and the 'Domestic Service Year' (*Hauswirtschaftliches Jahr*) (for girls, from 1934).

54 On the Hitler Youth generally, see A. Klönne (1984) *Jugend im Dritten Reich: Die Hitler-Jugend und ihre Gegner*, Köln. On the BDM, see D. Reese (1989) *'Straff, aber nicht stramm — herb, aber nicht derb: Zur Vergesellschaftung von Mädchen durch den Bund Deutscher Mädel im sozialkulturellen Vergleich zweier Milieus*, Weinheim, Beltz.

55 C. Kuhlmann, *Erbkrank oder erziehbar?*, pp. 202–7; D.J.K. Peukert, *Sozialdisziplinierung*, pp. 287–91.

References

The following abbreviations have been used in the references and notes:

AW = Arbeiterwohlfahrt
BA Koblenz = Bundesarchiv Koblenz
BA Potsdam = Bundesarchiv Potsdam
BWW = Blätter der Zentralleitung für die Wohltätigkeit in Württemberg
RG = Rundbrief der Gilde Soziale Arbeit
RGBl = Reichsgesetzblatt
RMdI = Reichsministerium des Innern
SP = Soziale Praxis
StAH = Staatsarchiv Hamburg
VO = Verordnung
WRP = Wohlfahrtspflege in der Rheinprovinz
ZStA = Zentrales Staatsarchiv Merseburg
ZBl = Zentralblatt für Jugendrecht und Jugendwohlfahrt

ACHINGER, H. (1932) 'Fürsorge und Wirtschaftskrise', *RG*, **23**, pp. 8–10.
BÄUMER, G. (1932) 'Die Jugendwohlfahrtspflege in der Krise', *Blätter des Deutschen Roten Kreuzes*, **11**, 7.
BONDY, C. (1930/1) 'Kritisches zur FE', *ZBl*, **22**, 5, pp. 145–9.
BONDY, C. (1931) *Scheuen*, Berlin.
BRANDT, A. (1929) 'Zwischenbilanz der Fürsorgeerziehungskampagne der IAH', *Proletarische Sozialpolitik*, **2**, 6, pp. 179–83.
BRAUNSCHWEIG, E. (1939) 'Die Situation von Fürsorgeerziehung und Jugendstrafvollzug vor und nach 1933', 2, *Die deutsche Sonderschule*, **6**, 4, pp. 281–9.
EHRHARDT, J. (1929/30) 'Cliquenwesen und Jugendverwahrlosung', *ZBl*, **12**, 12, pp. 413–18.
EHRHARDT, J. (1930) 'Arbeitslosigkeit und Jugendverwahrlosung', *Der Zwiespruch* **12**, 20, pp. 229–30.
EHRHARDT, J. (1932/3) 'Gefahren in der Jugendfürsorge', *ZBl*, **24**, 7, pp. 225–32.
FISCHER, C. (1983) *Stormtroopers: A Social, Economic and Ideological Analysis, 1929–1935*, London.

FRANCKE, H. (1932) 'Von Scheuen zu Strausberg', *SP*, **41**, 10, cols. 296–301.

FRIEDLÄNDER, W. (1931) 'Abbau der FE durch Notverordnung?' *AW*, **6**, 21, pp. 641–6.

GEARY, D. (1987) 'Unemployment and working-class solidarity: The German experience 1929–1932', in EVANS R.J. and GEARY, D. (Eds) *The German Unemployed.*

HARVEY, E. (1993) *Youth and the Welfare State in Weimar Germany*, Oxford, OUP.

HOMBURG, H. (1987) 'From unemployment insurance to compulsory labour: The transformation of the benefit system in Germany 1927–1933', in EVANS R.J. and GEARY, D. (Eds) *The German Unemployed.*

HUNDINGER, I. (1933) 'Zur Auswirkung der Notverordnung', *Evangelische Jugendhilfe*, **9**, 130–5.

KALL, G. (1931) 'Der Kampf um die Aufrechterhaltung der Jugendwohlfahrtspflege', *ZBl*, **23**, 10/11, pp. 341–6.

KESSLER, Dr. (1930) 'Wirtschaftskrise und Wohlfahrtsarbeit', *Blätter des Deutschen Roten Kreuzes*, **9**, pp. 576–82.

MAGNUS, E. (1927) *Werkheime für erwerbslose Jugendliche*, Berlin.

MUSER, H. (1933) *Homosexualität und Jugendfürsorge: Eine soziologische und fürsorgerische Untersuchung*, Paderborn.

NEUHAUS, A. (1932) 'FE und Bewahrung', *WRP*, **8**, 12, pp. 188–190.

OSWALT, A. (1932) 'Die Lage der Sozialarbeit', *RG*, **23**, pp. 5–8.

REICHSMINISTERIUM DES INNERN (Ed) (1932) *Notprogramme für die Jugendwohlfahrt*, Berlin.

RICHTER, K. (Ed) (1933) *Maßnahmen zur Betreuung der erwerbslosen Jugend: Handbuch der Jugendpflege*, **14**, Eberswalde, Berlin.

ROSENHAFT, E. (1983) *Beating the Fascists? The German Communists and Political Violence 1929–1933*, Cambridge, CUP.

SCHELLENBERG, E. (1931) 'FE und Proletariat', *Proletarische Sozialpolitik*, **4**, 1, pp. 21–3; **4**, 2, pp. 57–60.

WACHENHEIM, H. (1931a) 'Fürsorger und Fürsorgerinnen! Wo steht ihr im politischen Kampf?', *AW*, **6**, 23, pp. 727–30.

WACHENHEIM, H. (1931b) 'Arbeitshaus! die letzte Weisheit der Bürokratie', *Vorwärts*, 5 December.

WAUER, E. (1931) 'Maßnahmen der Stadt Berlin für die erwerbslose Jugend', *Berliner Wohlfahrtsblatt*, **7**, 5, pp. 33–39.

WEINDLING, P. (1989) *Health, Race and German Politics between National Unification and Nazism 1870–1945*, Cambridge.

WESSEL, H. (1931) *Lebenshaltung aus Fürsorge und aus Erwerbstätigkeit*, Berlin.

ZENGERLING, F. (1933/4) 'Die Fürsorgeerziehung in Preußen nach dem neuen Recht', *ZBl*, **25**, 4, pp. 125–30.

6   Emancipation or Social Incorporation: Girls in the *Bund Deutscher Mädel*

Dagmar Reese

Sometimes, when they play the old songs on the radio, E. tries to sing along, but something takes away her breath, rises in her throat. Her vocal chords refuse to clear, and it's not because she smokes. Even if she doesn't realize it straight away, the vague feeling is quicker, is always there, a feeling that 'that's not the way things are anymore, that used to be something'. (Sternheim-Peters, 1987, p. 264, translated)

Compared to the large amount of research on the male *Hitlerjugend* (Hitler Youth; HJ), the number of studies performed so far on the *Bund Deutscher Mädel* (League of German Girls; BDM) still seems sparse (Braun, 1981; Einfeldt, 1983; Jürgens, 1994; Gehmacher, 1994; Kinz, 1990; Klaus, 1980, 1983; Miller-Kipp, 1982; Möding, 1985; Reese, 1981, 1989; Willmot, 1980).[1] This is not just due to problems with historical sources, and it cannot be explained by a lack of interest in studying the history of girls under national socialism. In fact, the thoroughly positive memories of the women involved ensure that the phenomenon continues to raise enormous problems of judgment for a posthumous generation of researchers who are oriented toward female self-determination. One can hardly ignore the fact that the compulsory organization of girls in the BDM was accompanied by modernization phenomena. However, the historical preconditions and social conditions, which were in no way the same for all, still remain unexplained. A generally high acceptance of national socialist girls' organizations, as still claimed by most, is legend and presents a closed picture that has to exclude all those who say, 'Nobody ever wants to believe me, but I wasn't in the BDM' (B, pp. 9, 28).[2]

Nonetheless, compulsory recruitment had enabled the BDM to assert itself strongly after 1936, and there remains a need to explain why such a racist and sexist regime could be effective when women in retrospect felt hardly any discrimination and restriction to their freedom through national socialist policies. Therefore, all research findings on the BDM lead to an emphasis on the ambivalence of experiences. Miller-Kipp (1982, p. 94) describes this with terms such as 'integration' and 'free disposition'. Klaus (1983, p. 378) refers to the subject concept in 'critical psychology' and concludes that although girls obtained subjective meaning for life from the BDM, they remained objectively without identity. Finally, Möding (1985, p. 291) confirms a simultaneity of experiences of autonomy and subjection that first made it possible for a 'code shifting', understood as a 'change in the thought-, perception-, and action-generating impressions', to occur in the next generation, the generation of the daughters. Nowadays, the women's movement, as the most marked expression of such a 'code shifting', is a phenomenon that covers the whole of German society, and it is possible to trace it back to social changes during the 1960s (Beck-Gernsheim, 1983), rather than having to refer to continuities going back to the period before 1945. Nonetheless, I agree with Möding that mental preconditions for the changes in the female life context were created during national socialism, and that being reared in the extracurricular national socialist organizations such as the BDM but also the *Arbeitsdienst* (Labour Service), the *Pflichtjahr* (Duty Year) or *Landjahr* (Agricultural Year) played a central role.[3] However, whereas Möding emphasizes the precondition of the contradictory experiences of women growing up under National Socialism, who had to develop their individual personalities in the service of the national socialist community and could have been thwarted in this, the present text addresses the tense relationship between emancipation and sociation. It assumes that recruitment in national socialist organizations broadened the sociation of girls and women without intrinsically implying emancipation. Indeed, it supposes active participation of those involved, which was based on emancipatory needs. This links up with the question of the mechanisms through which it was possible to exploit these needs and create an illusion of satisfying self-realization that has lasted up to the present. Two sets of topics will be used to investigate this issue: Examining the example of the formation of constructions of femininity in the early history of the organization, I shall show that the way in which national socialists treated female youth was above all functional. The decisive aspect that made the BDM attractive for girls was its emphasis on youth and not on women.

In a second step, I shall consider the careers of female group leaders. This role was in no way reserved for a small committed elite, but was a phase in the life of large sections of this generation of female youth. The particular significance of the careers of female leaders does not lie in its mass distribution alone. Almost all autobiographical descriptions of the BDM have been written by former leaders whose experiences strongly mark our general view of childhood and adolescence under national socialism, while, nonetheless, remaining special (Finck, 1979; Gallwitz, 1964; Hannsmann, 1982; Maschmann, 1963; Stern, 1986; Sternheim-Peters, 1987; Wolf, 1984). These experiences had to be described and related to social criteria. However, it can also be seen that ideologies remained superficial and could be cast off at will. What was more essential and more far-reaching was the mental behaviour patterns that accompanied the recruitment of girls into national socialist organizations and which, for both those involved as well as those born after the war, continue almost imperceptibly but without a break into the present-day (Bude, 1987; Greiffenhagen, 1988; von Plato, 1994; Reese, 1994; Schörken, 1984, 1990; Wierling, 1993).

Gender-Specific or Youth-Appropriate?: Constructions of Femininity in the BDM

In 1937, Trude Bürkner, Reich Representative of the BDM, summarized the guiding images of national socialist 'girls' education' in the BDM in a trend-setting text:

> Over the work of the BDM, there are two educational phrases that the Fuhrer himself and the Youth Leader of the German Reich, Baldur von Schirach have given us. On Mayday 1936, at the Youth Meeting at Berlin, the Fuhrer stated: 'And you in the BDM, train the girls for me into strong and bold women!' And our Reich Youth Leader once expressed it in this way at the beginning of our work: 'In the BDM, the girls should be reared to be the representatives of the National Socialist ideology.' These two sentences, which sound so simple, encompass the entire educational work on all German girlhood. (p. 7, translated)

The quote reveals the scantiness of the 'educational' conception of the BDM. Hardly anything more profound can be found in the programmatic statements on the 'goals of education'. Rather, a violently verbal pathos is characteristic, behind which the inherent premises can be detected only with effort. The only inherently concrete statement that repeats itself regularly in the 'educational postulates' is the self-evident in any female existence.

However, a closer look at the programme of the BDM reveals that, apart from one or two global statements, hardly any intrinsic reference is made to motherhood. In a personal letter sent to me on 26 October, 1982, the former Reich Representative Jutta Rüdiger told me:

> In the education of girls — in which we were more self-determining than any previous generation — we hardly spoke about motherhood but, in our own interests and in the interests of the *Volk*, taught healthy lifestyles and prepared them for occupational and social work; but, above all, we encouraged a fresh and cheerful girlhood.

Apart from having a justifying character, this letter indicates not only that the BDM did not want to dedicate girls one-sidedly to the family but also that direct reference to motherhood played hardly any role in the girls' education itself. Other criteria were important here: 'physical training', health, and a sense of duty, as well as — and this seems to be the most important — an autonomous adolescent lifestyle for girls as well as for boys.

The strict separation between the adult world and that of youth, the assignment of girls to youth, indicates a central element of national socialist girls' education that is found repeatedly in almost all programmatic writings of the BDM. One can see how this idea of assigning girls to youth and not to women grew, first in order to fulfil the political ambitions of the male leaders of the HJ to expand the organization and make it more prominent, for, initially, girl membership in the HJ was a controversial topic. At a special conference of the HJ at Nuremberg in August 1929, a certain F. Bucher from Hamburg proposed a motion, the second part of which concerned the membership of girls in the HJ (Bundesarchiv Koblenz, NS 26/352). There exist two different replies to this motion that maintained that it was, above all, the girls themselves who wanted to amalgamate their groups with the HJ, which was rejected by both boys and women. The two replies came from the *Reichsleitung* of the National Socialist Party and the leadership of the HJ. While the party considered the 'formation of young girl groups in our youth movements to be dubious', the leaders of the HJ declared: 'The previous girl groups in the HJ, organized in the so-called sisterhoods of the HJ, should be praised and their formation should be further encouraged' (Bundesarchiv Koblenz, NS 26/336). This means that the party, guided by its interest in attracting the greatest support of the masses, freed itself from traditional ideas much more slowly than the power-hungry HJ, but basically did not act conservatively but opportunistically.

An analysis of the arguments introduced during the demarcation disputes between national socialistic women and the HJ from 1931 to 1932 casts light on several aspects of the character of the BDM. The differences, which ultimately were put forward as a pretext for the efforts of the two organizations — the National Socialist Woman's Movement and the HJ — to gain political power, concerned two issues: the organization and the contents of work. Whereas women campaigned in favour of girls' groups being part of the women's organization, the HJ maintained that 'youth must be led by youth'. The following citation reveals how this hid a purely opportunistic way of thinking:

> Germany was defeated not just by the political miseducation of its soldiers but also to a large extent that of its women. What is more appropriate than to exploit the new unified attitude of youth, which very obviously encompasses female youth, and use its expansion to train a new generation of young women in our sense, which will only be possible when the young perceive themselves as a certain [sic] contrast to the older female generation. This psychological element seems to me to be of extraordinary importance and deserves particularly strong attention. (Bundesarchiv Koblenz, Sammlung Schumacher, G VIII/251, Letter from Renteln dated 2.2.1932, p. 4, translated)

Thus the HJ exploited the politicization of female youth, their defensive attitude, and their scepticism toward the older female generation; attitudes that make it clear how much this generation was shaped by the youth movement, even without necessarily having been active members. These girls who were growing up during the 1920s no longer were determined by the duality of women related to the intimacy of the family and those stepping out into society that had been dominant before 1914, but by the image of the 'new woman' with a self-aware lifestyle and a search for recognition and the 'female comrade' who was committed to common ideals. Insofar, the political attitude of the NS women's organization was obsolete; viewed from the perspective of efficiency, it was no longer topical.

This becomes clear from a look at their actual work, in which clear differences existed between the girls' groups of the DFO (*Deutscher Frauenorden*) and those of the BDM. When in Berlin, for example, the DFO called for girls to wash clothes for the SA in the spring of 1931, the BDM countered:

> Indeed! Girls in the HJ! Despite all the warnings of the squares, we are calling out to you: Come to us. We must become one *Volk*! Nobody should be missing! Work on youth is the most positive work possible. (Angriff, 1 July, 1931, translated)

Trude Mohr, who later became the Reichs Representative of the BDM, revealed her position quite unequivocally in this article in which she promoted the founding of BDM groups in Mark Brandenburg as part of the NS youth organization, the HJ. The activities of the girls' movements were closely aligned to those already known in the youth movement and consisted of excursions, sport, and social evenings with handicrafts and song. This not only had programmatic significance, but, in addition, also significance in terms of political power. Trude Mohr, an experienced leader from the *Bündische Jugend*, was successful. With 155 girls, the '*Gau Brandenburg*' under her command was the second-largest sector of the BDM in the Reich at the beginning of 1932. Her appointment in 1931 to the post of leader of the BDM at the Berlin *Gau* has to be seen against this background. The subsequent decision in favour of the BDM as the only NS girls' organization in November 1932 also suggests that the BDM's emphasis on a youth programme had shown it to be a more attractive and powerful organization in line with the mass political concept of the Nazi party.

If one does not want to conceive the feminine in biological terms, one has to admit that the process of liberating women from their ascribed status implies the loss of a cultural difference that is bound to gender. This process commenced with the formulation of natural law at the beginning of modern times, and initially formed itself as a political will in the women's movement. On the one hand, it was accompanied by trends toward an objectification of the relationships between the genders, whereas, on the other hand, went along with forced gender-specific role assignments. By means of the concept of youth the sociation of women had been turning into a pedagogic programme since the beginning of the century. This leaves us with the question about the historical function of the concept of 'youth' as well as its significance and fascination for girls.

According to Harry Pross (1964, p. 121), the first youth movement groups for girls, like those for boys, formed at the turn of the century. However, whereas the boys' groups consolidated their organizations rapidly and thus extended their effective range, the girls lacked the self-confidence for autonomous activity and initially sought to amalgamate with existing boys' groups. Only around about 1910, when the presence of girls in the youth movement began to be taken for granted, was there a rapid increase in the number of girl members (Jahrbuch 15, 1984–5; Klönne, 1990; de Ras, 1988). However, the inclusion into youth simultaneously implied an abstraction from gender. The insistence on the ideal of comradeship — as described by Busse-Wilson (1963) for the girls in the youth movement and by Marianne Weber (1919) for the first women students — was not just due to a recognition of bourgeois morals, but was finally based on the idea of a life that was formally equal, whereas the concept of gender always carries a social connotation that indicates a history. The reference to youth among the girls therefore went along with the denial of a particular female history and a particular female fate. It expressed itself in the rejection of the world of mothers and their political organization, the women's movement. Aiming toward individual freedom, the Youth Movement resulted in isolation and alienation. To paraphrase a quote from Max Horkheimer (1967) on the process of individualization at the beginning of modern times, it can be stated that:

> In reality, for the majority of women (the concerned), liberation initially meant exposure to the frightful mechanisms of exploitation of society (manufactures). The woman (individual) who was thrown back on herself (himself), was confronted with an alien power with which she (he) had to come to terms. According to the theory, she (he) should not recognize the judgment of any human authority as binding without subjecting it to rational test, however, as a result, she (he) now stood alone in the world and had to adapt if she (he) was to survive. (Horkheimer, 1967, p. 31, adapted and translated, translation of original wording in parentheses)

'The purpose of the technological arrangement of the world is to liquidate fertility' writes Walter Benjamin (1982, p. 694, translated). This process was based on a need for freedom that represented a desire for equality in women. However, it forced them to deny their gender as the everyday reminder of their 'difference'.

Let us return to the programme of the BDM and compare it with that of the DFO. A presentation on the activities of the *Jungmädel* groups that were attached to the DFO stated that:

> The work of these young girls therefore touched on every aspect of female duty. Together with the women, they organized German culture evenings in a very refined manner, they cared for the German way, in particular, art and literature — they cared for German art, particularly through song, play, and dance. However, at the same time, they attended health courses in order to learn the basic concepts of nursing — or they also did needlework for the brown shirts. (Bundesarchiv Koblenz, Sammlung Schumacher, G VIII/251, p. 3, translated)

It was particularly the conception of the content of this work that was criticized by the HJ:

> Although I am not familiar with all the work of the women's organizations, I cannot suppress my serious reservations about whether these frequently older women are capable of carrying out a unified and comprehensive

> training of female youth because this calls for a corresponding understanding. Everybody who has performed intensive youth work knows that it is not enough to darn socks, cook soup for the SA, and sing songs, regardless of how important and urgent these things are. (Bundesarchiv Koblenz, Sammlung Schumacher, G VIII/251, Letter from Renteln dated 2 February 1932, p. 3, translated)

Compared to a programme in which the gender polarity appertaining to the nineteenth century served as a precondition and that offered an — in this sense — traditional range of female duties like that of the DFO the HJ in contrast put a strong emphasis on sport that was supposed to make up two-thirds of the work with girls. The HJ countered a gender-specific education with compulsory physical education for both girls and boys. When at the beginning of this chapter, I pointed to a conception of girls' education in the BDM devoid of substance, the reason for this was that it was no longer possible to define an autonomous idea of femininity. This went along with a range of national socialist images of womanhood, that were, in part, thoroughly contradictory. The arbitrariness of the ideologies formulated corresponded to a social reality that was dominated completely by the desire for a trouble-free order in which elements of otherness, of tension, were dysfunctional and subject to sanction.

This image of girls was subject to the dialectics underlying the wishes and needs of the girls themselves, the wishes and needs of the leaders of the HJ, and the ideas of the party, and this was still the case in the late 1930s, as the establishment of *Glaube und Schönheit* (faith and beauty, a section of the BDM for older girls) suggests.

Therefore, the work concept formulated by the BDM provides hardly any information for an analysis of the ideology and practice of national socialist education for girls. Far more characteristic was a practice resulting pragmatically from changing interests that, by appealing to youth, ensured the interest and the recruitment of girls. By assigning girls to youth, national socialism subordinated their striving toward emancipation without actually implying that they would become emancipated. Although being a member of the BDM meant the segregation from the traditional bonds to the family, paternal or maternal authority was always replaced by the authority of the state. Thus national socialist education for girls led to isolation and alienation and finally resulted in an increase in the power of society over women and girls. In this sense, by referring to the abstractly defined concept of youth, it completed the individualization process for the masses of women that had occurred for men at the beginning of bourgeois society. Just as the concept of the free and equal individual initially contained nothing more than the ruthless and pitiless exploitation of people by people, the formal equation of girls with boys through the concept of youth meant only that the freedoms that necessarily resulted from a gender polarity ceased to exist. With the concept of 'spiritual motherhood', the women's movement had turned the bourgeois female role into a weapon against the advances of technology. In contrast, now, the national socialists used all their powers to subordinate motherhood to technology. Therefore education through the

BDM did not contain education toward femininity, education toward motherhood, gender-polarized education but an education toward functionality that was based on individualization and focused for both boys and girls on mastery of the body, discipline, rationality, and efficiency. I shall now go into this in more depth with the example of the careers of female group leaders.

Careers of Female Group Leaders[4]

The national socialists repeatedly stressed the principle of the 'self-leadership' of youth. The reasons for this are obvious. When 'youth leads youth', one cannot talk retrospectively about a 'totalitarian state' or 'state youth'. Instead, this basic principle equipped youth with the right of autonomy. Indeed, the male and female leaders of the HJ actually were young. In clear contrast to the youth movement and the *Bündische Jugend*, they were generally only two or three years older than the boys and girls they led. In terms of the competencies and powers assigned to them, the male and female leadership corps were exceptionally young. At the time when he took up the post of *Reichsjugendführer* of the Nazi party, Baldur von Schirach was 24 years old; Jutta Rüdiger became Reichs representative of the BDM at the age of 27. Their 'youthfulness' helped make the HJ attractive to the young just as much as it was functional in terms of political power.

Nonetheless, this also had a completely material counterpart in the permanent shortage of male and female leaders. When it is assumed that approximately 4 million young persons were organized into the HJ at the end of 1935 (Kater, 1977, p. 170), a group size of about ten members meant that the organization required approximately 400,000 leaders. In the BDM alone with about half a million members, the smallest organization in terms of numbers (Bundesarchiv Koblenz, NS 26/358, Statistik der Jugend), there was a need for about 50,000 female group leaders in 1935. This need grew even more strongly in 1936 with the passing of the *Gesetz über die Hitlerjugend* (*HJ-Gesetz*, Hitler Youth Act)[5] that led to major increases particularly in the organizations for the under-14s, the *Jungvolk* and the *Jungmädeln*. It is obvious that such a large number of leaders could not be paid, that most of them had to work on a voluntary basis without any remuneration. However, this inherently means a high fluctuation rate, a reduction in selection criteria, and recourse to increasingly young girls as well as to institutions through which the old social order could be reinstated within the '*Volk* community of German youth' through the leadership elite.

As the youth of a totalitarian state, the HJ was, from its very beginnings, no voluntary organization. Nonetheless, its existence cannot be explained by the application of legal constraints and political violence alone. There is a considerable remainder of voluntariness and commitment that carried and stabilized the HJ. The male and female leaders played a decisive role in this. They provided the links through which membership in the BDM could either just remain a duty or become an enjoyable event. If we follow the reports of the BDM, the selection criteria were strict but at the same time diffuse, in that the selection of a leader should be based not only on qualities that could be tested but also take account of the entire personality of a girl. 'Character and achievement, not dead knowledge, but education and a model attitude should characterize the personalities of group leaders' (Rüdiger, 1983, p. 50, translated). This formulated high demands that remained remarkably undefined and, as a result, left a lot of scope. On the one hand, it is very clear that what was sought and desired was in no way limited to doctrine, to political conviction. Both more and less was called for at the same time in that the 'personality', the 'character', being a certain 'type of girl' should be decisive criteria. On the other hand, what kinds of 'personality', 'character', and 'type of girl' were meant remained undefined, so that the young persons were left with a free hand to a large extent. This, however, corresponded to a situation in which there was a permanent shortage of female leaders.

> And then I remembered that, of course, they were always on the lookout for some kind of group leader. Such a group leader always had 8 or 10 girls under her, for whom she was responsible, for whom she set the topics. I can still remember someone said to me, 'Now look, you go to high school, you can do some things better, and you're also a bit more intelligent than the others' — I don't remember whether there was any extra training; I couldn't say any more — 'Do it, I'll propose you, you can do it.' Naturally, I was horrified. (B 10, p. 26)

The girl who was proposed here was in no way an enthusiastic member of the BDM, a convinced national socialist. Before 1933, her father had been an active member of the Social Democratic Party (SPD), and, because of this, since 1933, his job as a public official had exposed him to increasing pressure from the national socialists. As a 'tribute' to the 'new times' with their 'new masters', the daughter finally joined the BDM at the request of her father. She had not wanted to join, and performed her 'service' unwillingly although without any thought of refusal. Now what does this imply when the organization was still willing to propose her as a group leader? Apparently, a lack of commitment, a lack of ideological conviction, and social democratic parents were no handicap. The contents of the BDM activities could be enforced, and were mostly preset through the introduction and dissemination of social-evening portfolios. It was something else that was essential. This girl lived in Wedding, a Berlin working-class district, there she was one of the few girls attending a higher secondary school. This distinguished her from the other girls in her group who were mostly working-class girls with little education and limited intellectual horizons.

Certainly, several of these girls were enthusiastic and committed members of the BDM, but this was not enough to become a group leader. The job required planning ability, authority, and the willingness to take on responsibility; qualities that are conveyed, on the one hand, by school, that is, academic education and, on the other hand, by family background.

> There was going to be an excursion, and the parents had to be told everything that they shouldn't do, what they should give the girls to take with

them, how everything was supposed to happen, and a sketch was put together in which I was the group leader, and I must have played my role so well that afterwards, the others said, 'She's the right one to be a group leader'. I was 10 years old then. I'd only just joined, and then I was sent to a leadership school. Now, I was also a lot taller than all the others of my age; people always thought I was older than I was. (B 15, pp. 6–7)

This girl also came from Wedding, had an academic family background, and attended a high school. This made her so obviously superior to the girls in her group that she was put forward for leadership training when she was only 10 years old. Once more, it was not her ideological beliefs that were decisive but completely pragmatic qualities revealed in the way she tackled a problem. Her suitability for group leadership arose from her technical competence. However, because the national socialists needed such abilities, they were forced to recruit from the old social elites. Particularly in small towns, it was conspicuous that the group leaders re-created the existing social differentiations within the 'community of youth'. Group leaders became, above all, those girls who attended a higher secondary school. This was obvious to all those girls who did not want to or could not make this 'promotion'.

Generally, girls were proposed for group leadership while they were still members of the *Jungmädeln*, that is, between the ages of 10 and 14. This had far-reaching consequences because the girls then remained leaders in the *Jungmädelbund* without ever passing through the BDM. This led not only to a drop in membership in the BDM but also to changes in its social composition compared to the *Jungmädelbund* that led to a further loss in attractiveness. There was hardly any way to counteract this trend, because, due to the afternoon meetings, the *Jungmädelbund* was in any case dependent on higher secondary school students who, because they had no lessons in the afternoons, were the only ones in a position to take over leadership tasks for 10- to 14-year-olds. The core of group leaders re-established the old social elites and shaped the social character of the organization. Nonetheless, the recourse to the old elites carried a new note; it was inseparable from the political system of national socialism. The fact that the social differentiation was based on objective criteria and contained hardly any *a priori* social connotations offered not only a scope for exclusion but also opportunities for upward social mobility. Although it was far from the pretended 'community of youth', it nonetheless increased social permeability. This is shown in the following statement in which a girl from Minden describes her relationship as a group leader to the male leadership.

I knew some of them, whom I still sometimes see today, who just came from another social class, but most of the ones we had contact with and who were also active as leaders naturally came from similar social classes. They attended the high school, and we also had dancing lessons together with them. (M 9, pp. 33–4)

Through the leadership in the Nazi Youth Organization, the social hierarchies re-established themselves, but not completely, and within another context. A position of leadership could not be achieved through social privilege alone. Personal commitment played an indispensable role. Although often identical in their membership, the new elites differed from the old in their awareness of a personal achievement: Careers were made. However, there were significant social differences in the type of advance. Not only the external conditions, such as work in the afternoons, but also the far-reaching dissociation from political content in favour of sport and play made the *Jungmädelbund* the most preferable vehicle for the ambitions of upper-class youth. The situation was different for the leadership positions in the BDM and paid work in the HJ. Insufficient social perspectives or even their complete lack were the preconditions to perform a paid leadership position in the BDM. However, this did not apply to upper-class girls. There was another picture here. Under the precondition of a more or less compulsory enrolment of youth, these girls entered the BDM either freely or against their wills. Naturally, many took the opportunity to become leaders. This extended their field of activity, and it was an incentive to try out their own powers and to prove themselves. In addition, it offered the possibility of avoiding tedious schooling as well as integration classification and subordination to group interests that were far from being their own. The leadership career became a terrain for thoroughly personal motives. One adapted oneself, and tried to exploit the political situation. However, this also involved not compromising oneself through more far-reaching identification: In the upper classes, commitment was of a precisely calculated amount.

In most girls, it could be seen clearly that personal interest was the primary motive for their decision to become a leader in the BDM. Few were 'true idealists' and lived out their beliefs, but naturally they amalgamated with national socialism the more strongly their own interests combined with those of this state. Nonetheless, personal motives frequently continued to remain in the foreground. In this way, the girls neither incorporated the aims of the state nor rejected them. Instead, they adapted themselves and exploited the conditions they found for their own purposes. Once more, this raises the question of the content of the work of a leader.

> It was just that, well, I never noticed it, that it had anything at all to do with Hitler. That was the way it was. We did needlework, we knitted these little samplers for a purpose, it used to be called Winter Aid, and we read a lot of the old books — as I said before — Rosegger, Storm, or Löns, and we played a lot of sports. And that was the daughter of the director of our school, and then there was another leader, and she just continued the same thing, and, I have to say, I was 15 then when I took over the group . . . and I led it just like the others and just did all those things, and we sang a lot of folk songs . . . (M 21, p. 3)

As a group leader, a girl took over responsibility for planning the content of a social evening. First of all, she had to turn up punctually; this was self-evident, and she also expected it of the other girls. Whether she intended to sing songs, make things, read a book together, or do sports, it was necessary for her to manage to plan this at least one afternoon or evening in advance. Once the group had assembled, she had to carry out the planned activities in the group. She had to establish quiet and order and encourage attention and cooperation. One can imagine it: Ten to fifteen girls, initially excited, later increasingly bored by compulsory attendance; before them a leader who was only slightly older, who more or less honestly tried to cope with her task. Naturally, there were talented leaders who managed to stimulate enthusiasm in their group, but just as naturally there were those for whom service deteriorated into a burden and those who spread anxiety and fear. Leaders also did not see themselves as free agents but viewed themselves as being forced to impart the required contents and to maintain discipline. It was 'achievements' that were performed by children and adolescents here. Their activity was lacking in any playful elements and anticipated the world of adulthood. These girls had to plan, organize, assert themselves, take on responsibility, decide, and judge. They had to adapt themselves to and find their way through a hierarchy of ranks and powers. The abstract aspect of their activity became more marked the higher they — and this quite consciously — climbed the career ladder. The rewards for such efforts were power and prestige. Naturally, the girls grew up into a system in which the relationship between children and adolescents was created through orders and sub-jugation, and it took only a little bit of will and skill and they were soon caught up in this system. Only too quickly, dreams now left the land of fantasy and took on a material face, and the shape of blue, red, and green cords — the different insignia of rank within the leadership. Ambition awakened so early recognized only itself, developed without inhibitions, and was beyond any morality. By participating in power, girls helped to retain power. Few perceived the burden that was placed on them, the heavy seriousness that prevented their joy in life and guided their lives into fixed lanes. Anxiety, nightmares, as in the following excerpt from an interview, are recalled rarely:

> For example, I had a terrible fear that some time I would have to go on a journey by myself with these little girls, and then, as I told you the last time, I stood up and took another look, and I thought that my accounts didn't balance, and I looked again, and then, I can still remember this exactly, my identity card had disappeared, that is, I woke up and thought, tomorrow, you need your identity card, where is it, and I was incredibly untidy and had no idea where it could be. This led to my mother waking up and helping me to look for it during the night. Nightmares, real nightmares, that may be the reason why I have forgotten many things. At some point in time, I said to myself that that was the end of my childhood, this decision to designate me as a leader. (B 15, pp. 9–10)

Most of them slipped, without noticing, into a world that was characterized by power, achievement, and social hierarchy. They adapted themselves, and prepared themselves for a life that could only be conceived as a struggle in which they wanted to succeed.

> I had never been that interested in becoming a leader. I was simply interested in looking after children, or, to put it better, later adolescents too,

> and that was something that had always interested me greatly, and I reckon
> that I brought that with me into my job. I never wanted to remain just a
> little preschool teacher, through further training, I slowly grappled my way
> upwards. (B 11, pp. 27–28)

The woman talking here hardly seems to have any interest in the contents of what
she was doing. Just as she hardly became a leader for the sake of the people she
led, even today, hardly any of her efforts are directed toward knowledge of the
children she is currently caring for in a preschool. At the centre of her activity there
is only herself: a person who has achieved something. The lack of conscience, the
lack of morals, that this reveals is not a personal 'problem', but the consistent
outcome of the 'education' of an authoritarian and racist state that also mercilessly
forced children to comply with its laws; that sought to make children into its
helpers at the price of their happiness. With little awareness of what was happen-
ing, children became part of an inhuman machinery, well functioning, but with
stunted souls.

> I have to say that much of what was done then may also have been bad,
> but there was something about it, in some way, one had another feeling of
> duty and another discipline, and you can still see it in those colleagues
> who went through the same times. (B 11, p. 28)

Emancipation or Sociation: Résumé

If we review these findings against the background of the issues raised in the
introduction, we can summarize as follows: Insofar as the organization of girls
through the BDM led to their increased integration into society, national socialist
rule was in line with the modernization of female life. However, to the same extent
that the girls participated in society, they were subject to its influence. If, in a
bourgeois world, women who were assigned to the private sphere could still incor-
porate a utopian other world at the turn of the century, such contradictions disap-
peared during the course of the twentieth century. National socialism played a
decisive role in this process. Because the state here penetrated by means of racist
legislation into the most intimate private spheres, in the area of the family, education, reproduction, and the body, it displaced the personal bonds and power relationships that were still dominant there and replaced them with new societal
authorities and state violence. Although the family remained, it was no longer the
area filled with intimacy in which bourgeois subjectivity should develop. Therefore,
it no longer differed essentially from the public sphere, but at best only in degree
and through the activities that remained in its domain. Anne-Katrin Einfeld illustrates these changes when she describes how the labour service, duty year, and land
year taught growing girls that rationality was their maxim of action, and how these
experiences were later applied by the young women to their own domestic sphere
(Einfeld, 1983). If the private sphere at the beginning of modern bourgeois society

is defined by its basic separation and distinction from the public sphere (Habermas, 1962; Hausen, 1977), the same societal strategies of an advanced modernization now increasingly penetrated in both spheres. Max Horkheimer (1967) was thinking of such trends when he wrote:

> The ideal modern mother plans the rearing of her children almost scientific-ally, from the carefully balanced diet to the equally carefully balanced ratio of praise and blame, as recommended in popular psychological literature. Her entire attitude toward the child becomes rational; even love is dealt with as a component of pedagogic hygiene. (Horkheimer, 1967, p. 277)

Max Horkheimer's observations were directed toward the American family. How-ever, what he was describing was modern forms of the family that could also be found elsewhere, and it was essentially the politics of national socialism that ena-bled them to be implemented in Germany. On the one hand, in Germany, this transformation process to the modern forms of the family differed from develop-ments in democratic countries through the violence with which a dictatorial regime forced people to comply with its will. Mass compulsory sterilizations (Bock, 1986) are just as much a confirmation of this as the encroachment into the intimate sphere of women through compulsory gynaecological examinations when applying for marriage loans (Czarnowski, 1985, 1991). However, the compulsory enrolment of children in extracurricular state organizations, the violent separation of adolescents from their families through drafting into the Duty Year, Agricultural Year, Labour Service, or Auxiliary War Service, and finally the multitude of war-related duties such as antiaircraft helpers or army helpers pointed in the same direction. On the other hand, developments in Germany were characterized by the instrumentalization of obstinate interests for the purpose of maintaining and stabilizing the rule of the state. However, this particularly concerned those women who belonged to the female generation recruited by the BDM. To explain this, it seems to be necessary to reconsider the concept of emancipation in more detail.

Emancipation originally described a technical term in Roman law and meant the discharge of the son from the hand of the *pater familias*. The meaning of the term changed during the eighteenth and nineteenth centuries, became reflexive, and solidified into a movement and goal concept in modern societies (Grass and Koselleck, 1975, p. 153). As such, the concept meant the release from those social circumstances that maintained minority rights. This definition finally gave the con-cept a political significance in the nineteenth century. Max Stirner (1845) differen-tiated between the promise of release and the giving of release, and thus contrasted the originally passive meaning of a given right, which he described as emancipation and evaluated negatively, with all active involvement for the extension and partici-pation in human rights that had become self-evident — self-emancipation — as is the case in modern emancipation movements. Stirner used this differentiation to indicate the internal connection between the form in which rights realize them-selves and the freedom that they permit, and additionally stressed the role of per-sonal will.

The one who has been given freedom is nothing more than one who has been left to be free; a libertine, a dog, who still carries a piece of his chain with him. He is an unfree person dressed in the clothes of freedom, like the donkey in the lion's skin. (Stirner, 1845, p. 221)

For Stirner, it is only rights that have been obtained through struggle that permit self-liberation and hence emancipation in the modern sense of the word.

If we now transfer this idea to the BDM, it can be seen that the recruitment of girls by national socialism could be effective particularly where needs for freedom and self-realization were present. The BDM could provide a place for this and protection for those who joined. However, national socialism largely took away the girls' own contribution toward their emancipatory desires and ideas. By forcing the departure without naming the destination, it prevented any reflected discussion and made the girls obedient to it. The instrumental dealings of a regime that was oriented only toward the maintenance of its own rule is therefore decisive for answering the question why experiences of autonomy were linked to the release of girls from traditionally derived contexts (Möding, 1985) without being accompanied by self-determination. Thus, after 1945, only memories of emancipatory feelings remained that seemed strangely lost because they were linked to no picture and recognized no end. For the girls in the BDM, political intentions were mixed up inextricably with subjective desires, and this turned them into willing accomplices. At the same time, the memory of their own departure combined with the catastrophe of genocide and national defeat left behind that fragmented self of which it was once said, 'The past is not dead; it is not even past. We separate it from ourselves and turn ourselves into strangers' (Wolf, 1984, p. 9, translated).

Notes

1 In the following, *Hitler Jugend* (HJ) is used to describe the complete organization of all young persons, both boys and girls. On the other hand, the HJ was the male national socialist youth movement encompassing the *Deutsche Jungvolk* (DJ), which organized 10- to 14-year-old boys, as well as the actual HJ, the organization for the 14- to 18-year-olds. I use the *Bund Deutscher Mädel* (BDM), in contrast, to cover the complete national socialist organization of girls. The *Jungmädelbund* organized 10- to 14-year-old girls; and the BDM, 14- to 18-year-olds. After 1938, voluntary groups were set up for 18- to 21-year-old young women in the BDM organization *Glaube und Schönheit*.

2 Both this and the following interviews are taken from a study in which I interviewed forty-seven women born between 1920 and 1930.

3 In 1938, a 'directive for increasing female labour in homekeeping and agriculture', the so-called *Pflichtjahr* (Duty Year), was introduced as part of the 4-year plan. This directive required all unmarried women under the age of 25 to provide evidence that they had worked for one year in domestic service or agriculture when applying for white-collar or blue-collar jobs in private or public companies or administrations. This duty year was restricted to certain trades and focused particularly on the clothing, textile, and tobacco industries, as well as sales personnel and office workers. Other work could be set off

against the duty year; that is, the obligation met through a homekeeping apprenticeship, an agricultural homekeeping or domestic work apprenticeship, the agricultural year, the homekeping year, or Labour Service. Although the duty year, just like the 'directive concerning the BDM's obligation to teach housekeeping' issued just previously, is interpreted as a move to make the girls' league more conventional (Klönne, 1982, p. 32), both measures were related closely to the anticipated war and aimed to thwart a labour shortage, particularly in agriculture and homekeeping, by establishing a legal framework for recruiting female youth into these economic fields (Deutschlandberichte der Sozialdemokratischen Partei Deutschland (SOPADE), 1938, pp. 494–5). Both measures lost their importance following the obligatory recruitment of female youth by the Labour Service (RAD w.J.) after 1940 (see Kleiber, 1981; Morgan, 1978; Willmot, 1990). The 'directive concerning the BDM's obligation to teach housekeeping' should not be confused with the 'homekeeping year' introduced jointly by the NS Women's League, the HJ, and the national job recruitment and unemployment insurance office in 1934. This was a call for all women and mothers to take girls into their own homes for a period of one year and train them in homekeeping. The idea behind the 'homekeeping year' was to counter mass unemployment in this age cohort of school leavers that was twice as high as that in 1933. The agricultural year was also introduced in 1934 and was intended to awaken the love of the land in school leavers, that is, encourage them to take up agricultural careers and thus counteract the exodus from the land. However, in terms of numbers, its impact was insignificant. Upon completion of this nine-month agricultural year, a agricultural year certificate was issued that was supposed to guarantee preferred treatment when applying for apprenticeships.

4 See, also, Möding and von Plato, 1986; Reese, 1991.
5 The passing of the *Gesetz über die Hitlerjugend* on 1 December, 1936 transformed the HJ into a state youth movement, a third childrearing authority alongside the parental home and the school. Using conscription lists, 10-year-olds were now 'drafted' into the HJ. The introduction of directives on implementing the *Gesetz über die Hitlerjugend* in 1939 provided a legal framework for punishing guardians who defied this 'draft'.

References

BECK-GERNSHEIM, E. (1983) 'Vom "Dasein für andere" zum Anspruch auf ein Stück "eigenes Leben": Individualisierungsprozesse im weiblichen Lebenszusammenhang', *Soziale Welt*, **34**, pp. 307–40.

BENJAMIN, W. (1982) 'Malerei, Jugendstil, Neuheit', in BENJAMIN, W. *Das Passagenwerk*, Gesammelte Schriften, Bd. V.2., Frankfurt/Main, Suhrkamp.

BOCK, G. (1986) *Zwangssterilisation im Nationalsozialismus: Studien zur Rassenpolitik und Frauenpolitik* (= Schriften des Zentralinstituts für sozialwissenschaftliche Forschung der Freien Universität Berlin Bd. 48), Opladen, Westdeutscher Verlag.

BRAUN, H. (1981) 'Der Bund Deutscher Mädel (BDM): Faschistische Projektionen von der "neuen deutschen Frau"', in FOCKE, H., REIMER, U. and KRULL, H. (Eds) *Sozialistische Erziehung contra Nazi-Verführung* (= Ergebnisse 15), Hamburg, pp. 92–124.

BUDE, H. (1987) *Deutsche Karrieren: Lebenskonstruktionen Sozialer Aufsteiger aus der Flakhelfer-Generation*, Frankfurt/Main, Suhrkamp.

BUSSE-WILSON, E. (1963) 'Liebe und Kameradschaft', in KINDT, W. (Ed) *Grundschriften der Deutschen Jugendbewegung*, Köln/Düsseldorf, pp. 327–34.

CZARNOWSKI, G. (1985) 'Frauen — Staat — Medizin: Aspekte der Körperpolitik im National-sozialismus', *Beiträge zur Feministischen Theorie und Praxis*, **8**, 14, pp. 79–98.

CZARNOWSKI, G. (1991) *Das Kontrollierte Paar: Ehe- und Sexualpolitik im National-sozialismus* (Ergebnisse der Frauenforschung, Bd. 24), Weinheim, Studienverlag.

DEUTSCHLANDBERICHTE DER SOZIALDEMOKRATISCHEN PARTEI DEUTSCHLAND (Sopade) 1934 –1940 (1980), Salzhausen and Frankfurt/Main, Petra Nettelbeck and Zweitausendeins.

EINFELD, A. (1983) 'Zwischen alten Werten und neuen Chancen. Häusliche Arbeit von Bergarbeiterfrauen in den fünziger Jahren', in NIETHAMMER, L. (Ed) *'Hinterher Merkt Man, Daß Es Richtig War, Daß Es Schiefgegangen Ist.' Nachkriegserfahrungen im Ruhrgebiet: Lebensgeschichte und Sozialkultur im Ruhrgebiet 1930 bis 1960*, Bd. 2, Berlin/Bonn, Dietz, pp. 149–90.

FINCK, R. (1979) *Mit Uns Zieht die Neue Zeit*, Baden-Baden, Signal.

FROMM, E., HORKHEIMER, M., MAYER, H. and MARCUSE, H. v.a. (Eds) (1936) *Autorität und Familie*, Forschungsberichte aus dem Institut für Sozialforschung, Paris, Félix Alcan.

GALLWITZ, E. (1964) *Freiheit 35 oder Wir Mädel Singen Falsch*, Freiburg.

GEHMACHER, J. (1994) *Jugend ohne Zukunft: Hitler-Jugend und Bund Deutscher Mädel in Österreich vor 1938*, Wien, Picus.

GRASS, K.M. and KOSELLECK, R. (1975) 'Stichwort: Emanzipation', VON OTTO, B., CONZE, W. and KOSELLECK, R. (Eds) *Geschichtliche Grundbegriffe. Historisches Lexikon zur politisch-sozialan Sprache in Deutschland hrsg*, Stuttgart, Ernst Kiett, pp. 153–97.

GREIFFENHAGEN, M. (1988) Jahrgang 1928. Aus einem unruhlgen Leben, München, Piper.

HABERMAS, J. (1969) *Strukturwandel der Öffentlichkeit: Untersuchungen zu einer Kategorie der Bürgerlichen Gesellschaft*, Neuwied and Berlin, Luchterhand.

HANNSMANN, M. (1982) *Der Helle Tag Bricht an: Ein Kind Wird Nazi*, Hamburg, dtv.

HAUSEN, K. (1977) 'Die Polarisierung der "Geschlechtscharaktere": Eine Dissoziation von Erwerbs- und Familienleben', in CONZE, W. (Ed) *Sozialgeschichte der Familie in der Neuzeit Europas: Neue Forschungen*, Stuttgart, pp. 363–93.

HORKHEIMER, M. (1967) 'Autorität und Familie in der Gegenwart', in HORKHEIMER, M. *Zur Kritik der Instrumentellen Vernunft: Aus den Vorträgen und Aufzeichnungen seit Kriegsende*, Frankfurt/Main, Fischer, pp. 269–87. (First edition New York 1947 *Eclipse of Reason*)

JAHRBUCH DES ARCHIVS DER DEUTSCHEN JUGENDBEWEGUNG (1984–1985) **15**, Witzenhausen.

JÜRGENS, B. (1994) *Zur Geschichte des BDM (Bund Deutscher Mädel) von 1923 bis 1939*, Frankfurt/Main, Peter Lang.

KATER, M.H. (1977) 'Bürgerliche Jugendbewegung und Hitlerjugend in Deutschland von 1926 bis 1939', *Archiv für Sozialgeschichte*, **XVII**, pp. 125–74.

KINZ, G. (1990) *Der Bund Deutscher Mädel: Ein Beitrag zur Außerschulischen Mädchen-erziehung im Nationalsozialismus*, Frankfurt/Main, Peter Lang.

KLAUS, M. (1980) Mädchen in der Hitlerjugend. Die Erziehung zur 'deutschen Frau' (Hochschulschriften 15), Köln, Pahl-Rugenstain.

KLAUS, M. (1983) *Mädchenerziehung zur Zeit der Faschistischen Herrschaft in Deutschland: Der Bund Deutscher Mädel*, 2 Bd., Frankfurt/Main, dipa.

KLEIBER, L. (1981) '"Wo ihr seid, da soll die Sonne scheinen!": Der Frauenarbeitsdienst am Ende der Weimarer Republik und im Nationalsozialismus', in FRAUENGRUPPE FASCHISMUSFORSCHUNG (Eds) *Mutterkreuz und Arbeitsbuch: Zur Geschichte der Frauen in der Weimarer Republik und im Nationalsozialismus*, Frankfurt/Main, Fischer, pp. 188–214.

KLÖNNE, A. (1982) *Jugend im Dritten Reich: Die Hitler-Jugend und Ihre Gegner*, Köln, Diederichs.

KLÖNNE, I. (1990) *'Ich spring' in diesem Ringe'* : *Mädchen und Frauen in der Jugendbewegung*, Pfaffenweiler, Centaurus.

MASCHMANN, M. (1963) *Fazit: Kein Rechtfertigungsversuch*, Stuttgart, DVA.

MILLER-KIPP, G. (1982) 'Der Bund Deutscher Mädel in der Hitler-Jugend — Erziehung zwischen Ideologie und Herrschaftsprozeß', *Pädagogische Rundschau*, **36**, Sonderheft August, pp. 71–105.

MÖDING, N. (1985) '"Ich muß irgendwo engagiert sein, fragen sie mich bloß nicht, warum." Überlegungen zu Sozialisationserfahrungen von Frauen in NS-Organisationen', in NIETHAMMER, L. and VON PLATO, A. (Eds) *'Wir Kriegen Jetzt Andere Zeiten.' Auf der Suche nach der Erfahrung des Volkes in Nachfaschistischen Ländern: Lebensgeschichte und Sozialkultur im Ruhrgebiet 1930 bis 1960*, Bd. 3, Berlin/Bonn, Dietz, pp. 256–304.

MÖDING, N. and V. PLATO, A. (1986) 'Siegernadeln. Jugendkarrieren in BDM und HJ', in *Schock und Schöpfung: Jugendästhetik im 20. Jahrhundert*, Darmstadt and Neuwied, Luchterhand, pp. 292–301.

MORGAN, D.G. (1978) *Weiblicher Arbeitsdienst in Deutschland*, Diss. Darmstadt.

NIETHAMMER, L. (Ed) (1983a) *'Die Jahre Weiß Man nicht, Wo Man die Heute Hinsetzen Soll.' Faschismuserfahrungen im Ruhrgebiet: Lebensgeschichte und Sozialkultur im Ruhrgebiet 1930 bis 1960*, Bd. 1, Berlin/Bonn, Dietz.

NIETHAMMER, L. (Ed) (1983b) *'Hinterher Merkt Man, Daß Es Richtig War, Daß Es Schiefgegangen Ist.' Nachkriegserfahrungen im Ruhrgebiet: Lebensgeschichte und Sozialkultur im Ruhrgebiet 1930 bis 1960*, Bd. 2, Berlin/Bonn, Dietz.

NIETHAMMER, L. and VON PLATO, A. (Eds) (1985) *'Wir Kriegen Jetzt Andere Zeiten.' Auf der Suche nach der Erfahrung des Volkes in Nachfaschistischen Ländern: Lebensgeschichte und Sozialkultur im Ruhrgebiet 1930 bis 1960*, Bd. 3, Berlin/Bonn, Dietz.

PROSS, H. (1964) *Jugend, Eros, Politik: Die Geschichte der Deutschen Jugendverbände*, Bern/München/Wien.

DE RAS, M.E.P. (1988) *Körper, Eros und Weibliche Kultur: Mädchen im Wandervogel und in der Bündischen Jugend*, Pfaffenweiler, Centaurus.

REESE, D. (1981) 'Bund Deutscher Mädel: Zur Geschichte der weiblichen deutschen Jugend im Dritten Reich', in FRAUENGRUPPE FASCHISMUSFORSCHUNG (Eds) *Mutterkreuz und Arbeitsbuch: Zur Geschichte der Frauen in der Weimarer Republik und im Nationalsozialismus*, Frankfurt/Main, Fischer, pp. 163–87.

REESE, D. (1989) *'Straff, aber nicht Stramm — Herb, aber nicht Derb.' Zur Vergesellschaftung der Mädchen durch den Bund Deutscher Mädel im Sozialkulturellen Vergleich zweier Milieus*, Weinheim, Studienverlag.

REESE, D. (1991) 'Verstrickung und Verantwortung: Weibliche Jugendliche in der Führung des Bunds Deutscher Mädel', *Sozialwissenschaftliche Informationen* (SOWI), **2**, pp. 90–103.

REESE, D. (1994) 'The BDM generation: A female generation in transition from dictatorship to democracy', in ROSEMAN, M. (Eds) *Generations in Conflict: Youth Revolt and Generation Formation in Germany 1770–1968*, Cambridge, Cambridge University Press, pp. 227–46.

RÜDIGER, J. (1983) *Die Hitler-Jugend und ihr Selbstverständnis im Spiegel ihrer Aufgabengebiete*, Lindhorst, Askania.

SCHÖRKEN, R. (1984) *Luftwaffenhelfer und Drittes Reich: Die Entstehung eines Politischen Bewußtseins*, Stuttgart, Klett-Cotta.

SCHÖRKEN, R. (1990) *Jugend 1945: Politisches Denken und Lebensgeschichte*, Opladen, Leske and Budrich.

STERN, C. (1986) *In den Netzen der Erinnerung: Lebensgeschichten zweier Menschen*, Reinbek bei Hamburg, Rowohlt.

STERNHEIM-PETERS, E. (1987) *Die Zeit der Großen Täuschungen: Mädchenleben im Faschismus*, Bielefeld, AJZ.

STIRNER, M. (1845) *Der Einzige und sein Eigentum*, Leipzig.

VON PLATO, A. (1995) 'The Hitler youth generation and its role in the two post-war German states', in ROSEMAN, MARK (Ed) *Generations in Conflict: Youth Revolt and Generation Formation in Germany 1770–1968*, Cambridge, Cambridge University Press, pp. 210–26.

WEBER, M. (1919) 'Vom Typenwandel der studierenden Frau', in WEBER, M. *Frauenfragen und Frauengedanken: Gesammelte Aufsätze*, Tübingen, pp. 179–201.

WIERLING, D. (1993) 'Von der HJ zur FDJ', *Bios*, **6**, 1, pp. 107–18.

WILLMOT, L. (1990) 'Nationalsocialistic Youth Organization for Girls: A contribution to the social und political history of the Third Reich', a thesis submitted for the degree of Doctor of Philosophy at Oxford University, Oxford.

WOLF, C. (1984) *Kindheitsmuster*, Darmstadt and Neuwied, Luchterhand.

7   Why Did Social Workers Accept the New Order?

Stefan Schnurr

Introduction

As recent research has shown, social work contributed to the implementation of national socialist (NS) social policy and the consolidation of NS power (a) through a selective promotion of the 'able' and a selective discrimination against the 'inferior' in the domain of public as well as voluntary welfare, and (b) through the production and stabilization of the images of the self and the world favoured by the state in the educational programmes of the intermediary mass organizations and the *Formationen* (Hansen, 1991; Kramer, 1983; Otto and Sünker, 1989; Sachße and Tennstedt, 1992; Schnurr, 1988). Although this was a very special kind of contribution, taken by itself, it cannot have been sufficient, though nonetheless an indispensable component in a set of facets of NS power.

The particular controversy in this topic is revealed when the 1930s are not viewed in isolation but as part of the continuum of development in the history of welfare and social work. The professionalization of social work in Germany, its legal embedment and institutionalization in the form of local public welfare offices and youth offices, the peak phase of the reform-oriented social-pedagogical movement, and the establishment of educational science at the universities — all these are trends that first became possible under the political and cultural framing conditions of the Weimar Republic. As a result, the 1920s have played a crucial role in academic and professional identity formation since the beginnings of the Bonn Republic, whereas the 1930s have long remained subject to taboo in the collective memory of social work. It was only the critical research of the 1980s that cast light once more on what was, for many persons, an astonishing and irritating fact: In the twelve years of national socialism following the reform period in the 1920s, communal social institutions were in no way dissolved, the welfare laws established in the Weimar republic remained in power, and the majority of personnel in welfare and social education were unaffected by political and anti-Semitic purges.[1] This raised the question of the continuity and discontinuity in the justifications and forms of activity in social work (Otto and Sünker, 1989).

For a research perspective interested in explaining social work through a critical confrontation with its history as a profession and as a state authority over itself — its opportunities and constraints, but also its risk potential — this situation represents a challenge. The question of the NS functionalization of social work and the conditions that permitted it to be functionalized directs research toward a complex explanatory context: the historical and systematic context of the legal foundations of welfare, the forms of institutionalization, the trends toward professionalism, its leading theoretical conceptions, and professional everyday practice. In other words, it is necessary to consider the elements of continuity and discontinuity in relation to the specific forms of rule and goals of the NS state, on the one hand, and social work in Germany at its historical stage of development, on the other; that is, in the way that it had developed under the influence of the women's movement, bourgeois social reform, social hygiene, and — after the 1920s — the youth movement, the social-pedagogical movement (*Sozialpädagogische Bewegung*), and humanistic educational science (*Geisteswisenschaftliche Paedagogik*),[2] and how it had finally became a profession and an authority through the welfare state laws and the accompanying legal framing of social work interventions in the Weimar Republic.

Several paths have been taken to transform this complex issue into accessible research questions. However, up to now, research has paid little attention to the professional everyday practice of social work as the societal location of transformation and the role of its personnel as co-producers of this transformation.[3] That is the topic of this chapter. It will attempt to advance the debate on the continuity and discontinuity of the grounds for social work and its forms of action against the background of the memories of former members of the profession. However, before turning to such subjective interpretations and problematizations of former (professional) reality, the NS transformation of the welfare state needs to be specified from a more theoretical perspective based on the concept of an NS functionalization of social work.

Social Selection and Social Education

Almost every contemporary NS publication that presents and justifies its concept of social policy and social work starts by criticizing the Weimar welfare state. This is not arbitrary: Particularly after 1930, the reality of welfare in the Weimar Republic offered a target that could not be missed: The ambitious project had failed and got itself into such an impossible situation that it could no longer free itself. Whereas, on the one hand, the expansion of the welfare state seemed urgently necessary to counter the threat of declining legitimacy, on the other hand, the glaring contrast between what was promised and what was delivered contributed 'decisively to the loss of legitimacy of the first republic' (Peukert, 1987, p. 132, translated). The attempt to provide a general social net guaranteed by the state (even though on an extremely low level) led to an increasingly legal, bureaucratic, and monetary welfare system. In the end, the need to extend welfare benefits under the pressure of social, economic, and political framing conditions surpassed the actual fiscal ability to cover them, because the 'normal conditions of the welfare state', namely, economic growth and full employment were never achieved. The final outcome was generous laws and an enormous bureaucratic apparatus — a 'welfare administration' that either administered no welfare, or distributed it under increasingly restrictive and rigid conditions. The Weimar Republic never managed to resolve or even reduce social problem and conflicts. Under the pressure of increasingly widespread social problems, it became impossible to complete the project of providing a general social net. This was precisely the point at which the NS criticism of the welfare state started, and, in the end, the NS transformation of the welfare state as well.

If the Weimar welfare state failed because of the material impossibility of attaining the normative postulate of the welfare state, national socialism performed a radical reversal of the welfare state's obligation to provide material benefits: The individual was placed under the obligation of providing 'assistance for the *Volk* and the state'. From this point on, the provision of benefits was measured fundamentally according to the achievement and good behaviour of the person in need in terms of criteria of race and *Volk* community. This did not just apply, for example, to the benefits provided by the NS *Volk* welfare (*Nationalsozialistische Volkswohlfahrt*, NSV), but also by public welfare institutions that weeded out the 'inferior' (*Minderwertige*), the 'antisocial' (*Asoziale*), and the 'alien within the community' (*Gemeinschaftsfremde*), or at least punished them with disadvantages in order to promote the 'irreproachable member of the *Volk*' with slightly higher benefits and advantages. The blessings of such care were only available for 'a useful member of the *Volk* as a whole who is willing to work' (Althaus, 1937, p. 11, translated); and not as assistance, but as investment and reward, as 'fair payment' and 'fair punishment' for achievement and loyalty. The welfare state was transformed into an educational state:

> We have . . . the great task of overcoming the materialist welfare system and restrengthening the soul of our *Volk* and its health through education in daily life . . . In our work, we must make it clear to each person we assist that not only his own fate but also that of his family as well as all his fellow men depends on the actions of every person in daily life. (Hilgenfeldt, 1937, pp. 11–12, translated)

The area of reproduction — as a context of fulfilment and as a medium for becoming a *Volk* with its political, racist, and social-romantic implications — became a centre of social modeling through education and control, through selective promotion of the 'able' and selective weeding out of the enemy, the 'unproductive', the 'alien to the community', and the deviant.

Whereas, on the one hand, this led to a policy of selection and separation by the public welfare institutions that was life-threatening for many, on the other hand, it involved an educational transformation of society within the framework of the mass organizations of national socialism, for example, in the women's league (*NS-Frauenschaft*, NSF), in the youth movements for boys (*Hitlerjugend*, HJ) and girls (*Bund Deutscher Mädel*, BDM), in the leisure-time and cultural activities of the NS leisure-time organization, *Kraft durch Freude* (strength through joy), in the educational camp organizations such as the national labour service (*Reichsarbeitsdienst*) and the land service (*Landjahr*), in the expansion of preschools and community health care centres (*Gemeindepflegestationen*) through the NSV (Hansen, 1991), and other institutions that were expressly directed toward an educational encroachment into daily life and the private sphere.

In this way, the reform of the welfare state represents an attempt to transform the bourgeois-welfare-state form of socialization into a new alternative social model. The (formal) universal character of the state-guaranteed social net should be transformed into the community character of direct mutual assistance among members of the *Volk*. That this would finally lead to a general lack of a social net was part of the programme. The only place where security should still be found was within the '*Volk* community'. Those who belonged should receive the signal that they were now secure (Theweleit, 1980, p. 397); however, individuals first had to show that they belonged by exhibiting their willingness to work and to make sacrifices. Therefore the programme was directed essentially toward mobilization (Haug, 1986). This was rounded off with the complementary element of an all-round educational programme. This should lead to the generation of a sort of *Volk consensus* and the willingness to work for the *Volk* community: in jobs and housework, in rearing healthy and able children, and in the war against the internal and external enemies of the *Volk*. In general, this all-round educational programme followed the idea that a preventive change in human attitudes and lifestyles would make material benefits, with very few exceptions, superfluous, because the programme would destroy social problems at their roots and awaken nonstate subsistence coping potentials that only had to be guided in the right direction through educational measures. When, finally, the eugenic measures for racial purity and the eradication of inferiors also started to bite, all 'nonproductive' state benefits would become completely unnecessary.

This is the context in which the role of social work in national socialism has to be located. The alternative social model of 'socialism of the *Volk* community', as well as the corresponding form of identity as a 'member of the *Volk*', did not just appear by themselves. To implement them, national socialism took advantage of social work and the social welfare institutions as an identity-forming and social-disciplinary technology, as an organized processing of problems of reproduction (Schaarschuch, 1990) through assistance and control and through social education. The interplay of rational-bureaucratic and (social-) educational strategies of guidance through assistance and control, selective encouragement and selective disciplining, was (and continues to be) the main constituent of the historical form of institutionalized social work. This was (and is) its function and determines its daily activities. For NS rule, based in structural analogy on the technique of exclusion extending as far as murder contrasted with integration in the form of 'permanent mobilization' (Prinz, 1989), social work provided a particularly accessible set of useful instruments. This is why social work was also 'promoted' in a particular way during national socialism. How far, with which motives, and with which conflicts professional social workers responded to this promotion will be addressed in the next section.

The Data

The data on which the following sections are based is the transcript of a group discussion with thirteen former members of the social work profession.[4] The participants, nine women and four men, had worked in various fields of social work during national socialism, and six of them had also worked during the Weimar Republic. Their work during this time was the topic of the group discussion. All these former social workers are members of the *Gilde Soziale Arbeit* (GSA, social work guild), an independent professional association founded in 1925 that disbanded in 1933 and reformed after 1946. Numerous persons who had had a strong impact on contemporary social education had been members of this association, and many more were close to it. Some of them had to emigrate from NS Germany or give up their jobs. In Dudek's (1988) historical study of this group, the GSA stands 'pars pro toto for the relationship between the bourgeois youth movement and social work and as the representative of the social-pedagogical movement in the Weimar Republic' (p. 7, translated).[5]

The GSA was not a political organization but an association of social-pedagogical professionals who avoided taking a political stance. In fact, political heterogeneity very much belonged to their self-concept — this also made it a legitimate heir of the German youth movement. Criticized by some contemporaries as being elitist, the GSA viewed itself and functioned as a centre for progressive and innovative trends in the new professional fields of social work and theory formulation in (social) educational science. Thus, the participants in this discussion are not a 'random selection' but a group representing a specific tradition and culture within German social work and social education: the tradition that West German educational science and social work took up again after the end of World War II.

The reason for drawing on reports of contemporary witnesses is to access the 'subjective, internal side of past reality' (Kocka, 1986, p. 74, translated), and not to assess the 'objective' external structures and action conditions in the various fields in which these former social workers were active. Instead, the contributions of these contemporary witnesses should be understood as source materials that can be used to derive and reveal the attitudes, interpretations, and behaviours (as well as forms of processing) of social workers caught between their professional ethical guidelines, their career ambitions, and institutional demands. Attention is focused particularly on the professional self-image, on guiding patterns of interpretation and action in professional practice, as well as behaviours in conflict situations, the estimation of institutional freedom of action, and the attempts to exploit such freedoms.

Hence, the research perspective in some ways follows assumptions from the field of oral history. However, its methodological operationalization is based on qualitative social research. The conversation protocol is viewed as a database from which aspects of subjective meaning are reconstructed by interpreting individual sequences with the method of hermeneutic text interpretation. Two of these case interpretations are presented in the following. The methodological procedure used in interpreting the text is oriented toward proposals based on the argumentation theory developed by Toulmin (1975).[6] Nonetheless, a hermeneutic approach has clear limits: 'Hermeneutic reflection is restricted to revealing opportunities for knowledge that would otherwise not be perceived. It does not itself provide a criterion of truth' (Gadamer, 1971, p. 300, translated).

Types of Coping and Career Biographies

In general, the materials reveal the following types of coping or career biography:

(a) Social workers who fell victim to the political and anti-Semitic purges directly following the seizure of power and later were unable (or unwilling) to return to jobs in line with their qualifications shifted to other activities, and some of them emigrated.[7]

(b) The majority of those working in public welfare institutions (at least those not holding senior posts) kept their jobs and continued their old daily routines under new conditions.

(c) A further group of professionals, particularly those who rejected a 'noneducational office job', profited from the NS emphasis on educating society because it led to a notable expansion in attractive career opportunities.

Members of the discussion group continuously revealed clear divergences in their retrospective interpretations of this phase of their careers. Whereas most who worked in public welfare institutions (as social workers) judged this phase negatively, the majority of those working in social-educational fields outside these institutions judged it positively. The decisive factor is how strongly individual social workers were involved in the NS policies of selection and active exclusion through the functional definitions and daily practices of their own fields of work. Whereas the conflict between theory and daily practice became even stronger for the social workers in the group (through the continuation of the professional disillusionment experienced in the Weimar Republic), for others, hopes came true. The fact that hopes for a positive professional future were met in the one group in no way means that they had not also been available for the other.

After experiencing the collapse of the Weimar welfare state, social workers were open to the NS promise to resolve the crisis, because they hoped that the catastrophic situation in the benefit institutions would be overcome and they would have more opportunities to do the sort of work they wanted to do. This certainly did not just apply to the practical workers in the profession. Among the representatives of the social-pedagogical movement, attitudes toward the national socialists were initially marked by a curious mixture of skepticism and hope. Rang (1989) arrives at this conclusion in his critical analysis of the reactions of Spranger and Flitner to the national socialists in the respected journal *Die Erziehung* in early 1933. The open letter of May 2, 1933, in which the board of the GSA publicized its voluntary disbandment to its members, is interpreted in the same way by Dudek (1988, p. 194). The board wrote:

If, as we all hope, the Guild is going to continue to perform useful work for welfare in the future, then this can occur only with complete approval for the revitalization of the state. Much of what we have always wished for as members of the youth movement can now be achieved. We are certain that for this reason and out of a feeling of responsibility toward one's work, every individual will place his or her full strength and practical experiences in the service of the new order. (cited in Dudek, 1988, p. 194, translated)

Professionals engaged in practical work were frequently called upon by their academic masters to use NS reforms in order to fulfil the goals of the social-educational inheritance, to support the new state with the strengths of their specific skills, and to intercept possible 'deviations'.

One could anticipate that the hopes awakened among the professionals would generally be disappointed as the NS system became established. However, this does not seem to be the case for those practitioners from the social-education movement who were active in social-pedagogical fields outside the state welfare institutions. To the extent that these were represented in the group discussions, their reports reveal no retrospective distancing. The prevailing perspective is that one was able to put genuine social-pedagogical ideas into practice in these areas, and that there was a degree of 'educational freedom' that was relatively unimpeded by regulations.

In the following, two cases will be used to illustrate the motives, interpretations, and activities of professionals in the practical fields of maternity training (*Mütterschulung*) and public welfare. Both the former full-time head of maternity training courses as well as the former social worker presented here had previously worked for several years under the Weimar Republic in social work and social education professions.

An Example from the Social Education Field: 'I Was Looking for Fields that You Were Free to Organize Yourself'

Maternity training courses had existed in Germany since the turn of the century. During the Weimar Republic, they were frequently one of the obligatory tasks of public welfare workers (see Zeller, 1987, p. 147). However, they were generally carried out in the voluntary sector and by Christian and political associations. The spread of the modern nuclear family and the accompanying forms of gender-specific division of labour led to an 'intensification and rationalization of housework' (Czarnowski, 1989, p. 130, translated). Taking on the role of housewife and mother, practising rational housekeeping, and the teaching of specific knowledge and skills thus also became part of the educational task of the experts in the new social professions created by the welfare state. On the one hand, the maternity training courses of the national mother service (*Reichsmütterdienst*; Dammer, 1981; Schiedeck, 1989), an auxiliary of the national socialist women's league and the German women's league (*Deutsches Frauenwerk*), reflect this continuity, whereas, on the other hand, they have to be located within the context of those women's or family and health policy measures of the national socialists whose intention and consequence was 'that welfare workers and physicians, more than ever before, were given the legal right [to enter] the internal sphere of the family in order to educate, to counsel, to monitor, and to select' (Czarnowski, 1989, p. 131, translated).

A typical pattern can be recognized in the extension of maternity training during national socialism:

(a) the expansion and weighting with ideological propaganda of an already tested measure aimed toward the greatest possible access to the target group for purposes of ideological and practical training;

(b) the centralized but all-encompassing implementation of the programme accompanied by the simultaneous exclusion of the prior providers of comparable measures;

(c) ensuring a monopoly and a clientele;

(d) deployment of appropriately trained or experienced full-time professionals and social workers (who were taken over selectively from the disbanded organizations), but also of the largest possible number of voluntary educators, who were, in turn, prepared for their task through special training measures.

Between 1934 and 1937, a total of 1,139,945 women were 'processed' in 53,977 courses. The curricula focused on the following contents: general schooling (NS philosophy on the role of the woman in the NS *Volk* community including racial and genetic theory); housekeeping; pregnancy, childcare, and childrearing; health education and care of the sick (Dammer, 1981, pp. 233–7). The educational starting point was the everyday life of the target group, housework, and reproduction. The focus was on teaching and practising methods of modern, hygienic, and economic subsistence work that should equip women to achieve the highest possible output of health and family harmony within the framework of the given wage level. In the propaganda used to present maternity training, the goal was always given as the levelling out of differences in status through the group experience. Dammer (1981) doubts whether this was actually achieved: 'What seems to have been more effective is the dissemination of bourgeois norms and values ... The ideals of harmonious family life were oriented toward bourgeois models' (p. 239, translated).

This background also explains the ability to link up with traditional professional standards of normality and normalization and the relatively high willingness of experienced (social) educators to apply their abilities to implementing these measures. The judgment that maternity training was a 'neutral space', which is maintained not only by the former full-time course leader but also by other participants in the discussion, lays implicit claim to a distancing of professional everyday practice within this measure from the 'actual' ideology and policy of the national socialists, and this is also emphasized repeatedly in explicit statements. In line with Dammer (1981), it is necessary to assume that the actual practice of maternity training — in contrast to the propaganda tracts of NS officials — did not focus on political and ideological topics. This would namely have tended to be irreconcilable with the national socialist (as well as the traditional bourgeois) image of women. The goal of maternity training courses was not political debate, and certainly not intellectual debate, but also not the dissemination of positive aspects of ideology that would go beyond the world of housework, but a subtle political encroachment into daily life in the sense of an education toward a specific attitude toward work as the essential expression of femininity. The relationship between maternity training courses and integration is also revealed through the fact that they were carried out more intensively in areas in which the influence of the workers' movement or the churches was particularly strong (see Dammer, 1981, p. 244).

The following comments of a former full-time head of maternity training courses reveal how far, in this case, the interests of a professional person corresponded with those of the NS service provider.

M.: [Hermann] Nohl, who didn't retire [from the university] until 1937, said that he liked to see his students join the movement [i.e., national socialism] so that something would come of it, right? And I had heard this call as well [laughter]. And then it was one of the first new professions for women — now, that also comes from my training. We were continuously trained to organize things and I was looking for fields that you were free to organize yourself and I didn't want to work in an administration. And then the first thing that came along was these maternity training courses; they were looking for professionals to run them and that in the *Gau* of Westphalia as well. So I applied, and I was summoned to a *Gauschule*, and they checked through all the papers there, whether I was Jewish, a member of the socialist party, and so forth; and as, by chance, there was nothing there about me [laughter], I was taken on. First of all, you were trained. You already knew all of that and judged it to be completely absurd. You know how it is, it goes in one ear and out the other, 'They were just doing their job' and so forth. But their only concern was to get people deployed. And I was told that I should set up maternity training courses in [name of a city], and several maternity training courses had already gone wrong there and it was a terribly difficult district, everything so catholic, and I should nonetheless give it a try, and so on.

One could finally say that both sides were in luck — an ideal correspondence between supply and demand for a specific competence profile that the speaker assigns herself. In the following sequence, the central motives of this generalizing retrospective interpretation are repeated and varied. The motive for distancing herself from social work in 'an administration' is reinforced and explicated as a distancing from all those professional colleagues who were active in public welfare institutions.

Now I wasn't in an administrative office, and it was a long time before I heard about these negative things. And, in addition, I was unemployed and I was also very committed to social-education work, especially the education part, and that was why I was so interested in maternity training. And, at the time, yes, one can say that, you can say that over and over again, it was something positive, that one was left a lot of freedom. Although you did receive training at the *Gauschule*, you just didn't listen to what they were saying, right? The important thing was the commitment to people, to the mothers whom I had got to know in the factories [the speaker's prior work field], and I knew that they urgently needed something where they would gain recognition, where they could get answers to their questions, and so on. And that is why I went into it positively. And my commitment was so strong that the NSDAP repeatedly gave me a good telling off. And I always just shrugged it off, and they always kept on employing me. Probably because I had so many women in my courses; and they always had to report the attendance figures to their superiors.

That the maternity training courses of the national mother service represented an ideal work field for the speaker is expressed very clearly here. She is simply advancing her career without any thoughts of compromising herself. Interpretations of her own professionality and that of the national socialists, of the specific work field and of the clients are woven together into a line of reasoning that follows the goal of showing that the speaker's professional commitment, which is what she is talking about, does not represent a break in her professional biography but is consistent and follows on from her training and the ethical norms and values guiding her profession: that it does not refer to an identification with the ideology and politics of the national socialists, nor to a naivety that could possibly be understood as culpable, but 'results' from her professionality itself.

First of all, attention should be drawn to those statements in which the speaker reconstructs not only her particular competence and disposition but also the professional field in a way in which a congruence should become apparent. Further data that should be understood within the context of this line of reasoning are the references to Nohl's appeal and to her unemployment. Not congruence, but contrast is the pattern of two further lines of reasoning that cannot be interpreted in full here but only sketched. By indicating her distance to the *Gauschule* and the NSDAP as the official forms of an 'actual national socialism', her work field and working practices are assigned to a space in which it is not the ideology and politics of national socialism but only her own professionality and the needs of the clients that determine activities. The same goal is followed with the distancing from 'offices', who are defined as the location of 'negative things'. With the emphasis that the speaker, in contrast to her conversation partner involved in this discussion, had not been involved in the exclusionist measures of NS social policy is used to legitimize her own practice and her positive interpretation. If values based on professional ethics are still kept implicit here, the speaker finally finds the focus of her reasoning in the ethical topos of her profession — that the interaction partner cannot question — that 'the important thing was the commitment to people', whose application to this context is justified in the accompanying construction of the clients as deficient, needing assistance, thankful, and so forth.

Idealization, namely of the field of work, one's own competence, and the fit between the two, is recognizable as the guiding motive in both sequences. In the context of the interaction situation, these idealizations have a legitimizing function. As Radtke (1983) has shown, speech acts within a circle of professional colleagues in which professional activity is the topic are shaped by forms of reasoning that correspond to the logic of the profession. If it is assumed that reasoning concerns 'the justification of practical conclusions in order to generate willingness to agree', which must be confirmed in standards of reasoning shared by speakers and listeners (Radtke, 1983, p. 64), talking about one's profession in front of professional colleagues must be guided by standards of interpretation and action that are, or were, also effective in the practice of the profession.

In the interaction situation that produced this protocol, those involved had to use the attitudes and perceptions of their professional culture in the (re-)constructive presentation of sections of their professional life. They had to fall back on patterns of interpretation and topoi to which they attribute validity within each specific professional culture of reasoning to which they belong. Thus, the use of reasoning standards and profession-specific topoi and premises is in no way arbitrary, but constrained by this membership of a professional culture and through the individual biographical range of interpretations available to the interaction partners in which the subjective interpretations can to be understood as spellings out of or case-related applications of collective patterns of interpretation. I have no doubt that the rationally linked interpretations in the present sequences also belonged to the existing contents of that range of interpretations of the past reality on which the speaker was dependent for the task of finding orientation within her profession. What seems to be more questionable to me is whether there was any need at all for legitimation at the time.

The sequences presented illustrate the ability to link professional standards and norms of activity among members of the profession from the field of the social-education movement to the fields of (social-) educational identity formation under national socialism. This could also be illustrated in the interpretations of the retrospective reports of a former land-service worker (*Landjahrhelfer*) that cannot be presented in detail here. The example of maternity training courses in their twin function of integration into the NS state through evoking an appearance of care (Mason, 1982) and the formation or stabilization of a functional women's role reveals that the use of the professional competence of experienced social workers by NS associations and formations made an important, if not indispensable contribution to the successful implementation of such target-group-oriented educational measures. The success of the maternity training courses run by the national mother service (measured in terms of this twin function) was to a great degree dependent on how successfully, starting from discussions of daily problems, they managed to link together the support and recognition of the women (see Dammer, 1981, p. 244) and normative definitions of a women's role in an educationally effective way that was 'acceptable' for the target group — a task that called for a specific professional knowledge and educational experience. A more distanced and/or careful approach to the ideological components of NS philosophy (an ability that officials in the women's auxiliary of the NS probably did not possess), but above all, the embedment of evaluations and practical action orientations within an apparently neutral professional competence probably tended to increase the educational impact as well as the integrative power of these measures in traditional, non-NS milieus.

An Example of Selection Practices: 'And then I Had to Make a List'

A further conversation sequence will be used to try to focus on the microcosm of a public welfare institution in an interpretation that is drawn more closely on the text. In the period discussed here, the speaker was simultaneously a district youth worker and city welfare worker, and in this latter function, she was also active as a welfare worker for the health department.

H (1) I was a city social worker, that is, I worked for the city administration and I was a district youth worker. (2) And there I had two confrontations with national socialism. (3) As a district youth worker, I was requisitioned, that is, I should be transferred to the national socialist youth organizations, and this meant I should be taken on with the rank of an *Untergauführerin* [district leader], Here . . .

D (D1) Oh! Oh, oh, oh!

H . . . Just think how high I could have gone! (amusement)

A (A1) Does that mean we have to stand up now?

H (4) . . . and I, fool that I was, refused and even made cheeky comments, saying 'We're allowed to show you how to do things and then we'll be given the boot.' (5) And that's also the way it would have been, but I didn't even try to show them what to do. (6) So I refused the transfer. (7) And then I had to make a list of the clients I knew who were suffering from hereditary diseases, and who should be registered for sterilization, no? (8) And among my clients, I was also a social worker for the health department, I knew a whole lot, a whole lot, well, more than two hands full, you know, who were suffering from hereditary diseases. (9) And I had to make a note of that. (10) So I wrote down their names for my medical officer, (11) there was no other way at the time, (12) because he also had to produce something and was not a fervent national socialist. (13) So, those were two situations that I can remember and that troubled me at the time.

The speaker, whom we shall simply call Mrs Herrmann in the following, is answering the interviewer's question on 'confrontations' and 'meetings' with national socialists within the context of professional work. Two situations are (re-) constructed here. However, they are not presented chronologically, but following aspects of reasoning.

First of all, Mrs Herrmann talks about her refusal to accept a leadership post in the NS youth organizations. She presents her case and names the rank of the official post offered *Untergauführerin* [district leader]. This causes one participant in the discussion to make direct noises of surprise and respect. Mrs Herrmann comments on the post offered with the words, 'Just think how high I could have gone!' This triggers general amusement and a further interjection 'Does that mean we have to stand up now?' The action in the recalled situation that follows becomes a self-assertion through the ironic self-criticism: 'and I, fool that I was, refused it and even made cheeky comments' (4). The speaker accounts for her actions by citing how she had spoken to an imaginary NS conversation partner in the situation constructed here 'saying "We're allowed to show you how to do things and then we'll be given the boot."'

The construction of the past situation is broken off here and the reported contemporary action and the reasons for it are confirmed from the current perspective: 'And that's also the way it would have been, but I didn't even try to show them what to do' (5). What should be emphasized here is the agreement between the interpretations of national socialism expressed at the time and the present-day ones: Mrs Herrmann did not let herself be instrumentalized, because becoming a *Untergauführerin* would have been an instrumentalization.

Together with this explicit justification for the contemporary action, another motive appears below the surface. Alongside the cleverness of her political estimation of the situation, which recognizes the attempted instrumentalization, Mrs H's irony about the official post offered exhibits a low estimation based on pride in her profession. This is understood immediately by the other colleagues present at the group discussion: a self-evident disparity between the qualifications and status of Mrs Herrmann as a district youth worker and city welfare worker and that assigned to a local district leader in the NS youth organizations. It is this discrepancy that leads to the comedy of the situation, which is perceived on all sides.

Drawing on historiographic context knowledge, the speaker's interpretation of instrumentalization can be understood as follows: It can be assumed that in the case reported here, the district youth officer of the community should be appointed to be a part-time local district leader of the *Bund Deutscher Mädel*, that is, the female NS youth movement. This job offer followed a strategy directed toward both integrating (and thus weakening) possible competitors as well as authorizing national socialism, that is, the strategy of 'nationalizing' NS youth work for which, in line with its totalitarian character, there should no longer be any competition. A BDM district leader would finally also have to fit into the internal hierarchy of the organization. This may be why the attempted instrumentalization of this request became obvious to Mrs Herrmann, and the necessary alignment with such a pecking order would then certainly have appeared unacceptable and even absurd.

The situation described is thus less a heroic act of ethically and politically motivated refusal than an expression of specific professional pride that is also shared by the other listeners. It corresponds to a topos expressed in several other places during the discussion regarding the 'boundless stupidity of the NS officials who did not understand anything about our work.' It is this pattern of interpretation that gives rise to the homogeneity of the group verbalized in the expressions of amusement and ironic comments.

Nonetheless, Mrs Herrmann becomes a group hero. In her self-citation she does not just speak for herself but in the 'we' form, and this stands for a 'common subject' — the profession: 'we' persons with social-education qualifications and professional experience and professional status. The demonstrated self-assertion then tends to become the assertion of a group identity through a discrimination based on professional pride. And the cleverness she demonstrates becomes a welcome example of how the listeners like to see themselves: as not letting themselves be instrumentalized and even making cheeky comments as well.

In the second part of the sequence, Mrs Herrmann reports on how she dealt with the command to name persons with hereditary diseases among her clients who would then be subject to compulsory sterilization in line with the act for the prevention of hereditarily diseased offspring (*Gesetz zur Verhütung erbkranken Nachwuchses*, GveN).[8]

(7) And then I had to make a list of the clients I knew who were suffering from hereditary diseases, and who should be registered for sterilization, no?

In terms of the way it is presented, this instruction has a completely different quality to the one presented before. The former was qualified as a 'requisitions'; here, she simply says 'I had to.' As above, she does not name a subject who issues this requisition or instruction. By using 'I had to', the speaker places herself retrospectively in an 'objectively compulsory position' that is then explained further in the following. The action itself, which Mrs Herrmann is ordered to perform, is presented as an administrative act.

(8) And among my clients, I was also a welfare worker for the health department, I knew a whole lot, a whole lot, well, more than two hands full, you know, who were suffering from hereditary diseases. (9) And I had to make a note of that.

This recollection (8–9) presents — almost repeatedly — the procedure for selecting persons according to set medical criteria. The fact that Mrs Herrmann can (and must be able to) apply these criteria within her area of responsibility as a welfare worker in the health department is not discussed as a problem, but taken for granted as a fact. It seems to be specifically the competence (as ability and responsibility) that becomes the grounds of justification here. The fact that, as a health worker, she 'knew a whole lot' of persons already sufficed. A refusal to obey the order seems to have been out of the question. The outcome of the situation is reported in (10):

(10) So I wrote down their names for my medical officer.

The completion of the action is presented as being harmless. Mrs Herrmann has passed on a memo — a 'neutral administrative act'. The speaker is aware that its consequences for those involved was anything but harmless. The legitimation for the action follows directly: (11) 'there was no other way at the time'. In this central final assertion, a temporally distanced perspective is used to presented the action situation witnessed in the past once more as an objectively compulsory position, as a situation in which no alternative actions were available. This assertion is, in turn, justified and further strengthened with new data. Here, the speaker refers back to the figure of the medical officer introduced in (10).

(12) because he also had to produce something and was not a fervent national socialist.

This emphasizes the embedment in the hierarchy and formal organizational structure of the health department. The selection and listing of persons for compulsory sterilization gains the quality of a dutiful fulfilment of a regular task within the context of the bureaucratic organizational structure. This dependent relationship is specified in the figure of the medical officer. However, the medical officer becomes a figure of legitimation in another way as well: With the indication that even the medical officer with his more far-reaching competencies had to discipline his personal feelings in order to fulfil his duties should underline the (relative) powerlessness of the lower-ranked welfare worker.

At the end of the sequence (13), the two narrated situations are related to each other and finally evaluated as 'two situations that I can remember and that troubled me at the time'.

In Mrs Herrmann's memory, the effects of national socialist reforms on herself as a practitioner in social work are interpreted as a worsening of crisis; she is confronted with expectations and action demands that conflict with her professional self-image (which includes her professional pride just as much as her professional ethics). In both situations, these are interpreted as instrumentalizations of her professional role that trigger professional and/or professional ethical conflicts. In the first situation, she risks open conflict and the intended instrumentalization is thwarted. When it comes to her involvement in compulsory sterilization, which has far more dramatic consequences for those concerned, she does not risk open conflict, apparently because no chances are seen of being able to refuse to comply with the order without risking her personal and material safety.

If the sequence is now regarded from the perspective that Mrs Herrmann is explaining and legitimizing her preferences and actions in confrontations with national socialism in the content of the group discussion, it can finally be interpreted as follows: Mrs Herrmann wanted to show that she had evaded NS attempts at instrumentalization when carrying out her professional role as far as each given or estimated action scope permitted.

Conclusion

This final summary will try to piece together general aspects of the profession and general aspects of this specific professional culture, the social-pedagogical movement, from the particularities of these cases, and then relate these general aspects to the NS functionalization of social work.

The retrospective interpretations of former members of the profession reveal a professional self-image that I personally consider to be typical for that generation of social workers whose choice of profession and training as well as professional background is related closely to the welfare state conception of social work in the Weimar Republic; in other words, that period of time during which the process of institutionalization and professionalization had been brought to a provisional conclusion, and the growing demand for professionals was frequently associated with a mood of reform among those for whom the new social professions and work fields provided an attractive and promising career prospect.

They viewed themselves as a professional group equipped with specific future-oriented competencies who tackled societal deficits by providing competent assistance in order to ward off trouble. The object of their professional pride, their professionality (understood in terms of their competencies, their action preferences, and their explanations) was oriented, on the one hand, toward the conventional ideas and concepts of social hygiene and, on the other hand, toward the idea of healing and renewing society in the spirit of the *Volksbildung* movement (educating the people to become a *Volk*) and the youth movement by applying social education. In this professional self-image, there was nothing wrong with turning people into clients or with educating them: It was viewed as a responsible act and as a precondition for saving people by applying an exclusive professional competence whose credibility and infallibility in solving problems were self-confidently taken for granted.

At the latest when the Weimar welfare state was in a crisis, which, in numerous ways, was also a crisis of its professions, many social workers began to perceive the situation of growing social difficulties, destabilization of society, social decline, and personnel cuts as an ideological and material threat. Any attempt to determine the relationship of the profession to national socialism certainly has to give due credit to the experience of crisis and the national socialist promise to overcome this crisis, particularly as far as the years between 1930 and 1938 are concerned. In this context, an examination of the conditions under which the national socialists could functionalize social work also has to pay attention to the social matrix of this profession, its typical historical ideals and claims to relevance, its ways of thinking and acting, and the practices used to implement, or intended to implement, its specific problem-solving competence. Competence in progress and a mood of reform, here one could find common interests with national socialism but also a degree of competition, and this to an increasing extent at a time when those in the social work professions, particularly women in the welfare professions, were having to accept further devaluations of their qualifications (see Dammer, 1989). One could distance oneself — from the position of professional superiority — yet discover opportunities for self-advancement in fields in which there was a demand for competence.

Even when the social-pedagogical milieu of the social workers surveyed here did 'not agree with everything' as far as the phenomenon and claims to power of the national socialists were concerned, there were nonetheless — with temporal and content-related differentiations — points of association and lines of affiliation for all on the level of profession-relevant concepts. A dichotomous discrimination of affinity and difference would not correspond to reality here. In the area of integrative and identity-forming national socialist programmes and measures, which drew on the handed-down forms of practice in camp education, culture work, and *Volksbildung*, there were particularly strong links to professional standards and professional dispositions. In the area of modernizing the public health system in terms of social hygiene — in contemporary terms: in the service of *Volksgesundheit* — there was generally a high level of agreement between social workers (and also welfare policymakers) shaped by the Weimar Republic and national socialists. The affinity on the level of conceptualizations of an appropriate way of dealing with social problems (through far-reaching education, publicity campaigns, and control) often resulted in a voluntary or willing functionalization for the new order promised by national socialism and anticipated from national socialism by the people. The memories recorded in the group discussion provide an insight into the variety of subjective and intersubjectively differing attitudes and patterns of legitimization that, even below the level of pure enthusiasm, reveal a broad range of forms of 'accepting and going along with' (Lüdtke, 1991), getting through, and protecting oneself from criticism and doubt. They show how social workers participated in the NS functionalization of social work. When the subjective interpretations of the former members of the profession implicitly address functionalization, it is only ever recognized as such at a point in time when it was 'already too late'. Only when collaboration turned into passive instrumentalization in their own eyes did professional pride and educational hubris seem to invert into a sudden recognition and admission of the weaknesses of their own status.

The estimation and exploitation of areas in which they had freedom of action and areas in which they had to adapt differed across situations and individuals. This can be seen by looking once more at the second case reported above. Estimated freedom of action seems to decline when the institutional density of regulations, hierarchies, and opportunities to exert control, as well as the degree of routine in the anticipated actions increases. Whereas the district youth work officer (responsible for youth work in the local district) could even make 'cheeky comments', as a social worker in the health department, the same person knew that 'there was no other way'. The internal rationality of the bureaucratically organized health department did not provide for a discursive consideration of compulsory sterilization that could have promoted and supported a refusal to obey orders through the united exploitation of action scopes. Under the threats of NS rule, the compulsion to obediently carry out one's duties was perceived more strongly than under other political systems. Nonetheless, both are there: the powerlessness of the subject against the power of the elites and their agents, and the subjective recognition of dominance through obedient self-constraint, because 'there was no other way at the time'. This turned the welfare worker into an object and subject of dominance combined.

To implement the policies of separation and eradication through the institutions of public welfare there was no need for those involved to identify with national socialism, either in terms of its political goals or the ideologies used to legitimize them. As with the development and implementation of genocide, these selections leading all the way to eliminations took place 'within the established routines of professional daily life'. A 'burning enthusiasm' was not necessary. What was necessary was ' "nothing more" than the usual "treatment of partial tasks in an absolute manner" in administrative actions' (Gerstenberger, 1988, p. 73, translated). The case-specific application of social and medical definition criteria belongs and belonged to the fundamental types of activity in routine daily work in the social work institutions. The discrimination between normality and deviance, the smooth sorting of cases into those for whom assistance is still possible and those to be redirected toward social disciplinary measures, the separation between active controlling subject and the client as object to be treated — this characterizes the classic social topic of social work as a 'power to establish order' (Brunkhorst, 1989, pp. 199–200).

The implementation of the interventions that were historically singular in terms of their content and consequences for the clients took place within the continuity of institutional forms of practice. Against this background, one has to view the historic form of the institutionalization of social work itself, namely, as a bureaucratic administration, as a decisive and necessary, but not sufficient, condition of its functionalization for NS race policy.

Even in the Weimar Republic, when the material limits to benefits in the welfare state had been reached, the controlling, disciplining, and excluding functions of institutions had already grown to be independent of their assistance functions. The establishment of social work as a defining power in relation to the need principle was soon followed by the hollowing out of state guarantees of benefits and security when the crisis of the welfare state led to a transformation of the need principle into a worthiness principle. It is only necessary to follow the debates in the publications and proceedings of annual conferences of the German Association of Public and Private Welfare (*Deutsche Verein für öffentliche und private Fürsorge*, DV) between 1926 and 1930 to find not only a drawing together of arguments attacking the universal character of the legalized welfare state guarantees to meet basic needs (which were in any case being limited systematically by the need principle) but also the seeds of those strategies for resolving the crisis that were later to dominate national socialism, though in a more radical form and one then modified by the ideologies of the NS *Volk* community and the race paradigm: increase in selection and control functions, appeal to self-help (and, associated with this, the demand for an energetic implementation of work and maintenance obligations), as well as demands for flanking prevention programs using the patterns for defining problems and processing them taken from social education, social hygiene, and finally, eugenics (Landwehr, 1983, p. 118). However, alongside the continuity of the normality and normalization discourse, there is one decisive difference: In the Weimar republic, the controlling and social-disciplinary attack on the subjects was still constrained by the protective barriers of civil rights, whereas the national socialists abolished these restrictions. Nonetheless, it is necessary to doubt whether the continuity of the sociopolitical crisis-resolving strategies discussed and partially applied against the background of the increasing crisis is already sufficient to explain the functionalization of the welfare state institutions for NS race policy.

In the radicalization of the exclusion function in national socialism, a specific difference in intention becomes apparent despite all potential and factual compatibilities and affinities with conceptualizations found in the historical form of professionalism. The professional development and application of social-disciplinary and educational forms of intervention as well as the measures for turning cases into objects and their authoritarian referral to forms of treatment was aimed toward the normalizing conversion of persons. Whether such interventions designed to process social problems damaged those involved more than they helped them (a question that can still be asked today) cannot be answered here. In the ideology and policy of national socialism, the racist and sociobiological maxims were used to tackle persons not only much more radically but also with a clear interest in eradication: Social problems should be overcome by murdering the problem groups involved; and the 'reproduction' of social problems by preventing the reproduction of persons defined as problematic through compulsory mutilation. The eugenic and racist explanation of social problems determined the form of intervention applied. Difference prevails not only on the level of forms of intervention but also on the level of the explanation of social problems. An interest in a rational application of racism and negative eugenics in social policy with such a marked orientation toward naked cost-utility calculations cannot be found in any of the leading conceptualizations of social work of the time. On the other hand, the opinion leaders and practitioners of social work hardly ever tried to prevent the political implementation or the practical application of NS selection and elimination policy.

Professional policy interests and individual concerns about personal job status were more important than the well-being of the clients or moral doubts. Even in the years of crisis in the Weimar Republic, one can already observe a clear trend toward the transformation of educational and welfare policy reasoning into arguments aimed at protecting the status of the profession. Within the movement in social work summarized here under the concept of the social-pedagogical movement, recognition of the political neutrality of assistance and education was a central component of the professional self-image and a criterion of exclusion — of both the political right and the political left — but, above all, against the political and in favour of the educational. In the years of crisis in the Weimar republic, the strict adherence to this concept of the political neutrality of assistance inverted in a particularly drastic way into political naivety and opportunism. Most contemporary witnesses recall the final phase of the Weimar Republic as a 'general emergency' and as a period of increasing politicization that also encroached on the fields of social policy and finally on social workers themselves in their professional role. This 'passive politicization' blamed on the historical situation did not lead to an 'active politicization' of professionals in anything more than a fragmentary way. The practitioners among this group were possibly too much involved in dealing with the pressure of problems; and although there has been some discussion of radical sociopolitical programmes in professional circles before 1933 as mentioned above, such a radical and intensified implementation as that carried out under national socialism lay far beyond the sociopolitical fantasy of those who belonged to the spectrum of the social-pedagogical movement. In any case, they would never have viewed an offensive and critical involvement in the public discussion on social policy as one of their urgent tasks. When the social-pedagogical movement entered the public discussion with critical intent, this was to oppose the 'social-pedagogical reaction' but not the sociopolitical reaction (see Dudek, 1988). The 'educational standpoint' of the social-education movement only managed to retain its critical potential as long as the welfare state continued to remain in a phase of expansion.

Notes

1 See Kramer (1983, p. 176). On 30 January, 1933, the day on which Hitler was appointed *Reichskanzler*, the terrorist rioting in the process of the NS struggle for power reached a peak. It is estimated that 100,000 persons were taken into custody, and between 500 and 600 persons were murdered (Longerich, 1989, p. 172). Welfare offices were also 'stormed' by the SA, and persons were abducted and mishandled. Most of the victims of terrorist actions were holders of high-ranking posts who were left-wing or Jewish or were viewed as such (Kramer, 1983, p. 200). The civil service reform act (*Gesetz zur Wiederherstellung des Berufsbeamtentums*) came into power on 7 April, 1933. All civil servants who were 'Jewish' or 'politically unreliable' according to a set criterion were dismissed. Social work was also affected by this. Particularly the prominent personalities, above all, those in high-ranking posts or involved in theoretical work or training such as Alice Salomon (1872–1948), Siddy Wronsky (1883–1949), Hedwig Wachenheim (1891–1969), Hildegard Gudilla Lion (1893–1970), Walter Friedländer (1891–1984), Curt Bondy (1894–1972), Carl Mennicke (1887–1959), and many others were forced by the national socialists to give up their political and professional careers and/or go into exile (Dudek, 1988; Wieler, 1989).
2 The main representatives of this development were Wilhelm Flitner (1889–1990), Theodor Litt (1880–1962), Hermann Nohl (1879–1960), Eduard Spranger (1882–1963), and Erich Weniger (1894–1961).
3 An exception to this is the papers of Knüppel-Dähne and Mitrovic (1989) and Mitrovic (1987).
4 The group discussion was carried out as part of a research project at the Faculty of Educational Science of the University of Bielefeld. The research team consisted of Hans-Uwe Otto (project manager), Hilmar Peter, Heinz Sünker, and Stefan Schnurr.
5 For a history of the GSA, see Dudek (1988). According to conservative estimations, it had between 600 and 800 members in the years 1930 to 1933. Most of these worked in the fields of child and youth welfare (Dudek, 1988, pp. 76–8). In comparison, national job statistics in 1933 counted 13,014 *Wohlfahrtspfleger*, the official title for social workers at the time, of whom 88.8 per cent were women (Statistik des Dt. Reiches, 1978 [1936], 2, p. 195). Men were disproportionately overrepresented in the GSA. This movement of men into social work, which began in the 1920s, was fed almost exclusively by the youth movement.

On the close relation between the youth movement and reform education (*Reform-pädagogik*), see Scheibe (1984) and the collection of sources in Flitner and Kudritzki (1961, 1962) and Kindt (1974). From the perspective of contemporary theory formulation in educational science, the work of Hermann Nohl (1933) on the education movement in Germany is exemplary for the raising of the status of the youth movement in educational philosophy in unity with its placement within a '. . . great internal movement. We call it the German movement' (Nohl, 1933, p. 308, translated). The *Gilde Soziale Arbeit* is specifically emphasized in this work as an interface between the youth movement and social-education work that had become an organization (p. 314). Nohl's text was reprinted in 1936 under the title *Die pädagogische Bewegung in Deutschland und ihre Theorie* (The education movement in Germany and its theory), and reached its seventh edition in 1970. This illustrates the bonds of continuity and the role of the 1920s in academic and professional identity formation, mentioned above. On the *Gilde Soziale Arbeit* see also the chapter of Elizabeth Harvey in this book.

6　See Radtke (1983), who uses a method of interpretation based on argumentation theory to analyse the professional (educational) interpretation and action standards in group discussions with teachers and school psychologists. Böhm, Mühlbach, and Otto (1989) also used Toulmin's (1975) approach to study how social workers use their knowledge of the social sciences in their formal and informal justifications for referral to residential care.

7　Two members of this group discussion, the head of a youth office and a teacher of social education at a teachers' training college, were dismissed in April 1933 as a result of the civil service reform act. The head of the youth office took up a job outside the profession. The college teacher managed to find a job in a 'polytechnic for women's professions' but was dismissed a second time for political reasons and then worked with female youth in the national labour service (*Reichsarbeitsdienst*).

8　This act, made law on 7 July 1933, called for compulsory sterilization of men and women in whom one of the following conditions had been diagnosed: innate feeble-mindedness, schizophrenia, manic depression, hereditary falling sickness (epilepsy), Huntington's chorea, hereditary blindness, hereditary deafness, severe hereditary physical deformation, severe alcoholism. Most sterilization proposals were made by state-employed medical officers in the new health departments established in 1934. They could also be made by hospital directors. The law formally obliged all persons working in welfare, medical, and care professions to report candidates for sterilization. Decisions were made by specially set up hereditary health courts composed of a judge, a state-employed physician, and a further person who 'is particularly well-informed about eugenics' (Paragraph 6, translated). The reason given for the law was the need to 'eliminate inferior genotypes'. It was directed particularly toward the so-called 'light cases'. The outcome was 400,000 compulsory sterilizations up to 1945. There were approximately equal proportions of men and women among the victims. The most frequent diagnosis used to justify sterilization was 'feeble-mindedness' (Bock, 1986, p. 88; see, also, 1992, pp. 103–5).

References

ALTHAUS, H. (1937) *Nationalsozialistische Volkswohlfahrt: Wesen, Aufgaben und Aufbau*, Berlin, Junker und Dünnhaupt.

BOCK, G. (1986) *Zwangssterilisation im Nationalsozialismus: Studien zur Rassenpolitik und Frauenpolitik*, Opladen, Westdeutscher Verlag.

BOCK, G. (1992) 'Frauen und Geschlechterbeziehungen in der nationalsozialistsichen Rassenpolitik', in WOBBE, TH. (Ed) *Nach Osten: Verdeckte Spuren Nationalsozialistischer Verbrechen*, Frankfurt am Main, Verlag Neue Kritik.

BÖHM, W., MÜHLBACH, M. and OTTO, H.-U. (1989) 'Zur Rationalität der Wissensverwendung im Kontext behördlicher Sozialarbeit', in BECK, U. and BONSS, W. (Eds) *Weder Sozialtechnologie noch Aufklärung?*, Frankfurt am Main, Suhrkamp.

BRUNKHORST, H. (1989) 'Sozialarbeit als Ordnungsmacht', in OLK, TH. and OTTO, H.-U. (Eds) *Soziale Dienste im Wandel, Bd. 2, Entwürfe Sozialpädagogischen Handelns*, Neuwied und Frankfurt am Main, Luchterhand.

CZARNOWSKI, G. (1989) 'Familienpolitik als Geschlechterpolitik', in OTTO, H.-U. and SÜNKER, H. (Eds) *Soziale Arbeit und Faschismus*, Frankfurt am Main, Suhrkamp.

DAMMER, S. (1981) 'Kinder, Küche, Kriegsarbeit: Die Schulung der Frauen durch die NS-Frauenschaft', in FRAUENGRUPPE FASCHISMUSFORSCHUNG (Eds) *Mutterkreuz und Arbeitsbuch: Zur Geschichte der Frauen in der Weimarer Republik und im Nationalsozialismus*, Frankfurt am Main, Fischer.

DAMMER, S. (1989) 'Nationalsozialistische Frauenpolitik und soziale Arbeit', in OTTO, H.-U. and SÜNKER, H. (Eds) *Soziale Arbeit und Faschismus*, Frankfurt am Main, Suhrkamp.

DUDEK, P. (1988) *Leitbild: Kamerad und Helfer: Sozialpädagogische Bewegung in der Weimarer Republik am Beispiel der 'Gilde Soziale Arbeit'* (Quellen und Beiträge zur Geschichte der Jugendbewegung, Band 31), Frankfurt am Main, dipa-Verlag.

FLITNER, W. and KUDRITZKI, G. (Eds) (1961) *Die Deutsche Reformpädagogik, Band 1, Die Pioniere der Pädagogischen Bewegung*, Düsseldorf-München, Küpper.

FLITNER, W. and KUDRITZKI, G. (Eds) (1962) *Die Deutsche Reformpädagogik, Band 2, Ausbau und Selbstkritik*, Herausgegeben und erläutert von Wilhelm Flitner und Gerhard Kudritzki, Düsseldorf-München, Küpper.

GADAMER, H.-G. (1971) 'Replik', in *Hermeneutik und Ideologiekritik*, Frankfurt am Main, Suhrkamp.

GERSTENBERGER, H. (1988) '"Das Warum steckt im Wie"', *Freibeuter*, **36**, pp. 73–8.

HANSEN, E. (1991) *Wohlfahrtspolitik im NS-Staat: Motivationen, Konflikte und Machtstrukturen im 'Sozialismus der Tat' des Dritten Reiches*, Augsburg, Maro.

HAUG, W.F. (1986) *Die Faschisierung des Bürgerlichen Subjekts: Die Ideologie der gesunden Normalität und die Ausrottungspolitiken im Deutschen Faschismus, Materialanalysen.* (Ideologische Mächte im deutschen Faschismus Bd. 2), Berlin, Argument.

HILGENGELDT, E. (1937) *Aufgaben der Nationalsozialistsichen Wohlfahrtspflege: Rede gehalten auf der NSV.-Tagung Anläßlich des Reichsparteitages der Arbeit 1937*, München und Berlin, Zentralverlag der NSDAP.

KINDT, W. (Ed) (1974) *Die Deutsche Jugendbewegung 1920 bis 1933: Die Bündische Zeit, Quellenschriften*, Herausgegeben im Auftrage des 'Gemeinschaftswerkes Archiv und Dokumentation des Jugendbewegung' von Werner Kindt. Mit einem Nachwort von Hans Raupach. (Dokumentation der Jugendbewegung III). Düsseldorf-Köln, Diederichs.

KNÜPPEL-DÄHNE, H. and MITROVIC, E. (1989) 'Die Arbeit von Fürsorgerinnen im Hamburger öffentlichen Dienst während des Nationalsozialismus', in OTTO, H.-U. and SÜNKER, H. (Eds) *Soziale Arbeit und Faschismus*, Frankfurt am Main, Suhrkamp.

KOCKA, J. (1986) 'Sozialgeschichte zwischen Strukturgeschichte und Erfahrungsgeschichte', in SCHIEDER, W. and SELLIN, V. (Eds) *Sozialgeschichte in Deutschland I*, Göttingen, Vandenhoeck and Ruprecht.

KRAMER, D. (1983) 'Das Fürsorgesystem im Dritten Reich', in LANDWEHR, R. and BARON, R. (Eds) *Geschichte der Sozialarbeit*, Weinheim und Basel, Beltz.

LANDWEHR, R. (1983) 'Funktionswandel der Fürsorge vom Ersten Weltkrieg bis zum Ende der Weimarer Republik', in LANDWEHR, R. and BARON, R. (Eds) *Geschichte der Sozialarbeit*, Weinheim und Basel, Beltz.

LONGERICH, P. (1989) *Die Braunen Bataillone: Geschichte der SA*, München, C.H. Beck.

LÜDTKE, A. (1991) 'Funktionseliten: Täter, Mit-Täter, Opfer? Zu den Bedingungen des deutschen Faschismus', in LÜDTKE, A. (Ed) *Herrschaft als Soziale Praxis*, Göttingen, Vandenhoeck and Ruprecht.

MASON, T. (1982) 'Die Bändigung der Arbeiterklasse im nationalsozialistischen Deutschland. Eine Einleitung', in SACHSE, C., SIEGEL, T., SPODE, H. and SPOHN, W. (Eds) *Angst, Belohnung, Zucht und Ordnung*, Opladen, Westdeutscher Verlag.

MITROVIC, E. (1987) 'Fürsorgerinnen im Nationalsozialismus', in EBBINGHAUS, A. (Ed) *Opfer und Täterinnen: Frauenbiographien des Nationalsozialismus* (Schriften der Hamburger Stiftung für Sozialgeschichte des 20. Jahrhunderts, Band 2), Nördlingen, Greno.

NOHL, H. (1933) 'Die pädagogische Bewegung in Deutschland', in NOHL, H. and PALLAT, L. (Eds) *Handbuch der Pädagogik, Band 1, Die Theorie und die Entwicklung des Bildungswesens*, Berlin-Leipzig, J. Beltz.

NOHL, H. (1970) [1935] *Die Pädagogische Bewegung in Deutschland und ihre Theorie*, Siebte, unveränderte Auflage, Frankfurt am Main, G. Schulte — Bumke.

OTTO, H.-U. and SÜNKER, H. (Eds) (1989) *Soziale Arbeit und Faschismus*, Frankfurt am Main, Suhrkamp.

PEUKERT, D.J.K. (1987) *Die Weimarer Republik: Krisenjahre der Klassischen Moderne*, Frankfurt am Main, Suhrkamp.

PRINZ, M. (1989) 'Wohlfahrtsstaat, Modernisierung und Nationalsozialismus: Thesen zu ihrem Verhältnis', in OTTO, H.-U. and SÜNKER, H. (Eds) *Soziale Arbeit und Faschismus*, Frankfurt am Main, Suhrkamp.

RADTKE, F.-O. (1983) *Pädagogische Konventionen: Zur Topik eines Berufsstandes*, Weinheim und Basel, Beltz.

RANG, A. (1989) '"Ja, aber". Reaktionen auf den Nationalsozialismus in der Zeitschrift Die Erziehung im Frühjahr 1933', in OTTO, H.-U. and SÜNKER, H. (Eds) *Soziale Arbeit und Faschismus*, Frankfurt am Main, Suhrkamp.

SACHßE, CH. and TENNSTEDT, F. (1992) *Der Wohlfahrtsstaat im Nationalsozialismus, Geschichte der Armenfürsorge in Deutschland Band 3*, Stuttgart-Berlin-Köln, Kohlhammer.

SCHAARSCHUCH, A. (1990) *Zwischen Regulation und Reproduktion: Gesellschaftliche Modernisierung und die Perspektiven Sozialer Arbeit*, Bielefeld, Karin Böllert KT-Verlag.

SCHEIBE, W. (1984) *Die Reformpädagogische Bewegung* (9. Aufl.), Weinheim und Basel, Beltz.

SCHIEDECK, J. (1989) 'Mütterschulung im Nationalsozialismus', *Theorie und Praxis der sozialen Arbeit*, **40**, 9, pp. 344–53.

SCHNURR, ST. (1988) 'Vom Wohlfahrtsstaat zum Erziehungsstaat: Sozialpolitik und soziale Arbeit in der Weimarer Republik und im Nationalsozialismus', *Widersprüche*, **8**, 26, pp. 47–64.

STATISTIK DES DEUTSCHEN REICHES (1978) Neue Folge, Band 453, *Die Erwerbspersonen nach Berufen, sozialer Stellung und Wirtschaftszweigen*, Neudruck der Ausgabe Berlin 1936, Osnabrück, Otto Zeller Verlag.

THEWELEIT, K. (1980) *Männerphantasien, Bd. 2*, Reinbek, Rowohlt.

TOULMIN, ST. E. (1969) *The Uses of Argument* (Reprinted), London, Cambridge University Press.

WIELER, J. (1989) 'Emigrierte Sozialarbeit nach 1933: Berufskolleginnen und -kollegen als politische Flüchtlinge', in OTTO, H.-U. and SÜNKER, H. (Eds) *Soziale Arbeit und Faschismus*, Frankfurt am Main, Suhrkamp.

ZELLER, S. (1987) *Volksmütter: Frauen im Wohlfahrtswesen der Zwanziger Jahre*, Düsseldorf, Schwann.

8   Social Work as Social Education

Heinz Sünker and Hans-Uwe Otto

Social work is today still largely disinterested in what it has inherited from National Socialism, the peculiarly German form of fascism. In this sense, it moves within the same spectrum of mentalities of repression as other professions and disciplines. Here, too, the attempts at exoneration reveal a variety of definitions of collaborators, with exculpating references to the apparent rationality of fascist power and the unavoidability of the totalitarian instrumentalization of social praxis, which meant that each individual was merely a little cog in the system. There is no lack of reference points for the analysis of the fascist past of precisely social work, when Adorno, for example, reflected on Auschwitz and its consequences:

> Hitler imposed a new categorical imperative on people in their unfreedom: to arrange their thoughts and actions so that Auschwitz will not be repeated, so that nothing similar will happen. In relation to finding its rationale, this imperative is as recalcitrant as once the Kantian had a particular 'givenness'. Dealing with it discursively would be an outrage: it gives us a bodily perception of the moral addendum. (Adorno, 1973, p. 365, translation modified)

Historicization of National Socialism?

Fifty years after the end of National Socialism it has become unavoidable to inquire into its relationship with both the forms and contents of social work — in its affirmation of, as well as its differentiation from, fascism. This also seems a good time after the dispute among historians and philosophers about how German history should be interpreted, as well as the discussion in a range of disciplines and professions which has made the concept of a 'helpless antifascism' entirely obsolete. This is why it is more than a historical reminiscence when Broszat comments insightfully on the state of historiography and everyday consciousness in relation to the study of National Socialism:

> The pseudo-religious affectation with which the 'unperson' Hitler charmed the majority of the German people, including its educated strata, drove not only German post-war historians to the explanatorily powerless solution of a demonising interpretation . . . At an intellectual level, it led from a mixture

of moral abhorrence and fascination with violence to the concept of the fascist aesthetic (Susan Sonntag), at the subcultural level to the worldwide popular literature on the Third Reich and the established genre of the Nazi adventure film. (Broszat, 1988, pp. 374–5)

An apologist tradition in historiography and politics (Fischer, 1983, p. 770), which anticipated aspects of the more recent historians' dispute, can be seen in Fest's book on Hitler and in a speech by Lübbe in connection with the fiftieth anniversary of Hitler's seizure of power, made in the Berlin *Reichstag*:

The aim of this speech was to delegitimate those sociological and social psychological theories, critical of capitalism, of fascism and the collective amnesia which the twelve years of dictatorship lapsed into in the context of reconstruction and the economic miracle, and to legitimate retrospectively the tight-lipped post-war community of unrepentant collaborators and poorly disguised perpetrators. Lübbe says all this from the heart, for all those who saw the resistance of the student opposition in 1968 as an unbearable offense, and who saw the current political constellation as offering a chance for revenge. Lübbe made use of a taboo-language, in which everything is rarely referred to with its proper name, in which we give each other broad hints, trip up opponents or jostle them into the background, rather than dealing with them openly. In this speech, the author of which argued against the well-known displacement thesis, what is displaced is diction. (Dahmer and Rosenkötter, 1984, p. 31)

The need to address the past thus remains, despite all the developments in the reconstruction of historical reality, its clarification and explanation in a multitude of versions, so that Adorno's warning about the use of slogans to deal with the past remains current:

Dealing with the past does not in this terminology mean that one takes the past seriously, breaking through its banishment with a clear consciousness. Rather, one wants to draw a final line underneath it and, where possible, brush it out of remembrance (1977, p. 555) Adorno closes his text with the words, that the part is only dealt with when the causes of what has happened have been established. Only because the causes continue, its banishment has to this day not been broken through. (Adorno, 1977, p. 572)

Broszat's plea for a historicization of National Socialism should be considered in this context, particularly when one considers his assessment that the history of the National-Socialist dictatorship has not yet become a history of the National-Socialist period (1985, p. 380). He comes to this desideratum even though, in his consideration of more recent historiography, he concludes:

Already at the beginning of the 1970s almost all political-moral, particularly 'sensitive' areas of NS-domination were more or less opened up, even if not completely explored. The documentation of the specific content of the National-Socialist world view stood in the foreground. Only gradually, with increasing academic interest, did something else come more clearly into the field of view: the inner structure and dynamics of movement of the regime, the motivation of the participants, the economic and social conditions, literature, the culture of art and leisure, *Volk* community and 'everyday life' in the Third Reich. (Broszat, 1988, p. 377)[1]

Social work, in its various administrative areas and fields of professional action, is certainly one of the elements of NS-domination which have so far been less opened up and studied.

Under these auspices, we will need to ask in the future, the exent to which the debates on social history and ideological production, on problems in the concrete implementation of domination in National Socialism, are able to contribute to the determination of the role of social work in this system. Further, there is the question of the ways in which social work, on the basis of its foundations, conditions and forms of domination, contributed to the establishment of normal and terrorist standards in National Socialism. In a general historiographical sense, the question then arises of the relation between the history of structure and of events, the relation of everyday life and history, and the relative importance of everyday life in a reconstruction of social relationships. However, so far the debate has taken the form of an opposition between the actual or supposed advantages and disadvantages of the various approaches (Lüdtke, 1982; Steinbach, 1984; Peukert, 1987; Gerstenberger and Schmidt, 1987).[2]

For Lüdtke, as a leading representative of this history of everyday life, which we feel does not, in this form, escape the critique of structural historians, this approach concerns the mediation of socio-economic conditions with experiences of class, age-groups and gender, with the associated cultural reference points and frameworks of meaning, to thus risk a view of the 'interior' of whole social structures or secular trends (1982, p. 327). In contrast to abstract representations of socio-historical relations, for Lüdtke the particular emphasis of the history of everyday life lies in the attempt to show the contradictory and uneven character of the forms and relations of production in the lives of those concerned — to explain them and make them more visible (1982, p. 328). The question of the production and reproduction of objective as well as subjective elements of society and sociability, therefore, stands in the foreground of attempts to explore the problem of how economic history can be conceptualized as a part of social history.

In relation to the potential for an analysis of the history of National Socialist society and domination, as well as of practices and suffering, Jasdhke poses, at the end of a very precise and enlightening work in which he thematizes the contradictory relation between the social basis and the social function of National Socialism, a postulate which has both theoretical and practical research implications. After establishing that there is still no satisfactory theory to explain adequately the rise of fascism in Germany, and that it cannot be created with new abstract theoretical debates on fascism, he offers the following perspective:

More promising appears to be social-historical and empirical development of Bonapartist analyses. Their thematic limitation to the complex of Fascism's 'social basis' and 'social function' has proved to make sense. In this framework, it is necessary for the assessment of the NS mass movement to investigate — within a middle-range research time-frame of 10 to 20 years — the 'civic culture' or 'political culture' which guided action, in which above all the life experiences of contemporaries need to be kept in view . . . A discussion of fascism which is in this sense orientated towards praxis would then ask, why and how fascism was able to hold greater fascination in people's everyday life in 1933 than bourgeois and socialist lifestyles . . . (Jaschke, 1982, p. 243)[3]

Social Policy and the Alliance of the Elites

Both traditional, classical historical and more recent social-historical and social-theoretical studies examine the social context of National Socialism, the establishment as well as the establishability of National Socialist rule, the preconditions, formations and consequences of these problems and developments on the relations between sociey and state, economy and politics, the production of knowledge and ideology. Also thematized at the same time are the limitations and possibilities, normality and terror (which can coincide) of the socially-mediated lifestyles of the members of this society.

In addition, the themes addressed here are related to the various analytical schools and streams of thought, which can be (roughly) divided into intentionalist, functionalist and undogmatic Marxist. Depending on the approach taken, there will be differing research emphases, differing results will be aimed for, and with differing understandings of the rise of National Socialism in German history with specific reference to precisely that history (Herf, 1984; Broszat, 1984; Michalka, 1985; Wehler, 1979) or general modernization processes within industrial (capitalist) development (Peukert, 1987; Schoenbaum, 1980; Moore, 1969). This question can be extended to the apparently surprising demonstration of the feudal aspects of National-Socialist rule; an insight which is essential for the analysis of specific ideologically-founded clientele relations and corresponding competing interests, as well as their establishment in the context of social policy and social work. Koehl thus comes to the conclusion, sometimes reached even by non-Marxists, that National Socialism was the offspring of an unholy alliance between robber-baron capitalists and reactionary land-owners, for which the right-wing romantics served as midwife (1960, p. 931).

The debate has been dominated by the argument between the traditionally oriented 'intentionalists' and social-historically oriented 'functionalists' of the polycratic position: if they put these social processes and political decisions precisely in their contradictoriness at the centre of their considerations, they assume that Hitler's will, his world-view was — in a monocratic way — decisive for the rise of NS-society

(Mason, 1995; Kadritzke, 1976, p. 115; Mommsen, 1981; Bracher, 1980; Hildebrand, 1983; Hüttenberger, 1976; Broszat, 1988, p. 382). In our view this debate is ultimately not an objective but a political one; for each position attaches different responsibilities to the participating groups and classes, with differing senses of historical compulsion and room for autonomous action. Even if this debate is not entirely resolved, nor even easily defined, the polycratic position still allows for elements of a description of the National Socialist inner constitution which seems useful for a complete picture of NS-society. The premise of all — albeit not unified — polycratic positions is the notion that National Socialism's principle of domination represents a binding of totality and chaos, the attempt at total domination can be understood as a disorganization and decodification of processes of social interaction (Siegel, 1978, p. 62; Michalka, 1985, p. 12; Schäfer, 1981, p. 114; Broszat, 1988).[4]

The alliance of elites (Fischer, 1979; Jasper, 1986) hold the roots of the relation between economy and politics, the structure of advantages of NS society as well as its domination, an approach to the majority of the subordinate groups and classes which was a combination of welfare and oppression (Mason 1995, pp. 258–61).[5]

In summary we can say the following: the securing of capitalist reproduction in the interests of the ruling groups (Siegel, 1978; Kadritzke, 1976, pp. 156, 177; Jaschke, 1982, p. 129) leads with National Socialism to a 'stratification' of society, with the abolition of the constitutive differentiation of society and state lying at the basis of bourgeois society, in which citizens are caught up in a friend-foe schema.

> The total state led not only to the abolition of the distinction between private and public spheres, private and public justice, for which the organic relations of classification left no room. It abolished, above all, also the possibility of state-defined fundamental rights. The new state could not allow itself to be limited by individual wills in its pursuit of its communal goals. Human rights, which arise from individuals, do not exist here. They thus experienced, even before the National-Socialist seizure of power, a state-sponsored reinterpretation (in the legal theory of the conservatives and reactionaries). (Grimm, 1985, pp. 45–6)

This securing of capitalist relations of production, the processes of reproduction, also relates to the paradoxical synthesis of modern technology and political irrationalism, which led to refeudalization of the relations of production and an authoritarian rationalization in industry (Herf, 1981, 1984).[6] This alliance and combination of interests led to a variety of forms of rule, although they were all aimed primarily at the 'containment of the working class' (Mason, 1995). These forms moved between a subjugation or shackling with the help of terroristic repression and a simulaneous ability of the regime, in the case of disturbances and discontent to also make concessions. The aim was at least the neutralization of potential for resistance among the working class through a politics of division, as well as the integration of parts of that class in the regime (Mason, 1995; Hüttenberger, 1976, pp. 438–40). At a more general level, Schäfer identifies elements of integration which are significant for the study of cultural politics and everyday life:

> The history of Swing and Jazz in Hitler's state reveal in an exemplary way four characteristic elements of National-Socialist rule which — alongside the pluralistic fanning-out of power — can be seen as responsible for the fragmented reality of everyday life: 1. Personalised censure; 2. Adaptability to the dynamics of the private sector economy; 3. Securing of power through toleration of a politics-free sphere; 4. Limitation of bureaucratic control in relation to the interests of majority groups. (Schäfer, 1981, p. 133)

These elements of rule demonstrated their explosive force in a differentiation between the social basis and social function of National Socialism: despite anticapitalist mass movements and mass mobilizations the securing of capitalist conditions of reproduction continued (Jaschke, 1982; Negt and Kluge, 1972; Rabinbach, 1976). While those groups being part of the ruling alliance pursued a policy of expansion and plunder within Germany as well as in the occupied countries (Borkin, 1979; Fischer, 1983; Hallgarten and Radkau, 1986, pp. 355–432), the possibility for total control over the productive part of the population as created with national labour legislation (AOG, 20.1.1934; Spohn, 1987; Lampert, 1983, p. 188; Kolb, 1983, pp. 270–3). Mason interprets this legislation as the decisive attempt to provide a solution to incipient social conflicts in the context of the development of German capitalism. He poses the thesis that the agreement between the German labour movement (DAF) with industry on an abandonment of union activities (November 1933) constituted 'an important stage in the taming process which turned the Nazi labour movement into a servant of the political and economic elites; and this was an important precursor of the events of 30 June 1934' (1995, p. 100).

With National Socialism, developments were brought to a head which stand completely within the continuity of German history (Fischer, 1979, 1983; Elben, 1965) — not only in social, but also intellectual fields (Lundgreen, 1985a; Grimm, 1985; Vosskamp, 1985; Mehrtens and Richter, 1980). The social changes, above all the development of the total state — linked to relevant changes in social and workforce conditions (Broszat, 1983; Tyrell, 1983) — corresponded above all with the long-confined hopes and strivings of the ruling class.[7]

The development towards a restrictive social policy in the last years of the Weimar Republic was realized in National Socialism (Peukert, 1987; Jaschke, 1982), linked with the possibility for total control over the working class, while at the same time the social power of capital in National Socialism was generally reinforced: 'Alongside violent repression, as in the case of the autonomous trade unions, there were forms of more or less nominal, cosmetic equalization, such as in the area of industrial umbrella organisations' (Broszat, 1983, p. 42).[8]

From this perspective National Socialism can accordingly be understood, on the one hand, as a crisis in the capitalist relations of accumulation, on the other hand as a conservative and reactionary cultural crisis, an opposition to the radicalization of culture.[9] Cultural critique as a form of organistic-romantic thought is anti-western, anti-Enlightenment, anti-intellectual, celebrate 'life', human inequality, criticizes the 'degeneracy' of city dwellers (Kalikow, 1980, pp. 193, 199–200; Vosskamp, 1985, pp. 14–15; Sennett, 1983, pp. 333–4).[10]

Postone investigates the logic and the functionality of this type of cultural criticism and makes it clear that National Socialist ideology was not just in the interests of capital because it presented itself as aggressively anti-Marxist and led to the disruption of working-class organizations. In his view, it was as much in the interests of capital to expedite the transition from liberal to a quasi state-capitalist system. The attack on the liberal state, as an expression of abstractness, advanced the development of an interventionist state, as an expression of concreteness. This form of anti-capitalism is thus only on the surface a yearning for the past; as an expression of the fetishism of capitalism, however, it is to be interpreted as a real forward movement. Postone closes his analysis with this statement:

> Modern anti-semitism is a particulary outrageous form of commodity fetish-ism. Its power and its dangerousness consists in the creation of a compre-hensive world-view in which the various types of anti-capitalist discontent take on a form and an expression which leaves capitalism intact by attacking the personifications of this social form. (Postone, 1980, p. 113)

Social Education: Dictatorship over the People

Hennig has formulated the claims of a political sociology of National Socialism as making National Socialism understandable as a system and a movement, within the Reich and in the regions, in state-political interests and in everyday life, which is particularly concerned with revealing the relations of tension between these two poles and to de-differentiate it through a subsumption of one opposition to the other (1982, p. xii).

The connection demanded by Hennig between the variously focused points of access to different parts of the National Socialist system can be achieved with the concept of the '*Volk* community' (*Volksgemeinschaft*). Its ideological elevation in National Socialism was symptomatic of the link to the utilization of the specifically German anti-Englightenment tradition of cultural criticism, but at the same time it gained real power, in that the ideology of the *Volksgemeinschaft* played a leading role in the field of social work: both in the form of welfare, and in the form of terror and murder.

The attempts at social modernization, without any change in social structure (Moore, 1969, pp. 506–7) are accompanied by a combination of reactionary pol-itics and technical progress, within which the socio-political and historical irration-alism, the late-romantic tradition, is brought to a head.[11] Decisive here is the fact that technology turned from an element of the alien, western civilization into an organic part of German culture; political reaction was thus linked with technolog-ical progress. While the German conservatives still spoke of technology or culture, the German right was taught by reactionary modernists to speak of technology and culture. This tied in with the call for a revolution from the right, which would firstly lead to the restitution of the primacy of the political, and secondly was able to connect the threads of romanticism and rearmament in Germany (as a national movement) (Herf, 1984, pp. 1–16).

The ideology of the *Volksgemeinschaft* linked up with the requirements of nationalism, organic thought, a fetishization of totality, which came together in a repressive social order (Koehl, 1960, pp. 928–31; Moore, 1969, p. 563; Sturm, 1942, pp. 11, 27–8, 61). Already among the Romantics there was a well-defined feeling of unease about the effects of the social relations of capitalism on individuals, which can be described as alienation or also the feeling of anonymity (Sennett, 1983, p. 331). According to Peukert, the ideology of the *Volksgemeinschaft* was built on this basis and mixed with the yearning of a population shaken by crises and unsure of its patterns of social orientation for normality. At the same time we must note explicitly that the much-heralded *Volksgemeinschaft* of the National Socialists in no way abolished the real contradictions of a modern industrial society; rather, these were inadvertently aggravated by the use of highly modern industrial and propaganda techniques for achieving war-readiness (Peukert, 1987, p. 246). Nonetheless, this ideology of *Volksgemeinschaft* established a framework for the goal of systematic integration, and thus represented the opposition to the real process of atomization of individual's social existence.[12]

For the areas of social work concerned with support — monetary and pedagogic — the potential of the *Volksgemeinschaft* idea is obvious. Since welfare as obligatory state assistance was seen in these terms as wasteful and unnecessary, and state assistance was the product of liberalism and socialism, which dissipated the individual, familial and community responsibility towards the poor, assistance became a task for every German in relation to other Germans, to reinforce the potential for self-help, create a community spirit and thus also overcome social divisions. In this way it is no longer individual welfare, individuals with their rights and needs which stand at the centre of attention, but that which is defined with the term national care, established as society's welfare — precisely in the departure from the Weimar Republic's 'welfare state project' (Schnurr, 1988). The functionalization of assistance was thus realized in its establishment. Assistance based not on compassion or sympathy, rights and needs, but on the conception that sick or impoverished members of an organic society affect the health of the whole social body and consequently also weaken national power and military potential.

> Ultimately welfare would become obsolete, since the Nazis interpreted poverty as primarily a racial problem which could be solved through preventive health care and economic assistance for the racially valuable — and politically reliable — citizen, therefore precluding welfare dependency.
> (de Witt, 1978, p. 260)

These conceptions and intentions were directly linked to a policy of control and selection, in the context of which the National Socialist People's Welfare (NSV) acquires a particular significance: on the one hand it was one of the transmission belts — as a mass organization connected to the party with 12.5 million members and roughly 1 million activists in 1939 — between the party and the people's movement; on the other hand it constituted an important precondition for the total incorporation of all national comrades (Zimmerman, n.d., p. 27).

H. Althaus, in charge of the NSDAP's Head Office for People's Welfare, presented the ideological foundations of the NSV's work: 'From the perspective of this world view, a welfare with a National-Socialist character is fundamentally oriented towards genetics and racial hygiene. Here the proposition that all citizens are equal has no validity. You know, that people's genetic make up makes them of unequal value for well-being of the whole. Environmental conditions are not the most decisive for the development of individuals' (1937, p. 14). The socio-political consequences of this position were made clear when he explained the genetic and racial character of National-Socialist welfare:

> A social welfare which is directed at the welfare of the people, would in contrast force the unfit into an eradicatory defense of heredity. Through the legislation on contraception against genetically inferior offspring, the National-Socialist state has on this basis led the way towards the removal of the genetically unfit from the national genetic pool. Living unfit individuals themselves should only be considered with a minimum level of care, in addition to, as far as necessary, being removed from national life in protective custody or secure containment in prison institutions. This applies above all to those individuals whose character as bearers of genetic sickness has not been established, but whose asocial behaviour leads us to suspect it. (Althaus, 1937, p. 15)

Corresponding legal regulations concerning the cooperation between the NSV and the municipalities point to the frankness of this policy. Under the heading 'Document Inspection by the NSV', the welfare ordinances stated:

> There is no objection to a direct exchange of such reports and information between municipal welfare offices and the NSV, which serves to reduce undesirable duplication of support and to improve the personal knowledge of the recipients. For example, when a municipality periodically sends the NSV a list with the names of those persons who have received assistance from the municipality, or when, particularly in cases of suspected asocial behaviour, the NSV is provided with further information about particular persons. To prevent possible legal objections, the NSV will henceforth include in the application forms for assistance an explicit authorization for the transmission of information by the municipalities. The NSV is prepared to send the municipalities the relevant information from its files. The confidentiality of the treatment of the information is also guaranteed by the NSV . . . (Linde, 1938, p. 100)

The cooperation between the NSV and the Youth Welfare Office was also secured as far as the administrative regulations, as the example of youth welfare shows. In the relevant regulations of the Youth Welfare Office it was recommended that the NSV be involved in the investigation (of the young people), because it is, as a result of its whole structure, in a better position than any other agency to provide an abundance of evidence (Axnick, 1939, p. 27). Further, it said that welfare agencies select the family care placements in consultation with the NSV and the welfare authorities. In the placement of a young person in family care, they will be allocated a youth worker, who will be responsible to the welfare authorities for the orderly education of the young person in every sense. These youth workers are selected by the NSV from the ranks of its helpers (Axnick, 1939, p. 25). Against this background, it is astounding that in the hitherto most comprehensive study of the NSV, the authors construct an image of the organization as oriented to the claims of a welfare organization. For Vorländer, the NSV operated correspondingly as an organization which in its activities bore the quite distinctive features of a welfare agency, and which was experienced as such by many people (Vorländer, 1988, p. 1). On the other hand, it is more a matter of making clear that the aspect of control had absolute priority in its practices, which is indicated not least in the NSV's administrative and ideologically secured leadership role in the German Association of Independent Welfare Agencies (Linde, 1938, p. 101).

For a realistic assessment of the social policy and social work execution of the 'selection' policy, it is necessary to show clearly that selection concerned not only the Jewish population, but that this policy presented itself far more explicitly as social selection based on the semantics of community suitability: it was, therefore, aimed at a variety of groups which were stigmatized as gypsies, criminals, homeless, workshy, genetically unfit, institutional inmates of all sorts, and so on (Noakes, 1987). The concepts of eugenics and racial hygiene, expressed in the talk of 'useless beings' (Zimmerman, n.d., p. 17), of the elimination of 'asocial elements' (Kirmeß, 1939, p. 43), had a practical dimension: 'planned improvement', the selection of 'community-suited national comrades' and the elimination — ranging from isolation through minimizing participation through to murder — correspond with and complement each other.

This constellation of racial hygiene and social questions aimed at the creation of a social policy field of action. Eugenics was a scientific technique of rule for splitting, division and selective intimidation (Aly and Roth, 1984, p. 142). The cleavage of society took place continuously: those who satisfied the requirements on the basis of racial and health policy, could in cases of need gain access to certain services. However, what was decisive was that the idea of these services was developed and also realized in the context of the notion of the *Volk* community as a 'performance-oriented community' (Mason, 1995, p. 93), so that it came both in the ideology and also the reality of national socialist welfare policy to relevant redefinitions of the formulation of claims on services and the resultant consequences (Kirmeß, 1939; Zimmerman, n.d.).

The central work of Zimmerman on National Socialist welfare and the Winter Relief Fund in 1938/9, as well as the conference papers of a gathering of the German Association for Public and Private Welfare in 1938, allow us to distil in an exemplary way the basic positions taken up in various fields of social work under

National Socialism. The foundation consists (self-evidently) of the ideology of *Volksgemeinschaft* from which emerges the specific aims and dynamics of social work (Zimmerman, n.d., p. 9). In this context anti-intellectualism and anti-individualism represent principles which were influential and formative in all the social work and pedagogic debates of this period. Accordingly, notions such as the 'end of pedagogic individualism' (Tiling and Jarausch, 1934) or Beyer's call to 'extract education from the clutches of liberal-individualist thought' (1933, p. 54), are no coincidence. These principles are determinant for the conceptions of the basis and range of social work, as well as for more concrete definitions of practice.

Tied up with this conception is the notion of a reversal of everything which used to be called welfare (Benzing, 1938, p. 7), so that:

> ... instead of a striving to exploit the public purse, as it was nourished and developed among the needy in the welfare state system through the unscrupulous agitation and election promises of the parliamentary parties, the feeling of one's place in the whole and one's obligation to the community also appears to a large extent among the needy. (Martini, 1938, p. 50)

Running like a *leitmotiv* through all discussions of the self-understanding and objectives of social work in National Socialism is the praise for 'self-help/self-responsibility', 'community service' and 'prevention'. In addition — again self-evidently — there was the central aim of social work as the education of the German people towards the maintenance of the healthy and the strong, and thus the securing of the people's future (Zimmerman, n.d., pp. 14, 18, 63, 154). The normalizing work in the social fields of action thus took place according to guidelines which were precisely formulated, ideologically mediated and to some extent mediatable — because they were long anchored in the professional discourses: the incorporation of the subject is complete.

All the instances and institutions of social work — such as public and independent agencies — had to subject themselves to this goal precisely in their real competition with each other, if not in actually playing a leading role themselves (Zimmerman, n.d., pp. 58–61; Ventzky, 1938; Martini, 1938).[13]

At the centre of it all stood the individual person, especially at those points where the possibilities for intervention could be precisely identified: Ventzky (1938, p. 29) formulated this position in an exemplary way, when he wrote that in the context of youth welfare it was no longer a matter of an 'established claim by young people on education to physical, psychological and social competence ... but exclusively [of] the *Volk* community's right and obligation to the maintenance and advancement of healthy offspring'. In a similarly decisive way, Martini made the essential feature of National-Socialist welfare clear; it is the view that:

> ... the obligation which emerges from national solidarity of the community to provide timely, extensive and effective assistance is complemented by the obligation of the needy person towards the community, which also, if it provides assistance, always controls the extent to which the needy

person or his family manages their own ability to help themselves, rather than patiently — as in the welfare state — expecting everything from the community. (Martini, 1938, p. 55)

It is certainly a task for future study to illuminate the conditions of fascist provenance and the ways in which they were realized in the various fields of social work, the extent to which the need for assistance was actually met within the system, which in turn could only be met in this form because of the splitting of society (Leibfried, Hansen and Heisig, 1984). However, what remains crucial for the history of social work is an explanation of the extent to which social work as a whole was embedded within the complex of National Socialist rule, and what consequences this has had for the post-fascist era.

Notes

1 On the question of the conditions, premises and consequences of a historicization of National Socialism in the context of a debate over German history, see Peukert (1987).
2 It seems striking that the discussions of the history of everyday life and of social structures, so far no reference has been made to the efforts in social theory to deal with the problem of the relation between everyday life and history, everyday life and social totality, as Agnes Heller and Henri Lefebvre have attempted (Sünker, 1988).
3 This argument links up with Bloch's (1973) analysis of fascism.
4 Mommsen (1981, p. 54) sees the form taken by National Socialism as determined by an increasing subversion of the state and the dissolution of the inner unity of the political system, now only integrated through propaganda, in the interests of particular holders of power; Hitler thus appears only as an extreme exponent of the system (1981, pp. 66–7).
5 These arguments are also linked to a relativization of the functionalist approach, as Mason suggests:

> What was permitted by conditions, or was possible, must be analysed, and it is here that marxism offers a more comprehensive framework than an approach which concentrates heavily upon political institutions and decision-making processes. We need to understand how it is decided what the available options are, which political leaders can choose among. Which alternative possibilities in the Third Reich were never even entertained as such by the leadership? Which got lost in the lower ranks of the bureaucracy or party and were thus never presented as policy options? These non-decisions are an important part of any system of power. They define the parameters of possible intentions at the top of the system, which are almost always narrow at that level. It is in this analytically difficult area that the economy and the state need to be taken as a whole in the study of the Third Reich, for the dynamic of economic development played a primary role in the filtering out of impossible options, in determining what it was that could be decided in terms of policy. (Mason, 1995, p. 227)

6 In relation to the problem, bound up with the question of the relations between economy and politics, of the state of the old ruling class, Jaschke establishes that:

> They were — measured against the peak industrial bodies — unwilling to delegate their political domination unconditionally to a fascist executive, it was more that they gave up their liberal creed of a division of state and economy for a state-interventionist economic policy. (Jaschke, 1982, p. 235)

See also the summary of his interpretation in Peukert (1987, p. 48), who maintains that National Socialism led to a regrouping of the hegemonic system while maintaining the capitalist structure.

7   On the role of state and municipal authorities in persecution and repression, see Kolb (1983); Adler (1974, p. 373); Caplan (1981).

8   In this context we can refer to the real living conditions of the working class: rising profits were accompanied by stagnating wages (Broszat, 1983; Michalka, 1985, p. 70).

Here we can point to Postone's (1980) analysis, where he goes into the question of the reasons for the divisions between industrial and finance capital, which was personified in relation to the Jews. On the basis of a marxist analysis of fetishism, he describes anti-semitism as a form of thought — arising from the specifically German, but also the general capitalist development, based on anti-capitalist elements — which redefined industrial capital as something highly valorized, and at the same time made the Jews the personification of capital in itself, and thus inferior, to be attacked and murdered. See also Herf (1981, 1984) and Goldhagen (1996).

9   See Sombart (1984, p. 181) with respect to cultural criticism in the context of a male-dominated society, the linkage of masculinity and the 'german conservative syndrome'.

10 See Oestreich (1947, p. 88) to the appeal of fascism for liberal educationalists.

11 On the problem of the relationship between Romanticism and modernity, and their social-theoretical and aesthetic implications, see Hohendahl (1974).

12 See Adorno (1977, p. 562) with respect to the social basis of the ideology of the *Volk* community.

13 It is very interesting to see that, for example, Ventzky (1938) strove to promote a strengthening of the NSV in its competitive relation to state social administration by applying elements of a critique of bureaucracy: proximity to clients, individual counselling, fighting the paper war, so that the Youth Welfare Office would actually become redundant. See also Matzerath (1970).

References

ADLER, H.G. (1974) *Der Verwaltete Mensch: Studien zur Deportation der Juden aus Deutschland*, Tübingen, Mohr.

ADORNO, TH.W. (1966) *Negative Dialektik*, Frankfurt/M., Suhrkamp.

ADORNO, TH.W. (1973) *Negative Dialectics*, London, Routledge and Kegan Paul.

ADORNO, TH.W. (1977) 'Was bedeutet: Aufarbeitung der Vergangenheit?', in ADORNO, TH.W. *Gesammelte Schriften*, Bd.10.2., Frankfurt/M., Suhrkamp.

ALTHAUS, H. (1937) *Nationalsozialistische Volkswohlfahrt: Wesen, Aufgaben und Aufbau*, 3, überarbeitete Aufl., Berlin, Junker und Dünnhaupt.

ALY, G. and ROTH, K.-H. (1984) *Die Restlose Erfassung: Volkszählen, Identifizieren, Aussondern im Nationalsozialismus*, Berlin, Rotbuch.

AXNICK, E. (1939) *Wegweiser durch die Öffentliche Jugendhilfe: Kurze Zusammenstellung der Wichtigsten Aufgabengebiete unter Besonderer Berücksichtigung der Zusammenarbeit der Kommunalen Jugendämter mit der NSV und HJ*, Berlin.

BENZIG, R. (1938) 'Die gesundheitsfürsorgerischen Aufgaben im Hilfswerk Mutter und Kind', in *Neue Familien- Und Arbeitspolitische Aufgaben Der Deutschen Wohlfahrtspflege*.

BEYER, K. (1933) 'Erziehung im leeren Raum', *Volk im Werden*, **1**, 4, pp. 54–62.

BLOCH, E. (1973) *Erbschaft dieser Zeit*, Frankfurt/M., Suhrkamp.

BORKIN, J. (1979) *Die Unheilige Allianz der IG-Farben: Eine Interessengemeinschaft im Dritten Reich*, Frankfurt/M., Campus.

BRACHER, K.D. (1980) *Zeitgeschichtliche Kontroversen: Faschismus, Totalitarismus, Demokratie*, **4**, Aufl. München, Piper.

BRACHER, D., FUNKE, M. and JACOBSEN, H.A. (Eds) (1983) *Nationalsozialistische Diktatur 1933 bis 1945: Eine Bilanz*, Bonn, Zentrale für politische Bildung.

BROSZAT, M. (1983) 'Grundzüge der gesellschaftlichen Verfassung des Dritten Reiches', in BROSZAT, M. and MÖLLER, H. (Eds) *Das Dritte Reich: Herrschaftsstruktur und Geschichte*, München, Beck.

BROSZAT, M. (1984) *Die Machtergreifung: Der Aufstieg der NSDAP und die Zerstörung der Weimarer Republik*, München, Deutscher Taschenbuch Verlag.

BROSZAT, M. (1988) Plädoyer für eine Historisierung des Nationalsozialismus, in Broszat, M. *Nach Hitler*, München, Deutscher Taschenbuch Verlag.

CAPLAN, J. (1981) 'Civil Service Support for National Socialism: An Evaluation', in HIRSCHFELD, G. and KETTENACKER, L. (Eds) *Der 'Führerstaat': Mythos und Realität: Studien zur Struktur und Politik im Dritten Reich*, Stuttgart, Klett-Cotta.

DAHMER, H. and ROSENKÖTTER, L. (1984) 'Jasager und Weißwäscher', in LOHMANN, H.-M. (Ed) (1984) *Psychoanalyse und Nationalsozialismus: Beiträge zur Bearbeitung eines unbewältigten Themas*, Frankfurt/M., Fischer.

ELBEN, W. (1965) *Das Problem der Kontinuität in der Deutschen Revolution*, Düsseldorf, Schwann.

FISCHER, F. (1979) *Bündnis der Eliten: Zur Kontinuität der Machtstrukturen in Deutschland 1871–1945*, Düsseldorf, Droste.

FISCHER, F. (1983) 'Zum Problem der Kontinuität in der deutschen Geschichte von Bismarck zu Hitler', in BRACHER, D., FUNKE, M. and JACOBSEN, H.A. (Eds) *Nationalsozialistische Diktatur 1933 bis 1945: Eine Bilanz*, Bonn, Zentrale für politische Bildung.

GERSTENBERGER, H. and SCHMIDT, D. (1987) (Eds) *Normalität und Normalisierung? Geschichtswerkstätten und Faschismusanalyse*, Münster, Westfälisches Dampfboot.

GEUTER, L. (1987) *Die Professionalisierung der Deutschen Psychologie im Nationalsozialismus*, Frankfurt/M., Suhrkamp.

GOLDHAGEN, D. (1996) *Hitler's Willing Executioners: Ordinary Germans and the Holocaust*, New York, Alfred A. Knopf Inc.

GRIMM, D. (1985) 'Die Neue Rechtswissenschaft: Über Funktion und Formation nationalsozialistischer Jurisprudenz', in LUNDGREEN, P. (Ed) *Wissenschaft im Dritten Reich*, Frankfurt/M., Suhrkamp.

HABERMAS, J. (1987) *Eine Art Schadensabwicklung*, Frankfurt/M., Suhrkamp.

HALLGARTEN, G. and RADKAU, J. (1986) *Deutsche Industrie und Politik von Bismarck bis in die Gegenwart*, Überarbeitete Neuauflage, Frankfurt/M., Syndikat/EVA.

HAUG, W.F. (1968) *Der Hilflose Antifaschismus*, Frankfurt/M., Suhrkamp.

HENNIG, E. (1982) 'Nationalsozialismus ist Bewegung und System: Zur Rekonstuktion einer Theorietradition und zur Konstruktion eines herrschaftssoziologischen Konzepts', in JASCHKE, H.-G. *Soziale Basis und soziale Funktion des Nationalsozialismus: Studien zur Bonapartismustheorie*, Opladen, Westdeutscher Verlag.

HENNIG, E. (Ed) (1983) *Hessen untem Hakenkreuz: Studien zur Durchsetzung der NSDAP in Hessen*, Frankfurt/M., Insel Verlag.

HERF, J. (1981) 'Reactionary Modernism', *Theory and Society*, **10**, pp. 805–32.

HERF, J. (1984) *Reactionary Modernism*, New York, Cambridge University Press.

HEYDORN, H.J. (1979) *Über den Widerspruch von Bildung und Herrschaft*, Frankfurt/M., Syndikat.

HILDEBRAND, K. (1983) 'Monokratie oder Polykratie? Hitlers Herrschaft und das Dritte Reich', in BRACHER, D., FUNKE, M. and JACOBSEN, H.A. (Eds) (1983) *Nationalsozialistische Diktatur 1933 bis 1945: Eine Bilanz*, Bonn, Zentrale für politische Bildung.

HIRSCHFELD, G. and KETTENACKER, L. (1981) *Der 'Führerstaat': Mythos und Realität: Studien zur Struktur und Politik im Dritten Reich*, Stuttgart, Klett-Cotta.

HOHENDAHL, P.U. (1974) 'Geschichte und Modernität: Heines Kritik an der Romantik', in HOHENDAHL, P.U. (Ed) *Literaturkritik und Öffentlichkeit*, München, Piper.

HÜTTENBERGER, P. (1976) 'Nationalsozialistische Polykratie', *Geschichte und Gesellschaft*, **2**, pp. 417–42.

JASCHKE, H.-G. (1982) *Soziale Basis und Soziale Funktion des Nationalsozialismus: Studien zur Bonapartismustheorie*, Opladen, Westdeutscher Verlag.

JASPER, G. (1986) *Die Gescheiterte Zähmung: Wege zur Machtergreifung Hitlers 1930– 1933*, Frankfurt/M., Suhrkamp.

KADRITZKE, N. (1976) *Faschismus und Krise: Zum Verhältnis von Politik und Ökonomie im Nationalsozialismus*, Frankfurt/M., Campus.

KALIKOW, TH.J. (1980) 'Die ethologische Theorie von Konrad Lorenz: Erklärung und Ideologie, 1938 bis 1943', in MEHRTENS/RICHTER.

KIRMEß, A. (1939) *Von der Wohlfahrtspflege zur Volkspflege*, Diss. München.

KOEHL, R. (1960) 'Feudal Aspects of National Socialism', *American Political Science Review*, **54**, pp. 921–33.

KOLB, E. (1983) 'Die Maschinerie der Terrors: Zum Funktionieren des Unterdrückungs- und Verfolgungsapparates im NS-Regime', in BRACHER, D., FUNKE, M. and JACOBSEN, H.A. (Eds) (1983) *Nationalsozialistische Diktatur 1933 bis 1945: Eine Bilanz*, Bonn, Zentrale für politische Bildung.

LAMPERT, H. (1983) 'Staatliche Sozialpolitik im Dritten Reich', in BRACHER, D., FUNKE, M. and JACOBSEN, H.A. (Eds) *Nationalsozialistische Diktatur 1933 bis 1945: Eine Bilanz*, Bonn, Zentrale für politische Bildung.

LEIBFRIED, ST., HANSEN, E. and HEISIG, M. (1984) 'Geteilte Erde? Bedarfsprinip und Existenzminimum unter dem NS-Regime', *Neue Praxis*, **14**, 1, pp. 3–20.

LINDE, F. (1938) *Fürsorge des Staates — Fürsorge der Partei: Eine Zusammenstellung aller Reichsrechtlichen Fürsorgebestimmungen mit Eingehender Erläuterung*, Braunschweig, Druck und Verlag der Waisenhaus-Buchdruckerei Braunschweig.

LOHMANN, H.-M. (Ed) (1984) *Psychoanalyse und Nationalsozialismus: Beiträge zur Bearbeitung eines Unbewältigten Themas*, Frankfurt/M., Fischer.

LÜDTKE, A. (1982) 'Rekonstruktion von Alltagswirklichkeit: Entpolitisierung der Sozialgeschichte?', in BERDAHL, R.M., LÜDTKE, A., MEDICK, H., PONI, C., REDDY, W.M., SABEAN, D., SCHINDLER, N. and SIDER, G.M. *Klassen und Kultur*, Frankfurt/M., Syndikat.

LUNDGREEN, P. (1985a) 'Hochschulpolitik und Wissenschaft im Dritten Reich', in LUNDGREEN, P. (Ed) *Wissenschaft im Dritten Reich*, Frankfurt/M., Suhrkamp.

LUNDGREEN, P. (1985b) (Ed) *Wissenschaft im Dritten Reich*, Frankfurt/M., Suhrkamp.

MARTINI, O. (1938) 'Die Aufgaben der öffentlichen Fürsorgen nach Beendigung der Massenarbeitslosigkeit', in *Neue Familien- Und Arbeitspolitische Aufgaben Der Deutschen Wohlfahrtspflege*.

MASON, T. (1974) 'Zur Entstehung des Gesetzes zur Ordnung der nationalen Arbeit vom 20. Januar 1934: Ein Versuch über das Verhältnis "archaischer" und "moderner" Momente in der neuesten deutschen Geschichte', in MOMMSEN, H. and WILLEMS, S. (Eds) *Industrielles System und Politische Entwicklung in der Weimarer Republik, Bd.II*, Düsseldorf, Droste.

MASON, T. (1982) 'Die Bändigung der Arbeiterklasse im nationalsozialistischen Deutschland: Eine Einleitung', in SACHSE, C., SIEGEL, T., SPODE, H. and SPOHN, W. (Eds) *Angst, Belohnung, Zucht und Ordnung: Herrschaftsmechanismen im Nationalsozialismus*, Opladen, Westdeutscher Verlag.

MASON, T. (1995) 'Intention and Explanation: A Current Controversy about the Interpretation of National Socialism', in MASON, T. *Nazism, Fascism and the Working Class*, Cambridge, Cambridge University Press.

MATZERATH, H. (1970) *Nationalsozialismus und Kommunale Selbstverwaltung*, Stuttgart, Kohlhammer.

MEHRTENS, H. (1980) 'Das Dritte Reich in der Naturwissenschaftsgeschichte', in MEHRTENS, J. and RICHTER, ST. *Naturwissenschaft, Technik und NS-Ideologie: Beiträge zur Wissenschaftsgeschichte des Dritten Reiches*, Frankfurt/M., Suhrkamp.

MEHRTENS, H. and RICHTER, St. (1980) *Naturwissenschaft, Technik und NS-Ideologie: Beiträge zur Wissenschaftsgeschichte des Dritten Reiches*, Frankfurt/M., Suhrkamp.

MICHALKA, W. (1985) *Das Dritte Reich, Bd. I: Volksgemeinschaft und Großmachtpolitik 1933 bis 1939*, München, Deutscher Taschenbuch Verlag.

MOMMSEN, H. (1981) 'Hitlers Stellung im nationalsozialistischen Herrschaftssystem', in HIRSCHFELD, G. and KETTENACKER, L. (1981) *Der 'Führerstaat': Mythos und Realität: Studien zur Struktur und Politik im Dritten Reich*, Stuttgart, Klett-Cotta.

MOORE, B. (1969) *Soziale Ursprünge von Diktatur und Demokratie*, Frankfurt/M., Suhrkamp.

MÜLLER, J. (1987) *Furchtbare Juristen: Die Unbewältigte Vergangenheit Unserer Juristen*, München, Kindler.

NEGT, O. and KLUGE, A. (1972) *Öffentlichkeit und Erfahrung: Zur Organisationsanalyse von Bürgerlicher und Proletarischer Öffentlichkeit*, Frankfurt/M., Suhrkamp.

NEUE FAMILIEN- UND ARBEITSPOLITISCHE AUFGABEN DER DEUTSCHEN WOHLFAHRTSPFLEGE (1938) Bericht über die Tagung des Deutschen Vereins für öffentliche und private Fürsorge am 23. und 24. Mai 1938 in Würzburg (*zit. als* NEUE AUFGABEN).

NOAKES, J. (1987) 'Social outcasts in the Third Reich', in BESSEL, R. (Ed) *Life in the Third Reich*, Oxford, Oxford University Press.

OESTREICH, P. (1947) 'Die Aufgaben der deutschen Lehrer', *Ost und West*, 1, pp. 87–90.

PEUKERT, D.J.K. (1982) *Volksgenossen und Gemeinschaftsfremde: Anpassung, Ausmerze und Aufbegehren unter dem Nationalsozialismus*, Köln, Bund-Verlag.

PEUKERT, D.J.K. (1987) *Inside Nazi Germany: Conformity, Opposition and Racism in Everyday Life*, New Haven, Yale University Press.

POSTONE, M. (1980) 'Anti-Semitismus and National Socialism: Notes on the German Reactions to "Holocaust"', *New German Critique*, 19, pp. 97–115.

RABINBACH, A.G. (1976) 'Marxistische Faschismustheorien: Ein Überblick', in *Ästhetik und Kommunikation*, 7, 26, pp. 5–19; 8, 27, pp. 89–103.

SCHÄFER, H.D. (1981) *Das Gespaltene Bewußtsein: Über die Lebenswirklichkeit in Deutschland 1933–1945*, München, Hanser.

SCHNELL, W. (1938) *Volksgesundheitspflege mit Rassen- und Erblehre*, München, Zentralverlag der NSDAP.

SCHNURR, ST. (1988) 'Vom Wohlfahrtsstaat zum Erziehungsstaat: Sozialpolitik und soziale Arbeit in der Weimarer Republik und im Nationalsozialismus', *Widersprüche*, 8, 26, pp. 47–64.

SCHOENBAUM, D. (1980) *Die Braune Revolution: Eine Sozialgeschichte des Dritten Reiches*, München, Dt. Taschenbuch Verlag.

SCHUMACHER, J. (1972) *Die Angst vor dem Chaos: Über die Falsche Apokalypse des Bürgertums*, Frankfurt/M., Maro.

SENNETT, R. (1983) *Verfall und Ende des öffentlichen Lebens: Die Tyrannei der Intimität*, Frankfurt/M., Fischer.

SIEGEL, E. (1981) *Dafür und dagegen: Ein Leben für die Sozialpädagogik*, Stuttgart, Radius.

SIEGEL, T. (1978) 'Thesen zur Charakterisierung faschistischer Herrschaft', *Ästhetik und Kommunikation*, **9**, 32, pp. 59–70.

SOMBART, N. (1984) *Jugend in Berlin 1933 bis 1945: Ein Bericht*, München, Fischer.

SPOHN, W. (1987) *Betriebsgemeinschaft und Volksgemeinschaft: Die Rechtliche und Institutionelle Regelung der Arbeitsbeziehungen im NS-Staat*, Berlin, Quorum-Verlag.

STEINBACH, L. (1984) *Ein Volk, Ein Reich, Ein Glaube? Ehemalige Nationalsozialisten und Zeitzeugen Berichten über ihr Leben im Dritten Reich*, Bonn, Dietz.

STURM, K.F. (1942) *Deutsche Erziehung im Werden: Von der Pädagogischen Reformbewegung zur Völkischen und Politischen Erziehung*, **5**, Auflage Osterwieck/Harz, Zickfeldt.

SÜNKER, H. (1988) *Bildung, Alltag und Subjektivität*, Weinheim, Deutscher Studien Verlag.

TILING, M. VON and JARAUSCH, K. (Eds) (1934) *Grundfragen Pädagogischen Handelns: Beiträge zur Neuen Erziehung*, Stuttgart, Steinkopf.

TYRELL, A. (1983) 'Voraussetzungen und Strukturelemente des nationalsozialistischen Herrschaftssystems', in BRACHER, D., FUNKE, M. and JACOBSEN, A.H. (Eds) (1983) *Nationalsozialistische Diktatur 1933 bis 1945: Eine Bilanz*, Bonn, Zentrale für politische Bildung.

VENTZKY, W. (1938) 'Die Neuformung der Jugendhilfe durch die NSV unter besonderer Berücksichtigung der NS-Jugendheimstätten', *Neue Familien- Und Arbeitspolitische Aufgaban Der Deutschen Wohlfahrtspflege*.

VORLÄNDER, H. (1988) *Die NSV: Darstellung und Dokumentation einer Nationalsozialistischen Organisation*, Boppard, Boldt (Schriften des Bundesarchivs 35).

VOSSKAMP, W. (1985) 'Kontinuität und Diskontinuität: Zur deutschen Literaturwissenschaft im Dritten Reich', in LUNDGREEN, P. (Ed) *Wissenschaft im Dritten Reich*, Frankfurt/M., Suhrkamp.

WEHLER, H.U. (1979) 'Der Aufstieg des organisierten Kapitalismus in Deutschland', in WEHLER, H.U. *Krisenherde des Kaiserreichs 1871–1918*, **2**, Auflage Göttingen, Vandenhoeck and Ruprecht.

WITT, TH.E.J. DE (1978) 'The economics and politics of welfare in the Third Reich', *Central European History*, **11**, pp. 256–78.

ZIMMERMANN, F.J. (n.d.) (1938) *Die NS-Volkswohlfahrt und das Winterhilfswerk des Deutschen Volkes*, Würzburg, Memminger.

9   After Auschwitz: The Quest for Democratic Education

Heinz Sünker

Education and Society

Against the background of the often devastating experiences of our century —
especially with respect to the German experiences — it may seem bold to deal in
a text with Democracy, Education, and Ethics in the Post-Auschwitz World, i.e.,
asking for a democratic pedgagogy and democratic education today.[1] So I would
like to declare at the outset that my concern here is simply to recall a number of
ideas from the history and present of the discipline of pedagogy, from the tradition of
democratic ideas, if possible to rethink them — with a social-theoretical and social
policy interest — and to examine their consequences for a democratic education.

   The focus of my deliberations are Adorno's (1903–69) thoughts on democratic
pedagogy (Adorno, 1977) and the starting point of his very famous text *Erziehung
nach Auschwitz* (Education after Auschwitz): 'The demand, that Auschwitz should
never reappear, is the very first one to be made of education' (Adorno, 1969, p. 85).[2]
This shows: Auschwitz is the salient sign of the decline of civilization. Adorno's
categories and postulate can serve as a focal point because they enable understanding of the relationships between social conditions, political culture, ethics and educational processes which are decisive for our topic.

   We can see what is most significant about the relationship between political
culture, democratic politics and subjectivity in the radio debate, which has since
become famous, between Theodor W. Adorno, the outstanding intellectual in post-
fascist Germany, and Arnold Gehlen, his counterpart — a 'mandarin', on 3 February 1965:

Gehlen   Yes, the child, who hides behind the mother's skirt, it has both
           anxiety and the minimum or optimum of security that the situ-
           ation produces. Herr Adorno, you of course again see here the
           problem of autonomy. Do you really believe that we should ex-
           pect everyone to bear this burden of a concern with principles,
           with excessive reflection, with the on-going after-effects of the
           confusions of life, because we have sought to swim free? That
           is what I would very much like to know.

> **Adorno** To that I can very simply say: Yes! I have a conception of objective happiness and objective despair, and I would say that as long as we unburden people [with authoritarian institutions, H.S.] and do not grant them full responsibility and self-determination, so long too will their well-being and their happiness in this world be a sham. And a sham which will one day burst. And when it bursts, it will have terrible consequences. (Grenz, 1974, p. 294f.)

Adorno responded to Gehlen's statement with the remark, I mean, the need which drives people to this unburdening is precisely the burden imposed by institutions, that is, the world's agencies which stand outside and over them. It is thus to a certain extent so: first they are chased out, sent out by the mother, into the cold, and are under terrible pressure; and then, afterwards, they flee into the lap of precisley the same mother, namely society, which chased them out. In the context of his view of the conditions of the constitution of subjectivity and its (in)capacity for action, he is here clearly speaking of the relation between autonomy — self-determination — accountability. This triad can be illuminated by an exploration of both individual and social history (Sünker, 1989a, 1993). In defending Adorno's position, intellectuals are the keepers of political culture in a democratic tradition and meaning. This means that, against the (neo-) Aristotelian tradition, not only a few people are able to reflect, to carry the burden of reflection and responsibility, but all are able to do so. It includes, today, the task to (re-)construct the public and, therefore, the political culture in a participatory model. Within this approach, 'the public sentiment which is encouraged is not reconciliation and harmony, but rather political agency and efficacy, namely the sense that we have a say in the economic, political and civic arrangements which define our lives together, and that what one does makes a difference' (Benhabib, 1989, p. 389).

Reflections on historical experience, which contains more than any gathering of knowledge, can lead to a socio-historical consciousness accompanied by a capacity for judgment which provides a capacity for action. Thus it can help serve this democratic, participatory goal.

Education — precisely in the ways it differs from 'knowledge' — has to derive its present from the past, to make it the content of educational processes (Benjamin, 1969; Wehler, 1988). For a democratic pedagogy this means, *inter alia*: learning from the history of this country or its regions, and — in my case — the history of German political culture. This requires, firstly, engaging with the question 'What does it mean to deal with the past?' (Adorno, 1977). And, secondly, posing the question, what form can be taken by an alternative to domination in individual action and social structures in democratic social conditions and an accompanying political culture in Germany.

In view of the frequently unsuccessful engagement, dominated by political majorities, with recent German history, and the accompanying consequences for the quality of political culture in Germany up to the present day (Mitscherlich and Mitscherlich, 1987; Brunkhorst, 1987; Stern, 1991), for the moment we can only say that this question, as a question for everyone interested in a substantial demo-cratization of all areas of life, must stay on the agenda.

The second question which follows from this is related to a problem which is decisive for the future of German society: that which currently appears as right-extremism and hostility to foreigners, as well as a re-activation of politically motiv-ated violence in this society, and in its adoption by a majority of the dominant political class exposes the latter, relates to traditions in German history and the history of the political culture which many overwhelmingly believed in (Lepsius, 1990).

In this situation it becomes clear that the question of democracy once again reappears on the agenda. Adorno maintained that the delay in German democracy also resulted in crucial problems in the way the past was dealt with: 'But demo-cracy had not taken hold in such a way that people really regarded it as their own affair, understanding themselves as subjects of political processes'. This is why, continued Adorno, democracy was evaluated according to the success or failure it brought with it (Adorno, 1977, p. 559).

In his lecture on the necessity of a return to the subject, his thesis education only makes any sense as critical self-reflection and his conclusion, the only true power against the principle of Auschwitz is autonomy, if I may be permitted the Kantian expression, the power of reflection, of self-determination, of non-participation (Adorno, 1969, pp. 87, 90), indicated the relationships between a democratic ped-agogy and a democratic education with which we should engage.[3]

An intial formulation of this question can be found in classical pedagogic conceptions, as they appeared in the reflective and wide-ranging early bourgeois theoretical debates. At the end of the eighteenth century Kant (1724–1804), in his lecture '*Über Pädagogik*', wrote perhaps education constantly improves, and every successive generation takes another step towards the full realization of humanity; for behind education lies the great secret of the realization of human nature (Kant, 1964, p. 700). He also tied this to a positive anthropology which placed social conditions, and thus the social conditionality of humans, in the foreground: Good education is precisely that which produces everything that is good in the world. The seeds which lie within people must be constantly developed. For the basis of evil cannot be found in the natural constitution of people. The only cause of evil is that nature is not brought under control. People contain only the seeds of good (Kant, 1964, p. 704f.). If, as Kant stresses, education constituted the most important and difficult question posed to humanity, it thus also led to this requirement: Children must be raised not towards the current, but the future possibly improved state of the human race, that is, the idea of humanity, and everything appropriate to its destiny. This principle is of great importance. Parents generally raise their children only so that they fit into the existing world, even though it may be ruined. They should, however, better raise them so that a future, better state is brought about (Kant, 1964, p. 704).[4]

In the first third of the nineteenth century Schleiermacher (1768–1834) — one of the discipline's founding fathers — also in a lecture titled '*Über Pädagogik*' said that education should be based on the intergenerational relationship, from which derives the task that the younger generation should be delivered to the main communities in which they have to become self-sufficiently active (Schleiermacher, 1983, p. 94). Because he was concerned with the category fundamental to the educational relationship, the future — thus the capacity for construction — he binds the perspective of the socially-based action of the rising generation to the dual task of conservation and change. At the same time this premise leads him to a crucial principle concerning the relationship between pedagogy and politics: Both theories, pedagogy and politics, strive towards what is most complete; both are ethical disciplines and require the same treatment. Politics will not reach its goal if pedagogy is not an integral part of it, or if a similarly developed discipline does not stand beside it. The more communal life within the state is practically disrupted — theoretically seen, misunderstood — the less it is possible for a correct approach to exist in relation to the influence of the older generation on the younger (Schleiermacher, 1983, p. 12; Mollenhauer, 1980, p. 103).

Democratic Education

The positions of Kant and Schleiermacher constitute a critique of the instrumentalization of people — foundational for all approaches to a criticial theory of society — to which Adorno's frosty conclusion, which in a certain sense describes a final stage in social relations, relates in a complementary way.[5]

This leads us to the task of examining social relations in their consequences for the relations between individuals and society. For the present this means, in an initial and general sense, the contradictory results of the capitalist framework of societalization for people, to dissect their conditions of existence. The relations between society and individual are constituted by a contradiction between a production and a destruction of the social, of sociality, which can be understood as a result of the capitalist framework of societalization, as inherent to it from the outset (Bowles and Gintis, 1987; Berman, 1988). This contradiction can be seen as both a general and a particular social problem, because it is generation-specific. What is interesting here in terms of ethics, education and pedagogy is that when one takes up this contradiction between the production and destruction of sociality, one can speak of a caesura or break in the development of the social potential for both control and communication (Sünker, 1996).

This finding is relevant within the framework of educational and pedagogic reflections if one poses the question, firstly, of possible determinations of the relationship between Education and Society[6], and secondly of the consequences for possible foundations and practices of democratic education.

What is of interest here is, of course, the question of the possibilities of a development of communicative potential within and opposed to social contexts which cannot free themselves of their hegemonic form. The issue then becomes one of the analysis of societalization and individualization, of democratic theory and its 'praxis' in the form of political culture, of the question of the constitutive conditions of subjectivity as a basis for the development of self-sufficient life orientations, and finally of a theory of educational processes, the social-theoretical and socio-political challenge of which still lies in the classical conception of every individual's capacity for education and reason.

This task becomes relevant precisely when one acknowledges Theunissen's comment, his reflection on social reality, that autonomy is complicated or even hindered, undermined to the same degree that the social deformation of individuals increases (Theunissen, 1989, p. 86). For in connection with classical and still-contemporary positions, which precisely in this way indicate their modernity, it is important to pose the problem of a contract based on the principle of communalization (Theunissen, 1989, p. 87) and thus the construction and principles of a relational reason (Geyer-Ryan and Lethen, 1987, p. 68). It seems to me to be crucial to establish a mediation between what Benjamin brought forward on the basis of his conception of the relevance of mutual recognition for processes of identity formation, that there is a coercion-free sphere of human agreement which is completely inaccessible to domination: the actual sphere of agreement, speech (Benjamin, 1966, p. 55), and the problem, how power can be criticized from a perspective which appears to profit from and out of it. The question is how reason in itself can establish that murder is worse than non-murder, if it is to one's advantage. In the light of a relational reason, murder becomes suicide, this is already the response of the Odyssey (Geyer-Ryan and Lethen, 1987, p. 69).

The systematic significance of these positions for the constitution of subjectivity and its consequences, is whether the issue is still the difference between a construction of knowledge which remains external to the individual, and the development of the individual themselves in constellations of educational processes (Koneffke, 1986, p. 72; Sünker, 1989, pp. 12–24), so that it can become clear how education, enlightenment and experience are interwoven with each other.

The thesis put forward by Adorno, discussed earlier, that people must experience democracy as their own affair, understand themselves as the actors in political processes (Adorno, 1977, p. 559), is complementary to the task of taking this up and spelling it out for institutionally-formed educational processes.[7] Opposed to one-dimensional, linear interpretations of the working possibilities in the institution of the school, we must insist that the contradiction contained within the dialectic of the institutionalization of education, between education and domination (Heydorn, 1979), indicates that the institution of the school in its diversely-determined structures, dimensions, levels of action encompasses possibilities for the promotion of emancipation and autonomy for all who work in these institutions. This raises the question, firstly of professionalization, the self-understanding of pupils and the consequences contained therein for praxis, that is, the initiation or promotion of educational processes (Bernfeld, 1969). Secondly that of the relationship between the individual being educated and the inner structures of educational processes and their objects (Holzkamp, 1994). This requires a pedagogy of recognition which, as Heydorn — taking up the Socratic maieutic — made clear in his emphasis on the significance of the Other in educational processes (Heydorn, 1979), lies in the promotion of the formation of subjectivity — and then simultaneously of potential for contractual communication.

To remove from pedagogical processes — as far as is possible in society and history — the existing formation of subject and object also means making it possible for the rising generation to live and experience democracy in everyday life and in institutions such as family, school, work (Bowles and Gintis, 1987, pp. 204, 208). This holds fast to the possibilities for dealing with individuals and associations of individuals — against the pedagogization of socially produced problems — within social relations, that is within social relations of power. This understanding certainly depends on a culture of hope (Benjamin, 1966), an ideal of education, as Kant formulated it; but it also refers to the necessity of building up new social movements to confront the experiences of domination in the various areas of life with experiences and life-forms orientated towards communication. Therefore principles of universalization and reciprocity are on the agenda. As Heller (1984) concluded the perspective is 'To create a society in which alienation is a thing of the past: a society in which every person has access to the social "gifts of fortune" which can enable her or him to lead a meaningful life . . . True "history" is pregnant with conflict and continually transcending its own given state. It is history consciously chosen by people and molded to their design that can enable everyone to make their everyday lives "being for them" and that will make the earth a true home for all people' (1984, p. 269).

In opposition to those who would coercively impose social integration (Adorno, 1969, p. 89) and patterns of meaning (Schlaffer, 1990, p. 136ff.) from outside, we can hold fast to the potential for autonomous actors, people who are aware of their societal contextualization, actors with a strong interest in a living democracy.

Notes

1   An initial thread to this discussion is today the theme Youth and Violence, which reveals this in its various facets and brings forwards very diverse findings in relation to the question of the conditions (Otto and Merten, 1993, Schubarth and Melzer, 1993; Hey, Müller and Sünker, 1993; Heitmeyer, Möller and Sünker, 1992; Bielefeld, 1993; Breyvogel, 1994). A second thread relates to the theme 'The 68ers and Youth Violence Today', in which the thesis itself is not very interesting, but rather the question of the role which can be played in hegemonic struggles by such a nonsensical proposition such as the responsibility of the 68ers for today's youth violence (Bohleber, 1994; Eisenberg, 1994).

Otherwise it seems to me to be worth referring to a conception of the problem of education similar to that of S. Bernfeld (1892–1953) over seventy years ago:

The educative role of the family is now everywhere in question, and the old pedagogical remedies on which our grandparents still relied have ceased to be effective, or at least have lost most of their authority. With regard to moral and social questions, a general insecurity prevails, robbing parents of the courage to enforce their will and lay down the law. Beset by a host of feelings, which include guilt and hostility to family and children, parents are caught in a situation of psychic stress and reach out for whatever help tested educational doctrines may give them. Even if these should not quite bring the desired results, they would at least permit the parents to justify themselves: they could say that they had done what was possible. This situation indeed creates a considerable interest in education, but not necessarily a high appreciation of it. On the contrary, there are indications that predict an early fatigue and disappointment in the parts of the parents. For the plain fact is that educational theory does not meet the expectations people set on it. (Bernfeld, 1993, pp. 3–4)

2 For a controversy over the range of this thesis of Adorno's see Dudek (1990, p. 364) and Koneffke (1990, p. 131ff.). Koneffke maintains, and thus implicitly opposed to Dudek, the primacy of the principle of education, which guarantees a possible humane future (p. 132).

3 A. Siemsen (1882–1951) has long ago — in agreement with many of the works of critical theory — in his research established the social foundations of education as essential for an analysis of the development of western Europe:

> I see the causes far more in the fact that our consciousness has become exclusively technically oriented, aimed at the tremendous success in the mastery of nature and in material technology, and thus completely neglects the realm of social relations. The objective result has been the degeneration and chaotic confusion of our social relations, which have exposed people to political emancipation, but simultaneously to social isolation and uncertainty, which has given rise to severe complexes of loneliness, anxiety and hate. . . . The struggle for existence becomes for them a competitive struggle with equals, in which ultimately every means is justified. Until finally the unbearability of this condition and this state of consciousness leads to flight into some social bond, whether it be that of the blind subjection to a state, a party or a leader. (Siemsen, 1948, p. 5)

The emphasis on the role of social relationships, reflection and working through them, makes it clear that every democratic pedagogy must today have an anti-fascist and anti-stalinist, and thus anti-totalitarian, orientation (Kershaw, 1994).

4 Interesting too is Kant's observation that parents and authorities are to be considered as obstacles to the road to an improvement of the human condition:

> 1 Parents namely generally ensure only that their children do well in the world and
> 2 Monarchs regard their subjects only as instruments for their goals. Parents care for the house, monarchs for the state. Both do not have as their aim the welfare and the completeness for which humanity is destined and for which it is capable (Kant, 1964, p. 704).

5 This diagnosis of the frost also throws a characteristic light on the question of the preconditions of National Socialism, as the German form of Fascism, in people themselves: It [the Hitler period, H.S.] violently anticipated current crisis management, a barbaric experiment in state administration of industrial society. The oft-mentioned integration, the organization intensification of the social net, which caught everything, also guaranteed protection against the universal anxiety about falling through the holes and sinking away. For countless people the chill of their alientated condition seemed to be removed by the ever-manipulated and artificial warmth of togetherness; the folk community of the unfree and unequal was, as lie, at the same time also the realization of an old, indeed ancient bad bourgeois dream. Certainly the system offering such gratifications contained within itself the potential for its own destruction (Adorno, 1977, p. 562).

6 Socio-historical and socio-political analyses of the relationship between education and

society can be found in an extremely interesting Anglo-Saxon discussion, which revolves around the concept new sociology of education and critical pedagogy (Giroux and McLaren, 1989; Wexler, 1990; Apple, 1993; Sünker, Timmerman and Kolbe, 1994). On the German-language discussion see Heydorn (1979), Lenhart (1987) and von Friedeburg (1989).

7 It is understandable that this emancipatory perspective is far more difficult to represent in the framework of school socialization process (Wexler, 1994) than in the context of educational labour which is not based in the school context (Peter, Sünker and Willigmann, 1982). In view of debates on global society and interculturalism, such an approach to the task of schooling seems even more relevant (Richter, 1994).

References

ADORNO, T.W. (1969) 'Erziehung nach Auschwitz', in ADORNO, T.W. *Stichworte, Kritische Modelle II*, Frankfurt/M., Suhrkamp.

ADORNO, T.W. (1977) 'Was bedeutet: Aufarbeitung der Vergangenheit', in ADORNO, T.W. *Gesammelte Schriften*, Bd. 10.2. Frankfurt/M., Suhrkamp.

APPLE, M.W. (1993) *Official Knowledge: Democratic Education In A Conservative Age*, New York/London, Routledge.

BENHABIB, S. (1989) 'Autonomy, modernity, and community: Communitarianism and critical social theory in dialogue', in HONNETH, A., MCCARTHY, Th., OFFE, C. and WELLMER, A. (Eds) Zwischenbetrachtungen. Im Prozeß der Aufklärung. Jürgen Habermas zum 60. Geburtstag, Frankfurt/M., Suhrkamp.

BENJAMIN, W. (1966) 'Zur Kritik der Gewalt', in BENJAMIN, W. *Angelus Novus: Ausgewählte Schriften II*, Frankfurt/M., Suhrkamp.

BENJAMIN, W. (1969) 'Geschichtsphilosophische Thesen', in BENJAMIN, W. *Illuminationen*, Frankfurt/M., Suhrkamp.

BERMAN, M. (1988) *All That Is Solid Melts into Air: The Experience of Modernity*, New York, Basic Books.

BERNFELD, S. (1967) *Sisyphos oder die Grenzen der Erziehung*, Frankfurt/M., Suhrkamp.

BERNFELD, S. (1969) 'Kinderheim Baumgarten: Bericht über einen ernsthaften Versuch mit neuer Erziehung', in BERNFELD, S. *Antiautoritäre Erziehung und Psychoanalyse I*, Frankfurt/M., März.

BIELEFELD, U. (1993) 'Nationalismus, Nationalstaat und die anderen', *Sozialwissenschaftliche Literatur Rundschau*, **16**, pp. 7–24.

BOHLEBER, W. (1994) 'Autorität und Freiheit heute: Sind die 68er schuld am Rechtsextremismus?', *Psychosozial*, **17**, pp. 73–85.

BOWLES, S. and GINTIS, H. (1987) *Democracy and Capitalism: Property, Community, and the Contradictions of Modern Social Thought*, New York, Basic Books.

BREYVOGEL, W. (1994) 'Die neue Gewalt Jugendlicher gegen Fremde 1990 — 1993: Zur Kritik der Arbeiten des "Bielefelder Erklärungsansatzes"', *Sozialwissenschaftliche Literatur Rundschau*, **17**, pp. 14–26.

BRUNKHORST, H. (1987) *Der Intellektuelle im Land der Mandarine*, Frankfurt/M., Suhrkamp.

DUDEK, P. (1990) 'Antifaschismus: Von einer politischen Kampfformel zum erziehungstheoretischen Grundbegriff', *Zeitschr. f. Päd.*, **36**, pp. 353–70.

EISENBERG, G. (1994) 'Das moralische Ozonloch: Versuch über das Verhältnis von Markt und Moral', *Psychosozial*, **17**, pp. 97–114.

FRIEDEBURG, L. VON (1989) *Bildungsreform in Deutschland: Geschichte und Gesellschaftlicher Widerspruch*, Frankfurt/M., Suhrkamp.

GEYER-RYAN, H. and LETHEN, H. (1987) 'Von der Dialektik der Gewalt zur Dialektik der Aufklärung: Eine Re-vision der Odyssee', in VAN REIJEN, W. and SCHMID NOERR, G. (Eds) *Vierzig Jahre Flaschenpost: 'Dialektik der Aufklärung' 1947–1987*, Frankfurt/M., Fischer.

GIROUX, H. and McLAREN, P. (1989) (Eds) *Critical Pedagogy: The State and Cultural Struggle*, Albany, SUNY Press.

GRENZ, F. (1974) *Adornos Philosophie in Grundbegriffen Auflösung einiger Deutungsprobleme: Mit einem Anhang: Theodor W. Adorno und Arnold Gehlen: Ist die Soziologie eine Wissenschaft vom Menschen? Ein Streitgespräch*, Frankfurt/M., Suhrkamp.

HEITMEYER, W., MÖLLER, K. and SÜNKER, H. (1992) (Eds) *Jugend — Staat — Gewalt: Politische Sozialisation von Jugendlichen, Jugendpolitik und politische Bildung*, 2. Aufl. Weinheim/München, Juventa.

HELLER, A. (1984) *Everyday Life*, London, Routledge and Kegan.

HEY, G., MÜLLER, S. and SÜNKER, H. (1993) (Eds) *Gewalt — Gesellschaft — Soziale Arbeit*, Frankfurt/M., ISS.

HEYDORN, H.-J. (1979) *Über den Widerspruch von Bildung und Herrschaft*, Frankfurt/M., Syndikat.

HOLZKAMP, K. (1994) 'Antirassistische Erziehung als Änderung rassistischer "Einstellungen"?', *Das Argument*, **203**, pp. 41–58.

KANT, I. (1964) 'Über Pädagogik', in Kant, I. Band 10, *Werke in 10 Bänden*, Darmstadt, Wiss. Buchgesellschaft.

KERSHAW, I. (1994) 'Totalitarianism Revisited: Nazism and Stalinism in Comparative Perspective', *Tel Aviver Jahrbuch für Deutsche Geschichte*, **23**, pp. 23–40.

KONEFFKE, G. (1986) 'Revidierte Allgemeinbildung', *Widersprüche*, **6**, pp. 67–75.

KONEFFKE, G. (1990) 'Auschwitz und die Pädagogik', in ZUBKE, F. (Ed) *Politische Pädagogik*, Weinheim, Deutscher Studienverlag.

LENHART, V. (1987) *Die Evolution Erzieherischen Handelns*, Frankfurt/M., Peter Lang.

LEPSIUS, M.R. (1990) *Interessen, Ideen und Institutionen*, Opladen, Westdeutscher Verlag.

MITSCHERLICH, A. and MITSCHERLICH, M. (1987) Die Unfähigkeit zu trauern. Grundlagen kollektiven Verhaltens, München, Piper.

MOLLENHAUER, K. (1980) 'Einige erziehungswissenschaftliche Probleme im Zusammenhang der Erforschung von "Alltagswelten Jugendlicher"', in LENZEN, D. (Ed) *Pädagogik und Alltag*, Stuttgart, Klett Clotta.

OTTO, H.-U. and MERTEN, R. (1993) (Eds) *Rechtsradikale Gewalt im Vereinigten Deutschland: Jugend im Gesellschaftlichen Umbruch*, Opladen, Leske and Budrich.

PETER, H., SÜNKER, H. and WILLIGMANN, S. (1982) (Eds) *Politische Jugendbildungsarbeit*, Frankfurt/M./Aarau, Sauerländer/Diesterweg.

RICHTER, E. (1994) 'International education as the responsibility of the school', *Education*, **49/50**, pp. 40–60.

SCHLAFFER, H. (1990) *Poesie und Wissen: Die Entstehung des Ästhetischen Bewußtseins und der Philologischen Erkenntnis*, Frankfurt/M., Suhrkamp.

SCHLEIERMACHER, F. (1983) *Pädagogische Schriften I. Die Vorlesungen aus dem Jahre 1826*, Frankfurt/M., Ullstein.

SCHUBARTH, W. and MELZER, W. (1993) (Eds) *Schule, Gewalt, Rechtsextremismus*, Opladen, Leske and Budrich.

SIEMSEN, A. (1948) *Die Gesellschaftlichen Grundlagen der Erziehung*, Hamburg, Oetinger.

STERN, F. (1991) *Im Anfang war Auschwitz: Antisemitismus und Philosemitismus im Deutschen Nachkrieg*, Gerlingen, Bleicher.

SÜNKER, H. (1989a) 'Heinz-Joachim Heydorn: Bildungstheorie als Gesellschaftskritik', in

HANSMANN, O. and MAROTZKI, W. (Eds) *Diskurs Bildungstheorie II: Problemges-chichtliche Orientierungen*, Weinheim, Deutscher Studien Verlag.

SÜNKER, H. (1889b) *Bildung, Alltag und Subjektivität*, Weinheim, Deutscher Studien Verlag.

SÜNKER, H. (1993) 'Education and enlightenment, or, educational theory contra postmodernism?', *Education*, **48**, pp. 39–57.

SÜNKER, H. (1994) 'Pluralismus und Utopie der Bildung', in HEYTING, F. and TENORTH, H.-E. (Eds) *Pädagogik und Pluralismus*, Weinheim, Deutscher Studien Verlag.

SÜNKER, H. (1996) 'Violence and Society-Violence in Society', in FREHSEE, D., HORN, W. and BUSSMAN, K.-D. (Eds) Family Violence against Children: A Challenge for Society, Berlin, New York, de Gruyter.

SÜNKER, H., TIMMERMANN, D. and KOLBE, F.-U. (1994) (Eds) *Bildung, Gesellschaft, Soziale Ungleichheit*, Frankfurt/M., Suhrkamp.

THEUNISSEN, M. (1989) 'Möglichkeiten des Philosophierens heute', *Sozialwissenschaftliche Literatur Rundschau*, **12**, pp. 77–89.

WEHLER, H.-U. (1988) *Aus der Geschichte lernen?*, München, Beck.

WEXLER, P. (1990) *Social Analysis of Education: After the New Sociology*, New York/London, Routledge.

WEXLER, P. (1994) 'Schichtspezifisches Selbst und soziale Interaktion in der Schule', in SÜNKER, H., TIMMERMANN, D. and KOLBE, F.-U. op.cit.

Notes on Contributors

Peter Dudek is Professor of Education at the University of Frankfurt/Main. His research interests include History of Education, Political Education, Youth, Right-Wing Extremism in Europe. His most recent publications include (with H.-E. Tenorth) 'Transformationen der deutschen Bildungslandschaft. Lernprozeß mit ungewissem Ausgang', Weinheim/Basel 1994 (Beltz), 'Der Rückblick auf die Vergangenheit wird sich nicht vermeiden lassen. Zur pädagogischen Verarbeitung des Nationalsozialismus in Deutschland', Opladen 1995 (Westdeutscher Verlag), and 'Peter Petersen: Reformpädagogik in SBZ und DDR 1945–1950', Weinheim 1996 (Deutscher Studien Verlag).

Elizabeth Harvey is a Lecturer in History at the University of Liverpool. She has researched and published on the history of social policy and on women and young people in Weimar Germany, and she is currently carrying out research on women's involvement in National Socialist Germanization policies in the 'German East'. She is the author of *Youth and the Welfare State in Weimar Germany* (Oxford University Press, 1993), and she has coedited two volumes of essays: (with Jennifer Birkett) *Determined Women: Studies in the Construction of the Female Subject, 1900–1990* (Macmillan, 1991) and (with Lynn Abrams) *Gender Relations in German History: Power, Agency and Experience from the Sixteenth to the Twentieth Century* (UCL Press, 1996).

Hans-Uwe Otto is Professor of Social Pedagogy at the University of Bielefeld. He has researched and published on social work professionalization, social administration, youth welfare, the welfare state. He is editor of main journals in social work *neue praxis* and *Sozialwissenschaftliche Literatur Rundschau* and coeditor of the *Handbuch der Sozialarbeit/Sozialpädagogik*, Neuwied 1995 (Luchterhand, fifth edition). He is author and coeditor of many books including *Sozialarbeit zwischen Routine und Innovation*, (Berlin/New York, 1991 de Gruyter), (with B. Dewe) *Zugänge zur Sozialpädagogik* (Weinheim, 1996 Juventa), (with G. Flösser) *How to Organize Prevention*, (Berlin/New York 1992 de Gruyter).

Dagmar Reese is a Historical Sociologist based in Berlin and currently engaged in a project about Georg Simmel's philosophy and sociology of gender in its historical context financed by the Förderprogramm Frauenforschung des Senats von Berlin. She is author of *Straff, aber nicht stramm — Herb, aber nicht derb. Zur Vergesellschaftung der Mädchen im Bund Deutscher Mädel im sozialkulturellen Vergleich* (Weinheim/Basel, 1989 Beltz) and coauthor of *Rationale Beziehungen? Geschlechterverhältnisse im Rationalisierungsprozeß* (Frankfurt/Main, 1993 Suhrkamp).

Jürgen Schiedeck is the Head of an Adult Education Institution in Northern Germany and he is lecturer in education at the University of Kiel. His research interests are adult education, and history of education. He has published on various educational topics and he is coauthor (with M. Stahlmann) of *Erziehung zur Gemeinschaft — Auslese durch Gemeinschaft. Zur Zurichtung des Menschen im Nationalsozialismus* (Bielefeld, 1991).

Stefan Schnurr is a Researcher in the field of education and social pedagogy at the University of Bielefeld. He has published on social policy, social work and education in the Third Reich. He is currently completing a book on the German 'Sozialpädagogische Bewegung in the transition from the Weimar Republic to National Socialism', and he is currently carrying out research on the consequences of the recent implementation of 'lean administration' and 'new public management' models in social welfare organizations on the professional identity and the professional knowledge of social workers.

Martin Stahlmann is a Lecturer in Education and Social Peagogy at the Fachschulen für Sozialpädagogik und Heilpädagogik in Neumünster. He has published on social pedagogy, special education, residential care, history of education. His publications include (with J. Schiedeck) *Erziehung zur Gemeinschaft — Auslese durch die Gemeinschaft. Zur Zurichtung des Menschen im Nationalsozialismus* (Bielefeld, 1991), and Die *berufliche Sozialisation in der Heimerziehung* (Bern, 1993).

Heinz Sünker is Professor of Social Pedagogy at thc University of Wuppertal. He has researched and published on critical social theory, philosophy of education, theory and history of social work, social work and social policy, childhood, and youth. His books include a study of Western Marxism *Bildung, Alltag, Subjektivität* (Weinheim, 1989 Deutscher Studienverlag), and he has edited or coedited many books including (with R. Farnen) *Politics, Sociology, and Economics of Education* (Basingstoke, 1997 Macmillan), (with W. Marotzki) *Kritische Erziehungswissenschaft — Moderne — Postmoderne*, 2 Vol. (Weinheim, 1992, 1993 Deutscher Studienverlag), and *Soziale Arbeit und Faschismus* (Frankfurt, 1989 Suhrkamp).

Index